# George Orwell Studies

Volume Nine

No. 2

# George Orwell Studies

**Publishing Office**
Abramis Academic
Eagle House
Sudbury Road
Great whelnetham
Bury St edmunds
Suffolk
IP30 0UN
UK

Tel: +44 (0)1284 717884
Fax: +44 (0)1284 717889
Email: info@abramis.co.uk
Web: www.abramis.co.uk

**Copyright**
All rights reserved. No part of this publication may be reproduced in any material form (including photocopying or storing it in any medium by electronic means, and whether or not transiently or incidentally to some other use of this publication) without the written permission of the copyright owner, except in accordance with the provisions of the Copyright, Designs and Patents Act 1988, or under terms of a licence issued by the Copyright Licensing Agency Ltd, 33-34, Alfred Place, London WC1E 7DP, UK. Applications for the copyright owner's permission to reproduce part of this publication should be addressed to the Publishers.

© 2025 George Orwell Studies & Abramis Academic

ISSN 2399-1267
ISBN 978-1-84549-848-1

# Contents

**George Orwell**

### Editorial
Congrats to Darcy Moore on Winning Major Research Award — Richard Lance Keeble — Page 1

### Front Cover
The Fun of Playing with AI and Orwell's Portrait — David Ryan — Page 5

### Papers
The Significance of Goldstein in *Nineteen Eighty-Four* — G. Alexander Denning — Page 6

Echoes from the 'Beasts of England': Orwell's 1947 BBC Radio Adaptation of *Animal Farm* — Peter Marks and Simon J. Potter — Page 25

Orwell and Fisher: Rebellion and Realism — Patrick Homes — Page 41

High Praise and Critique: Tom Hopkinson's Early Assessment of George Orwell — Tim Crook — Page 48

Wyndham Lewis Reading (and Misreading?) George Orwell — Nathan Waddell — Page 63

### Articles
Dear Charoux: Revealed — Orwell's 13 Letters to his Artist Friend — Darcy Moore — Page 91

Throwing Light on Darkness — Paul W.B. Marsden — Page 106

'Our command is "Thou art:"' Winston Smith's Fabricated Life in George Orwell's *Nineteen Eighty-Four* — Jan-Boje Frauen — Page 112

### Interview
L.J. Hurst interviews Nathan Waddell, author of *A Bright Cold Day: The Wonder of George Orwell* — Page 123

### Poetry Inspired by Orwell
'The special patient', 'He rose above', 'Class', 'Room 101' and 'Railroad to Wigan' — Rob Joyson — Page 138

### Short Stories
Two extracts from *Holding Up His Sky: Stories of Women in the Life of George Orwell* (plus Foreword) — Ann Kronbergs — Page 143

### Review Essays
John Newsinger on *'Perfidious Albion': Britain and the Spanish Civil War*, by Paul Preston — Page 160

Paul Flewers on *George Orwell and Russia*, by Masha Karp — Page 167

### Book Reviews
L.J. Hurst on *A Jura for Julia*, by Ken MacLeod; Jackson Ayres on *Orwell's Ghosts: Wisdom and Warnings for the Twenty-First Century*, by Laura Beers; D. Harlan Wilson on *1948: A Critical and Creative Prequel to George Orwell's* 1984, by Brian May; Hassan Akram on *Believe Nothing until It Is Officially Denied: Claud Cockburn and the Invention of Guerrilla Journalism* — Page 185

### And Finally
A special diary column for Orwellians — by New Pitcher — Page 202

**Editors**
Richard Lance Keeble — University of Lincoln
Tim Crook — Goldsmiths, University of London

**Reviews Editor**
Megan Faragher — Wright State University

**Production Editor**
Paul Anderson — University of Essex

**Editorial Board**
Kristin Bluemel — Monmouth University, New Jersey
Dorian Lynskey — Author, journalist
Peter Marks — University of Sydney
John Newsinger — Bath Spa University
Marina Remy — Paris Sorbonne
John Rodden — University of Texas at Austin
Jean Seaton — University of Westminster
Peter Stansky — Stanford University, US
D.J. Taylor — Author, journalist, biographer of Orwell
Martin Tyrrell — Queen's University, Belfast
Nathan Waddell — University of Birmingham
Florian Zollmann — Newcastle University

With editorial assistance from Marja Giejgo

# EDITORIAL

# Congrats to Darcy Moore on Winning Major Orwell Research Award

## RICHARD LANCE KEEBLE

Darcy Moore's status as one of the world's leading authorities on Orwell's life and writings was recently confirmed by his winning the Orwell Society's Peter Davison Award for 2024. This was rightly given to Darcy in recognition of his 'outstanding' contribution to Orwell Studies, Peter Davison being the editor of the 20-volume *Complete Works*.

Darcy has been contributing regularly over the last eight years to *George Orwell Studies*. Much new Orwellian scholarship offers original interpretations of his work. Some researchers have privileged access to newly discovered Orwellian letters and these help provide new insights into his writing routines, ideas, psychology and relationships. But Darcy's writings are very different. They are based on entirely original research in the archives, in specialised (and often very complex and difficult to access) web-based databases and on interviews with authoritative, important sources. Or they emerge from travels to places around the world of special Orwellian interest where again he delves deeply into the archives – and also interviews relevant sources. As a result, he is able offer new and important insights but also to highlight areas in which Orwellian scholarship to date is often based on inaccuracies.

Darcy's extraordinarily deep knowledge of all things Orwellian emerges in part from his possession of a unique and substantial collection of first editions, translations and books of interest for the Orwell enthusiast (see https://www.darcymoore.net/orwell-collection/). In fact, in his first essay for *George Orwell Studies* ('Collecting Orwell'), which appeared in Vol. 2, No. 2 pp 14-19 in 2018, Darcy reflects on what he has learned from his collecting 'compulsion'. In his next paper ('Orwell and the appeal of opium'), Darcy is typically unafraid to tackle sensitive, controversial aspects of Orwell's life when he explores his possible relationship with opium. Did he ever smoke opium in Burma? Darcy, drawing on letters, interviews, the memoir of Captain Herbert Reginald Robinson and

**RICHARD LANCE KEEBLE**

his novel, *Burmese Days*, argues that this is likely – particularly given his father's lifelong involvement in the British opium industry in India.

Very little is known about Orwell's years in Paris during the late 1920s and early 1930s. So filling in the gaps has become one of Darcy's major preoccupations. One of his friends there was Ruth Graves. But who was she? Only two of Orwell's biographers – D.J. Taylor and Gordon Bowker – mention her, but only briefly. In his essay for Vol. 3, No. 2 pp 55-70, Darcy uses a wide range of original sources to provide a fascinating and colourful profile of Graves. They include ancestry.com, Special Branch files on Eric Blair, a memoir of living in Montparnasse, Paris, Orwell letters, a 'remarkable' article written by Graves and published in the *Wichita Beacon* on Christmas Day 1916, and another article in the *Wichita Eagle* newspaper on 13 June 1926 which reports her exhibiting paintings at the prestigious 'Salon de Paris'.

Following Darcy's original research, it is clear that the importance of his Aunt Nellie to Orwell has been somewhat under-estimated by biographers. His 2020 *GOS* paper (published in Vol. 4, No. 2 pp 30-44) draws on letters by prominent Esperantists (including Nellie and her husband Eugène Lanti), registers at the Library and Museum of Freemasonry in London, British Library archives, a death certificate from Wandsworth Register Office, electoral registers and *The Times of India* to argue persuasively that 'Blair may never have travelled far down the path to becoming the writer Orwell without his Aunt Nellie's encouragement, support and literary contacts'.

More recent papers have examined in detail:

- the deep involvement of his Scottish ancestors in the slave trade (Vol. 4, No. 2 pp 6-19);
- Orwell's relationship with fellow old Etonian Eric Seeley and the problematic representation of Seeley's 'Indian lady' in Orwell scholarship (Vol. 5, No. 2 pp 6-24);
- his wide reading and acquaintances in Paris (Vol. 6, No. 1 pp 7-31);
- the origins of his obsession – reflected in his fiction, reportage, correspondence, diaries and essays – with rats (Vol. 7, No. 1 pp 92-106), and
- the significance of Orwell's Anglo-Indian family connection to Polperro, in Cornwall (Vol 8, No. 1 pp 142-158).

During a six-week research trip to India, Darcy discovered a long-lost transcript of a talk, 'The meaning of scorched earth', given by Orwell on the BBC in January 1942. It forms the basis for his 2024 paper in Vol. 8, No. 2 pp 20-31.

And his essay in Vol. 9, No 1 pp 135-144 offers more typical Darcy Moore original research. Working with previously ignored sources such as *Bath Record Office, Dorset County Chronicle and Somerset Gazette, English Chronicle and Whitehall Evening Post* (1823), *Indian Daily News* (1875), *London Gazette* (1909), the National Archives, *Thacker's Directory* (1873), *Times of India* and the UCL Department of History archives, Darcy is able to argue persuasively that the new biographical information connecting Orwell's father, Richard, with his uncles Arthur and Horatio, 'goes some way to explaining why Mr Blair was so adamant that his son would join the Indian Imperial Police and follow in Arthur Blair's footsteps'.

This summary of Darcy Moore's contributions to *GOS* gives an indication of the range and originality of his writings that are transforming Orwellian scholarship and winning him plaudits from academics and commentators around the world. Darcy also shares his insights and discoveries regularly on the Orwell Society Facebook page and he has given a number of fascinating, Zoom-based 'George Talks' for Orwell Society members. And he has an essay on *Nineteen Eighty-Four*'s Newspeak (exploring originally the impact of two invented languages, Basic English and Esperanto) for a 41-chapter *Routledge Companion to Orwell* I am currently co-editing with Tim Crook. Well done, Darcy!

## HOW *GEORGE ORWELL STUDIES* IS FOREVER EVOLVING

*GOS* is constantly introducing new elements becoming perhaps a *Horizon*-like, Orwell-focused cultural journal. Academic, peer-reviewed papers, shorter articles, book reviews together with an 'And Finally' diary by the anonymous New Pitcher are our staples. Recently, we carried our first, specially commissioned short story (by Orwell biographer D.J. Taylor). This issue carries the first two stories in Ann Kronbergs' excellent *Holding Up His Sky: Stories of Women in the Life of George Orwell*. As Ann explains in her Foreword, the title 'argues an untold truth about these women's lives: that just as influential men in high places, like Sir Richard Rees or David Astor, helped smooth Orwell's entry into the world of letters, so too, collectively, these women were also significant at crucial times in his journey as a writer, providing a degree of psychological and moral support, secretarial and editorial input, sexual pleasure and cultural companionship, domestic and even nursing care up to the last days of his life'. We look forward to carrying more of Ann's beautifully crafted stories in future issues.

We also in this issue feature more poems inspired by Orwell: 'The special patient', 'He rose above', 'Class', 'Room 101' and 'Railroad

**RICHARD LANCE KEEBLE**

to Wigan', by Rob Joyson. The 'review essay' format allows for a more discursive approach to the text than the typical review. In this issue, John Newsinger, one of the founding editors of the journal, uses the format to take a detailed, critical look at Paul Preston's latest book on the Spanish Civil War and Orwell's role in it.

According to Newsinger, Masha Karp's recently published *Orwell and Russia* is 'one of the most important books on Orwell of the last few decades'. Our last issue (Vol. 9, No. 1: 111-117) featured a fascinating and deeply probing interview with Masha by L.J. Hurst. We follow it up here with Paul Flewers' wide-ranging review essay on the book.

Richard Lance Keeble,
University of Lincoln

FRONT COVER

# The Fun of Playing with AI and Orwell's Portrait

## DAVID RYAN

In a recent tweetalong to BBC Four's screening of *Nineteen Eighty-Four* – the Nigel Kneale-scripted TV play from 1954 – a poster on X (formerly Twitter) made a wry comment about the Fiction Department's 'Pornorite' machine. Here, it seemed, was another Orwell prediction come true: that artificial intelligence would eventually write books.

Still, AI has its attractions. By running the portrait from Orwell's National Union of Journalists' card through the Dzine website, for instance, I generated a string of colourful, and sometimes irreverent, variations on that well-known copyright-free image. If nothing else, it's given this magazine an eye-catching cover.

Unlike other AI platforms I could mention, Dzine (pronounced 'design') boasts an image-to-image function that transforms photographs into a variety of preprogrammed styles, from Cartoon Anime to Apocalyptic Horror. Crucially, it retains the pictures' structure and faces.

For all I know, this innovation may be a short-lived novelty. Having said that, I do like the fresh perspective that these revamped images of Orwell offer us. Goodness knows, there are precious few photographs of the man in existence. If technology can bring us new variations of these – with colour in his cheeks, or the illusion of a modern studio setting – then I'm all for it.

It's not perfect, of course. Many of the images I generated showed Orwell's eyes as brown, when in fact they were a steely blue. If only I were more tech-savvy, I may have used a prompt to achieve better results (or changed the colour afterwards in Photoshop).

I've also played around with Dzine's image-to-video option, which produces fake clips lasting five or ten seconds. I've used it on family photos, to eerie effect, and would feed it pictures of Orwell if it were not for the Orwellian overtones.

*David Ryan is the author of* George Orwell on Screen: Adaptations, Documentaries and Docudramas on Film and Television

PAPER

# The significance of Goldstein in *Nineteen Eighty-Four*

## G. ALEXANDER DENNING

*This paper investigates the importance of Emmanuel Goldstein to the plot of George Orwell's* Nineteen Eighty-Four. *It specifically addresses the influences of Leon Trotsky and James Burnham on the teachings of Goldstein, with particular interest in where they differ. It confines itself primarily to the text of the novel, referring to Orwell's other writings where they enhance the meaning behind what became his last and greatest work. The paper also examines where Orwell's views differ from the teachings of his fictional character, particularly regarding his hope that the Marxist revolution would bring about a free and just society. The conclusion focuses on Orwell's struggle to reconcile hope with the uncertainties which he believed were facing a post-war world caught in the grip of a totalitarian nightmare.*

Key words: Orwell, *Nineteen Eighty-Four*, Goldstein, Trotsky, Burnham

## ORWELL'S USE OF FICTION

*Nineteen Eighty-Four* does not directly refer to historical characters (e.g. Marx, Engels, Lenin, Trotsky, Stalin, Hitler, Churchill) nor to historical events (e.g. the Russian Revolution, both world wars, the nuclear bombing of Hiroshima, the Cold War) of Orwell's time. And there is no direct reference to James Burnham's *The Managerial Revolution*, to Leon Trotsky's *The Revolution Betrayed* nor to *The Communist Manifesto*, of Karl Marx and Friedrich Engels. This was probably done so that he could more easily critique the communist and socialist agendas vying for control in post-war Europe without being accused of betraying the socialist cause.[1] He was outraged by the way journalists (represented by Winston Smith whose job is to re-write history in the records department at the Ministry of Truth) and the British intelligentsia (represented by the philologist Syme, a specialist in Newspeak, whose job involves the destruction of language) had developed what he called 'a nationalistic loyalty towards the USSR' and were 'dishonestly uncritical of its policies'

(*CWGO* XVI: 365). Edward Crankshaw says that his argument 'was not with Communism, which was self-evidently a disaster, but with the left-wing intellectuals who rushed to be deceived by it' (1971: 119).[2] Alok Rai makes the important point that the Goldstein interpolations are necessary 'in order to say what the novelist wishes his novel to say but cannot by the same token allow it to say' (1988: 116), because of the requirement for Winston Smith to be, what Crankshaw calls, the 'recalcitrant protagonist' (1971: 119). Rai argues that Orwell 'invents the language of Goldstein – different alike from Newspeak and from the language of the novel – as a means ... whereby Winston (and we) can gain a critical perspective on the oppressive society' (1988: 133). In these ways, it can be said that Orwell found fiction an effective medium through which to express his political views.

ARE GOLDSTEIN AND HIS BOOK REAL?

The first mention of Emmanuel Goldstein is telling. We are told he is:

> ... the Enemy of the People ... the renegade and backslider who once ... had been one of the leading figures of the Party, almost on a level with Big Brother himself, and then had engaged in counter-revolutionary activities, had been condemned to death and had mysteriously escaped and disappeared ... He was the primal traitor, the earliest defiler of the Party's purity. All subsequent crimes against the Party, all treacheries, acts of sabotage, heresies, deviations, sprang directly out of his teaching. Somewhere or other he was still alive and hatching his conspiracies ... (Orwell 1989 [1949]: 13-14).

The Party depicts him as 'the commander of a vast shadowy army, an underground network of conspirators which it calls "the Brotherhood" dedicated to the overthrow of the State' (ibid: 15). However, Winston thinks that even 'a child' could see through the propaganda (ibid: 14), and that he is the 'sole guardian of truth and sanity in a world of lies' (ibid: 16-17). O'Brien refers to him in his apartment as 'our Leader' (ibid: 178), and when Winston asks him if he exists, he replies: 'Yes, there is such a person, and he is alive. Where, I do not know' (ibid: 179). When asked whether the secret Brotherhood exists, he is adamant: 'You will never learn much more about the Brotherhood than that it exists and that you belong to it' (ibid). In his apartment, O'Brien says that the book is 'indestructible' and could be reproduced 'word for word' if required (ibid: 185). When it is successfully smuggled into Winston's possession, we are told it is 'a heavy black volume, amateurishly bound, with no name or title on the cover. The print also looked slightly irregular. The pages were worn at the edges, and fell apart easily, as though the book had passed through many hands' (ibid: 191).

However, during the torture sessions O'Brien throws doubt on the Brotherhood, describing its existence as 'an unsolved riddle' in Winston's mind (ibid: 272). He also denigrates the authenticity of the book by admitting to 'collaborating' in its writing (ibid: 274). Goldstein, he argues, will live forever because he is simply a political invention to focus hatred against the heretic (ibid: 281). Alok Rai concludes that when Goldstein and his book are finally revealed to be an invention of the state, the novel becomes 'consumed in the effulgence of its perfection' (1988: 117), leaving Winston with no escape from the nightmare which imprisons him (ibid: 133). Similarly, Philip Bounds argues that Orwell uses the figure of Goldstein and his secret Brotherhood to illustrate how 'dictatorships can only survive by greatly exaggerating their vulnerability', which they do by creating the impression 'that the state is under imminent threat of being overthrown, either by external conquest or internal uprising' (2009: 149). Consequently, it is tempting to conclude that these fictional creations of the Party become the ultimate irony of the novel.

This somewhat cynical conclusion does not explain certain key aspects of the plot. Firstly, there is the sabotage scene during the processional parade on the sixth day of Hate Week (Orwell 1989 [1949]: 187-189), which has all the hallmarks of an unexpected event that catches the speaker by surprise and is beyond the power of the Party to stop. Secondly, the idea that the Goldstein book is a forged document of the Party does not fit the description of the well-worn book that Winston receives, which is more like the underground publication which O'Brien spoke of in his apartment (see above). Thirdly, the meticulous planning required for Winston to be given his copy (see ibid: 184-189) seems unnecessarily complicated for an all-powerful regime to have to orchestrate. More importantly, it cannot explain the apparent defeat of the Party by '2050' (ibid: 312) unless there was an actual underground movement.[3]

THE INFLUENCE OF TROTSKY ON THE CHARACTER OF GOLDSTEIN

The first description of Goldstein highlights his Jewishness:[4]

> It was a lean Jewish face, with a great fuzzy aureole of white hair and a small goatee beard – a clever face, and yet somehow inherently despicable, with a kind of senile silliness in the long thin nose near the end of which a pair of spectacles was perched. It resembled the face of a sheep, and the voice, too, had a sheeplike quality (ibid: 14).

The most likely influence on the character of Goldstein is Leon Trotsky (born Lev Davidovich Bronstein). Tosco Fyvel recalled how

Orwell told him that he gave the Jewish name to the rebel Goldstein as a reference to Trotsky because he thought 'the most likely man to stage a hopeless last revolt against a possible totalitarian regime would be some Jewish intellectual' (quoted by Tim Crook in Keeble 2021: 249). But the actual name was probably taken from a poem Orwell included in an 'As I Please' column of 1944, which ends: 'The first American son-of-a-bitch to get four new tyres from the Ration Board was Abe Goldstein' (ibid). However, Ian Bloom, in his essay, 'The ever-present antisemitism of George Orwell' (2023), cautions that Orwell never satisfactorily resolved the Jewish question. While he distinguished antisemitism from anti-Zionism, he 'never explained the distinction with his normal moral clarity'. Bloom says that Tosco Fyvel became his 'Jewish conscience' in enabling him to 're-examine his antisemitism', though in the end Orwell combined 'ignorance with insight.[5]

According to Janice Ho, Goldstein's Jewishness acts as 'the scapegoat upon which all the threats of Oceania are concentrated and displaced' (2020: 145). She cites the 1945 essay by Orwell, 'Antisemitism in Britain', which links anti-Jewish discrimination with the increasing extremes of nationalism (ibid: 143-144)[6]. However, Ho fails to mention that Goldstein, having declared that there is no racial discrimination in Oceania, ironically proceeds to outline a far more pervasive form of discrimination based not on 'blood-ties' and 'hereditary' but, rather, a form of regimental citizenship which he calls 'adherence to a common doctrine' (Orwell 1989 [1949]: 217) which discriminates against both Jew and Gentile.[7]

Trotsky and Goldstein also share a similar political destiny. Goldstein is heard crying hysterically during the Two Minutes Hate session that, '*the revolution had been betrayed*' (ibid: 14, italics inserted), which is a clear reference to Trotsky's seminal work, *The Revolution Betrayed* (1936). There is also the reference to Goldstein having been 'one of the leading figures of the Party, almost on a level with Big Brother himself' (ibid: 13), which corresponds to the power struggle which erupted between Trotsky and Stalin upon Lenin's death in January 1924. According to Erika Gottlieb, the ritualistic Two Minutes Hate sessions in *Nineteen Eighty-Four* parallel the demonisation of Trotsky by Stalin (1992: 107). Significantly, the novel notes that by 1970 Goldstein 'had fled and was hiding no one knew where', while many of his followers 'had been executed after spectacular public trials at which they made confessions of their crimes' (Orwell 1989 [1949]: 78). Allowing for the projection of the novel into 1984, this would correspond to Stalin's spectacular show trials of 1936-1938 which ended in Trotsky's exile in Mexico where he was assassinated in August 1940.

G. ALEXANDER DENNING

Dorian Lynskey reminds us that Orwell, in *Animal Farm* (1945), had already developed elements of the Goldstein character in his portrayal of Snowball, who serves to represent Trotsky and 'a younger version of the "sinister enchanter" Goldstein' (2019: 138). However, Gordon Bowker quotes Orwell's essay 'Catastrophic gradualism' (*CWGO* XVII: 342-345) in which he writes critically of Trotsky: '… all the seeds of evil were from the start and … things would not have been substantially different if Lenin or Trotsky had remained in control' (2004 [2003]: 316).

## INFLUENCES ON THE TEACHINGS OF GOLDSTEIN

Before analysing the Goldstein book, it is important to realise that Winston appears never to read all of it. He reads Chapters 1 and 3 but none of Chapter 2. In fact, we are not sure if he reads all the first and last chapters, or that there are only three chapters (though the book follows the three slogans of the Party).[8] Significantly, O'Brien says during the torture scenes: 'You have read *the book*, Goldstein's book, *or parts of it*, at least' (Orwell 1989 [1949]: 274, italics inserted). This may simply be the result of his eagerness to obtain a copy, which may also explain why he begins the first chapter twice (ibid: 192 and 209). Then again, he may simply have dropped off to sleep (ibid: 226) and is arrested before he can finish the book (ibid: 230). Of greater perplexity is why Orwell should withhold from the reader parts of a document which clearly form part of his own critique of totalitarianism – unless Chapter 2 is contained elsewhere in the novel (see below).

## THE INFLUENCE OF MARX AND ENGELS

Even though little has been written about the influence of *The Communist Manifesto*, by Marx and Engels, on the Goldstein book, its significance should not be overlooked, if only for its importance in the development of the socialist movement in the second half of the nineteenth century, which led to the revolutionary period in the first half of the twentieth century of which Orwell was writing. Bowker states that Orwell regarded the *Manifesto* as 'a powerful and elegant piece of rhetorical prose' (2004 [2003]: 101). Of significance is his observation: '*Nineteen Eighty-Four* was completed in the hundredth anniversary year of the publication of *The Communist Manifesto*. (Had Orwell finished it the previous February, as originally intended, it would have been the hundredth anniversary month!)' (ibid: 383).

Though the Goldstein Book is not based on the *Manifesto*, it does refer to the revolutionary stirrings of the second half of the nineteenth century as 'Socialism' (Orwell 1989 [1949]: 211), by which it means the communist movement. Further, the *Manifesto* describes the struggle between the bourgeois (the benefactors of the new industrial economy) and the proletarians (the workers who must sell their labour for the wealth to be created), singling out a middle group of 'petty bourgeoisie' (1999 [1848]: 65-77). This approximates to Goldstein's three divisions of High, Middle and Low which have fought for supremacy throughout history (Orwell 1989 [1949]: 210).

The two documents differ in their perception of how the struggle will end. The *Manifesto* builds the case for how the proletariat became a political force for the overthrow of their oppressors, ending with a clarion call to international action: 'The proletarians have nothing to lose but their chains. They have a world to win. Proletarians of all countries, unite!' (1999 [1848]: 96). In contrast, and in the wake of two world wars and various failed attempts to set up a communist system, Goldstein builds a case for why this utopian vision is not achievable. He ends with anything but a clarion call to action. It is more like a permanent truce between the three warring super-states: 'A peace that was truly permanent,' says Goldstein, 'would be the same as a permanent war' (Orwell 1989 [1949]: 208).

## THE INFLUENCE OF TROTSKY

The Goldstein book is titled *The Theory and Practice of Oligarchical Collectivism* (ibid: 191) and is referred to in the novel simply as *'the book'* (ibid: 184, italics in original).[9] According to Goldstein, 'the only secure basis for oligarchy is collectivism' (ibid: 214), which recalls the notion of 'bureaucratic collectivism' first advanced by Trotsky in his seminal work *The Revolution Betrayed* (1936). His argument is summarised in Chapters 1-4: the 'proletarian revolution' was meant to bring about the 'socialisation of the means of production'; the Russian economy was backward compared with the West, especially America; the Russian economy could only be modernised by a regime of bureaucratic managers who could lift the people out of poverty; this bureaucratic group of managers would be transitional and would diminish with time, leaving the socialist state envisaged by Marxism to flourish. Trotsky is critical of the fact that the bureaucracy under Stalin did not give way to Soviet democracy, but caused the Revolution to transform into a 'dictatorship of the bureaucracy' which stifled the freedom of the proletariat. He blames this period of decline on what he calls 'the Soviet Thermidor' which he describes in Chapters 5-9. In Chapters 10-11 he stresses the need for a workers' counter revolution which, unlike the first – which was essentially an attempt to change the economic foundation of society – would be a political attack on what he calls a 'bureaucratic oligarchy' which had 'betrayed the revolution'.

G. ALEXANDER DENNING

Chapter 1 of Goldstein's book ('Ignorance is Strength') traces the emergence of an 'elite aristocracy' of salaried bureaucrats like Trotsky's bureaucratic elite, who openly 'abandoned' (Orwell 1989 [1949]: 211 c.f. Trotsky's 'betrayed') the revolution, leading to the rise of the totalitarian world of Ingsoc in Oceania. This group seized upon the socialist idea of 'collectivism' to wrest the wealth of the people to itself. It could be said that the term 'oligarchical collectivism' is an oxymoron, like the other three slogans of the Party, in that the Marxist sense of collectivism was meant to be ownership of the means of production by the collective group of workers and not an elitist group of rulers.

Despite their agreement that the revolution had been betrayed, Goldstein and Trotsky differ in what effect it has on the population, though the difference is one of emphasis rather than essence. While Trotsky attacks the bureaucracy's impact on the Russian economic and social structure, Goldstein is more concerned with its indoctrination of the people. This does not mean that Goldstein is not interested in the people's economic wellbeing. As Philip Bounds contends, unlike Trotsky, Orwell was not inclined to blame the collapse of the revolution on Stalin's 'inexpert response' but rather saw its fundamental flaw as being its attraction for authoritarian figures to use the absolute control of economic resources to dominate the individual (2009: 140-141). According to Goldstein: 'Political domination can only exist in the midst of widespread poverty' (ibid: 150). Just as Orwell wrote in his 'As I Please' column in *Tribune* on 29 November 1946, 'the desire for pure power seems to be much more dominant than the desire for wealth' (*CWGO* XVIII: 504).

At the core of Goldstein's argument is the belief that the poverty resulting from continuous war robs the people of their power to revolt. It does this in two ways. Firstly, it robs them of an education which would enable them to realise that the privileged minority have no function and can be swept away (Orwell 1989 [1949]: 198). Secondly, it produces fear which causes them to hand over their power to a small group which they misguidedly think will protect them from their enemies (ibid: 199-200). In this way, Goldstein argues that war 'helps to preserve the special *mental* atmosphere that a hierarchical society needs … to keep the structure of society intact' (ibid: 20, italics inserted for emphasis). Goldstein, then, says more about the robbing of the 'mind' than the 'pocket'.

Goldstein and Trotsky also differ in their analysis of the role of the bureaucracy. Goldstein is more interested in the bureaucracy as an 'institution' promoting ideological conformity whereas Trotsky's critique is primarily directed at Stalin. Understandably, Trotsky focuses on the failings of Stalin because he had lived under his rule and had personally fallen out of favour with him. But Goldstein is writing later, when the Party's machine is more entrenched around what might be called the cult of 'ideology' rather than the cult of 'personality'. Goldstein certainly describes Big Brother in almost 'godlike' terms:

> Nobody has ever seen Big Brother … he will never die, and there is considerable uncertainty as to when he was born. Big Brother is the guise in which the Party chooses to exhibit itself to the world … Oceania has no capital, and its titular head is a person whose whereabouts nobody knows … it is not centralised in any way. Its rulers are not held together by blood-ties but by adherence to a common doctrine … membership… is not hereditary (ibid: 216-217).

But what the citizens of Oceania have come to fear is not the presence of a fallible dictator who could be defeated in a revolution, but an infallible authority – described by Bounds as a 'panopticon' (2009: 146) – which Goldstein argues can demand 'complete uniformity of opinion on all subjects' (Orwell 1989 [1949]: 214) and from which there is no way that 'discontent can become articulate' (ibid: 216).

Despite their different criticisms of the bureaucracy, Goldstein agrees with Trotsky that it has betrayed the revolution. Where Trotsky writes: 'The ruling Soviet stratum has learned to fear the masses with a perfectly bourgeois fear' (2015 [1936]: 194), Goldstein stresses: 'The Party rejects and vilifies every principle for which the Socialist movement originally stood, and it chooses to do this in the name of Socialism' (Orwell 1989 [1949]: 225). Far from supporting the subject of its title (*The Theory and Practice of Oligarchical Collectivism*), the Goldstein book appears to be its chief critic.

## THE INFLUENCE OF BURNHAM

Though James Burnham may have originated the term 'managerial revolution', his theory was greatly dependent on the criticisms which Leon Trotsky (his mentor) levelled against the bureaucratisation of the state under Stalin. They both agreed that a bureaucratic/managerial style of government was needed to direct an emerging technological economy. Burnham argued that just as the workers in a socialist state had lost their power because they were not able to run a more sophisticated economy (2021 [1941]: 65-69), the leaders of the capitalist society – especially the youth – had lost heart in those ideologies which were not able to solve the economic and social problems of the inter-war period (ibid: 26-33). Neither side anticipated, he said, the rise of a middle class of salaried, executive-styled bureaucrats who were neither 'capitalist' nor 'workers' (ibid: 45-46). Though drawn initially from 'private enterprise', gradually they had been taken over by government departments which had, in turn, been taken over by what he called the 'executive branch of government' so that sovereignty had moved from parliament to 'administrative bureaus' (ibid: 138-140).[10] In effect, Burnham argued that both capitalists and the proletariat had forfeited individual property rights and ownership of the means of production to this governmental class of managers, so that neither capitalism nor socialism would survive, but would be replaced by the managerial society.

The influence of Burnham is primarily seen in Chapter 3 ('War is Peace') of Goldstein's book where he describes a world divided into 'three super-states'[11] in which none 'could be definitely conquered even by the other two in combination' (Orwell 1989 [1949]: 194). This is similar to Burnham's description of a world split into *'three primary super-states'* (2021 [1941]: 163, italics in original) of which 'it does not seem possible for any one of these to conquer the others; and even two of them in coalition could not win a decisive and lasting victory over the third' (ibid: 166).

However, when Burnham speaks of the 'struggle for power' (ibid: 65), he is thinking beyond the military struggle of World War Two to the economic struggle which would follow. This economic struggle would be fought over what he called, 'state ownership of the major instruments of production', whereby the state would become the 'property' of the managers (ibid: 66). This, he argues, would bring about an economic transformation because state-owned economies were not handicapped by the profit incentive of capitalism (ibid: 102-127). He cites the managerial model of nazi Germany and Stalinist Russia as examples of such countries which were better able to use the production of armaments to turn around their economies (ibid: 121-124). The war effort, in other words, was more a business opportunity for making an economy more competitive in the post-war world. 'If it were really true,' he wrote, 'that the Nazi economy were solely an "armament economy", no one in the United States would be so worried, as all serious economists are worried, about Nazi *economic* competition *after* the war' (ibid: 123, italics in original). In this way, Burnham saw war as the catalyst for the world to split into three economic regions where conflict would be more about trading with one's enemy than seeking to annihilate them.

Although Burnham wants to believe that the 'dictatorial phase' of managerialism will enter a less dangerous 'democratic phase' (ibid: 159), he concedes that violence may be necessary because a managerial society was inevitable (ibid: 255). Alternatively, Hannah Arendt (a contemporary of both Burnham and Orwell) argues that 'violence' should not be used as 'the accelerator of economic development' (1970 [2023]: 6).[12] Similarly (as argued above),

Goldstein states that there is no economic advantage from war when it leads to psychological deprivation:

> War ... not only accomplishes the necessary destruction, but accomplishes it in a *psychologically acceptable* way. In principle it would be quite simple to waste the surplus labour of the world by building temples and pyramids, by digging holes and filling them up again, or even by producing vast quantities of goods and then setting fire to them. But this would only provide the *economic* and not the *emotional* basis for a hierarchical society (Orwell 1989 [1949]: 200, italics inserted for emphasis).

It is on the issue of the political abuse of power where Goldstein differs markedly from Burnham. Burnham was an advocate of Machiavelli (1469-1527), who theorised that politics could be reduced to the pursuit of power and that the end justifies the means.[13] This is why Burnham was quick to link war with economic growth. But unlike Machiavelli's interest in the power of political leaders (which he develops in *The Machiavellians*), Burnham is more interested in the power of technocrats (those who control the means of production) which he sees in Stalinist communism, nazi fascism and the New Dealism of the USA (2021 [1941]: 182). Orwell accuses him in his 1946 essay, 'Second thoughts on James Burnham' (*CWGO* XVIII: 268-284), for the journal, *Polemic*, of being 'fascinated by the spectacle of power' and of having a 'fascinated admiration' for Stalin and his atrocities against his own people. This he attributes to his Americanism: that being a great power, America was not as intimidated as the British by the totalitarianism of Russia and Germany because America would always survive.[14] In the same essay, Orwell places Burnham in the camp of the intelligentsia, who also worship power and who see in the Russian regime, 'a system which eliminates the upper class, keeps the working class in its place, and hands unlimited power to people very similar to themselves' (ibid: 282). Orwell proceeds to criticise Burnham for never asking the question: 'why do people want power', but he makes sure that O'Brien puts the question to Winston (see below), and in the dialogue which follows, Winston is given a shocking insight into how the Party is able to hold on to its power.

## GOLDSTEIN AND THE DYNAMICS OF POWER

The last words Winston reads from the Goldstein book are '*why should human equality be averted? ... Here we reach the central secret ... the mystique of the Party ... that first led to the seizure of power ... This motive really consists ...*' (Orwell 1989 [1949]: 225-226, italics in original). And here Winston stops reading as his attention turns to the sleeping Julia. The narrator confides: 'He had still … not learned the ultimate secret. He understood *how*; he did not understand *why*. Chapter I, like Chapter III, had not actually told him anything that he did not know' (ibid: 226, italics in original). Presumably, if he had continued and had read the second chapter, Goldstein would have given him the answer to *why* the Party seeks power. While undergoing torture, O'Brien reminds Winston he had written these very words in his diary: 'I understand *how*: I do not understand *why*' (ibid: 274, italics in original), before telling him: 'You understand well enough *how* the Party maintains itself in power. Now tell me *why* we cling to power …' (ibid: 274, italics in original). This duplication of the words 'how' and 'why' by O'Brien and Goldstein (and their repetition in Winston's diary) forms the conduit to understanding the missing chapter in the Goldstein book. This is confirmed when O'Brien raises the title of the second chapter to begin his diatribe on the meaning of power: 'You know the Party slogan: "Freedom is Slavery"' (ibid: 277, repeated 290).

In effect, what follows is a summary of the missing second chapter. Its content forms the 'understanding' part of the three stages of what O'Brien refers to as Winston's 're-integration' (ibid: 273). The first is 'learning', which is contained in the initial stage of his torture when he learns that reality and truth are what the Party decreed (ibid: 261). This second stage of 'understanding' relates to what could be called the 'dynamics of power'. It is summarised in O'Brien's answer to his own question: 'we are interested solely in power. … Power is not a means, it is an end … The object of power is power' (ibid: 275-276). O'Brien isolates two aspects to this power. Firstly, that it is 'collective' (ibid: 276). This is not an accidental use of the word considering its context in a passage about the corrupting effect of a collective group of oligarchs. As O'Brien explains:

> The individual only has power in so far as he ceases to be an individual. You know the Party slogan: 'Freedom is Slavery.' Has it ever occurred to you that it is reversible? Slavery is freedom … if [the human being] can make complete, utter submission, if he can escape from his identity, if he can merge himself in the Party so that he *is* the Party, then he is all-powerful and immortal (ibid: 276-277, italics in original).

Erika Gottlieb describes this transformation as the 'private self' being enslaved by the 'collective self' (1992: 80) to produce what she calls 'collective insanity' (ibid: 81), or 'collective immortality' (ibid: 95). In other words, the individual is trapped into believing they are most powerful when they are at their weakest, having relinquished their individual consciousness to the Party mindset.

And Hannah Arendt cautions that bureaucratic power is the most formidable form of dominion in that no-one is held responsible because it is never the property of an individual (1970 [2023]: 32, 37).

The second aspect to the Party's use of power is that it is 'over the mind' (Orwell 1989 [1949]: 277) – what is commonly called 'mind control' – and it is only achievable through the pain of suffering: 'If you want a picture of the future,' says O'Brien, 'imagine a boot stamping on a human face – for ever' (ibid: 280).

But there is a third aspect to the Party's use of power. It is never directly stated in the text but is cleverly inferred in the torture scenes. Thus, Winston experiences this knowledge 'existentially' and not 'intellectually' through reading Goldstein's book or listening to O'Brien's pontifications. This third aspect to the Party's use of power could be called 'incarnational'[15] in that its ultimate source lies in the ability to convince the individual to find (surrender) their identity (their humanity) in the Party. Inevitably, this is played out in Room 101 when Winston relinquishes his love for Julia – what might be called, his love for 'the other': 'Do it to Julia! Not me! Julia!' (ibid: 300) – and finally in the Chestnut Tree café where he relinquishes his love for 'the self': 'He loved Big Brother' (ibid: 311). This is tantamount to a denial of that 'spirit of Man' which was his final defence before O'Brien: (ibid: 282).

Of course, Winston had always known that 'to die hating them' was the ultimate 'freedom' (ibid: 294) and, hence, the ultimate power over the Party. The fact that he fails is not the point, because others will come – and others did come according to the Appendix (see below) who did not fail.

## GOLDSTEIN AND THE FUTURE OF TYRANNY

Goldstein differs from Trotsky and Burnham in his prognosis for the socialist movement. Trotsky believed that the bureaucratic apparatus of the state 'begins to die away the first day of the proletarian dictatorship' (2015 [1936]: 35) and riled against it for not doing so. A second revolution was needed to rid the Soviet regime of the extremes of Stalinism. Unlike the first, which was an attempt to change the economic foundation of society, the second would be a 'political' attack on 'bureaucratic oligarchy'. It would be 'international' in the spirit of Marxism and a more 'permanent' and 'democratic' form of socialism to that of Stalinist totalitarianism (ibid: 204-208).

Unlike Trotsky, Burnham did not believe that socialism and capitalism were the sole alternatives. 'Russia's motion,' he writes, 'has been toward neither capitalism nor socialism, but toward *managerial society*' (2021 [1941]: 44, italics in original). Again, in

**G. ALEXANDER DENNING**

his essay 'Second thoughts on James Burnham', Orwell agrees with Burnham that socialism (as defined by Marxism) is 'not going to come'; that capitalism is 'doomed'. But he does not believe that managerialism will be their automatic replacement, principally because it relies upon the idea that:

> ... certain rules of conduct have to be observed if humanity is to hold together at all ... The huge, invisible, everlasting slave empire of which Burnham appears to dream will not be established, or if established, will not endure, because slavery is no longer a stable basis for human society (*CWGO* XVIII: 283).

Bernard Crick says that Orwell 'parodies' Burnham's idea that the two great ideologies of the super-powers would one day 'converge' with the 'commissars and congressmen' being taken over by 'technocrats' (2007: 155).

It is not surprising that Goldstein sees no future in either Trotsky's return to a purified socialist revolution, or Burnham's faith in a new style of managerial revolution, even though the Goldstein book takes its title from Burnham's work. The question is whether Goldstein sees an end to the tyranny of Big Brother. It might be assumed that he does. The narrator tells us this is what Winston concludes: 'If there was hope, it lay in the proles! Without having read to the end of *the book*, he knew that that must be Goldstein's final message' (Orwell 1989 [1949]: 229, italics in original). But the sections which Winston reads say nothing about hope nor how the Party can be overthrown. The problem is exacerbated by O'Brien's earlier words when he promised Winston a copy of the book: 'you will learn the true nature of the society we live in, and the strategy by which we shall destroy it' (ibid: 181-182). Yet contextually, one would expect Goldstein's book to imply a way to defeat the Party, otherwise there would be no reason for the secret Brotherhood to exist.

This problem is resolved if the secret to the Party's defeat – its 'weakest link' – is the subject of the missing chapter. But for this to be the case, it must be inferred. In other words, O'Brien inadvertently divulges the Party's weakness in what he says about its use of power.[16] Which is this: the only way to defeat the Party is to resist the urge (even under great suffering) to define one's identity (one's humanity) by one's allegiance to the Party. By reconstructing the missing chapter in this way, it is possible to argue that Goldstein does see an end to the Party's tyranny.

Goldstein is primarily concerned with the Party's indoctrination of its people and shows little concern for its effect on their standard of living (as argued above), other than to show that they are left alone because they pose no revolutionary threat. By contrast, Orwell dwells at length on the economic plight of the working-class. In an 'As I Please' column in *Tribune* on 14 January 1944, he criticises the managerial class's 'contempt for the common man' (*CWGO* XVI: 61). Philip Bounds reminds us that Orwell was concerned about the 'totalitarian perversions' to which socialism was susceptible (2009: 1), arguing that the system which replaced it would not be socialism, but 'an extreme form of Stalinism' (ibid: 27). Orwell, he says, believed that socialism often attracted people with dictatorial ambitions. He writes: 'By equating social justice with state ownership of the means of production, it naturally appeals to doctrinaire intellectuals who recognise that one of the surest ways of dominating the individual is to establish absolute control of his economic resources' (ibid: 140).[17]

Similarly, while Goldstein gives no alternative to a world stuck in an endless war which no-one can win, Orwell, as Glenn Burgess comments, was hopeful that the patriotism inspired by the war would create an opportunity for a genuine mass movement in favour of socialism (2023: 81).[18] He also reminds us that while Orwell was writing *Nineteen Eighty-Four*, he became an advocate for a broader-based 'Socialist United States of Europe' (ibid: 241). Similarly, Hannah Arendt argues that violence and power are antithetical: that violence destroys power and can never produce it (2023 [1970]: 46). She writes: 'Terror is not the same as violence; it is, rather, the form of government that comes into being when violence, having destroyed all power, does not abdicate but, on the contrary, remains in full control' (ibid: 47). This is the world of Big Brother that Orwell warns could be our future.

Alok Rai maintains that Orwell 'wrestles with the crisis at the heart of twentieth-century liberalism itself' (1988: 1); that at the end of his career there was still an 'unfinished radicalism' (ibid: 164).[19] This struggle is particularly evident in Orwell's criticism of Burnham in 'Second thoughts on James Burnham', where he says his thesis is at face value 'extremely plausible' since the USSR 'is not Socialist' and capitalism is 'obviously doomed'. For Orwell, the question is whether the system which replaces them will have an oligarchical power base or whether it will be what he calls 'true democracy'.

It could be argued that Goldstein represents the sensible intellectual, as opposed to those members of the intelligentsia whom Orwell despised.[20] But it is not enough to have intellectual

G. ALEXANDER DENNING

sensibility. Enter, Winston Smith – whom we might call 'Goldstein with a heart' – the fallible anti-hero, courageous enough to defy the Party, but unable to maintain his rage to the end. He could well be more representative of a troubled Orwell, lying on his sickbed, trying to make sense of the 'cold war' era.[21] The difficulty for Orwell was two-fold. Firstly, as Crick argues, how to reconcile the typically socialist mould of seeing the proles as an instrument for revolutionary change when they are too debased to do anything about it (2007: 153). But a second and more profound problem is what this debased condition of working people says about Orwell's belief in the common decency of man and the need for democratic socialism to deliver a free and just society. As he writes in 'Second thoughts on James Burnham': '… the question is whether capitalism, now obviously doomed, is to give way to oligarchy or to true democracy' (*CWGO* XVIII: 272). Until the end of his life, Bounds concludes, Orwell believed that totalitarianism could still be averted by the action of libertarian socialists in the spirit of what he called, 'international communism' (2009: 28).

GOLDSTEIN AND THE APPENDIX[22]

Although Goldstein is not mentioned in the Appendix 'The principles of Newspeak' (Orwell 1989 [1949]: 312-325), its importance for understanding his role in the novel should not be underestimated. Margaret Atwood draws attention to the fact that the essay at the end of the novel 'is written in standard English, in the third person, and in the past tense, which can only mean that the regime has fallen' (2005: Chapter 41). There is also the fact that Winston Smith's name (Orwell 1989 [1949]: 320) and the year 1984 which he wrote in his diary (ibid: 9) and which is repeated in the Appendix (ibid: 312, 323), are remembered some sixty or so years after all trace of him should have been erased. This provides strong evidence that O'Brien, who was the only person who knew of the diary's existence, is not 'an agent provocateur' (as D.J. Taylor argues [2003: 403]), but is an actual member of an active secret Brotherhood led by Goldstein.[23]

Glenn Burgess disagrees that there is any evidence that the regime had fallen, postulating that the Appendix may have been written after 2050 'by Oceania's scholars, or by those of its perfected successor regime, looking back on how the final obliteration of all heterodoxy had been achieved, and with the confidence to write in an Oldspeak now no more threatening than ancient Greek' (2023: 255). Patrick Homes takes a middle ground, suggesting that Goldstein and his book function as 'cultural zones' of rebellion which make one 'feel rebellious when true rebellion is impossible', and that similarly, Winston's actions are 'mere dissidence, and not rebellion'.[24]

Orwell uses the Appendix as a literary device for altering the time frame of the story. Suddenly, the reader is transported into the future. The year is 'about the year 2050' (Orwell 1989 [1949]: 312, see also 326), when the Party had predicted that Newspeak would have superseded Oldspeak (ibid: 54, 55, 56). But this has not happened, as is indicated by the difficulty it has had in eliminating the literary works of Shakespeare etc., and the American Declaration of Independence (ibid: 325). The reader can now see that Goldstein's criticisms of oligarchical collectivism have been vindicated, even though there is no evidence that his resistance movement was confident that the regime would be defeated. However, given the context of the story (and we can only argue from what Orwell has provided), there is every reason to believe that Goldstein and his teachings formed the basis of the revolutionary groundswell (of which Winston – if not O'Brien himself – were a part) which must have led to the downfall of Big Brother.

## CONCLUDING REMARKS

We, the modern readers, live in the world which Orwell anticipated in the Appendix. It is our generation that can assess whether he was right in his condemnation of totalitarianism. Without the figure of Goldstein and his movement, Winston Smith would have been just another voice crying in the wilderness, with no guarantee of being heard. But through the literary construct of Goldstein and his book, Orwell was better able to deconstruct the way power works in a totalitarian system to control its citizens. He could have used the narrator's voice to achieve this end – like a journalistic report or an academic lecture – but this would have been less engaging than his choice to use the more dramatic voices of fictional characters to tell the tale of how victory over oppression was finally won, even though we never get to meet Goldstein in person.

Despite the wretchedness of life under Big Brother (as symbolised in Mrs Parson's blocked drain) and the endless war and the distortion of truth and the watchful eye of the Party, the novel speaks of hope. For there are still people like Goldstein – the 'unsung hero' of the story – who 'dare to be a Daniel'[25] and can lead a movement which will allow the spirit of Man to flourish again. Ironically, Orwell's message – like Winston's diary which was written 'For the future, for the unborn' (ibid: 9) – is that the collective voice of the majority will overcome the oppressive power of the minority. Not only is Orwell warning future generations of the dangers of authoritarianism, but he is also sharing with us his vision that man will prevail against those forces which seek to suppress him.

## NOTES

[1] John Newsinger writes that Orwell has been unfairly criticised by those on the left who hijacked his anti-Stalinist stance as an attack on socialism which was never his intention (2018: 136-139); Philip Bounds makes a similar point that Orwell was often critical of his own side of politics, and was especially indebted to people on the left to whom he was most opposed politically (2009: 2)

[2] See also Keeble, Richard Lance (2020: 8-9); Gottlieb, Erika (1992: 50-51)

[3] See discussion of the Appendix below

[4] For a summary of Orwell and antisemitism, see Tim Crook's essay (2021: 243-258)

[5] John Newsinger argues that Orwell was more concerned with Stalinist tyranny than with nazism because of his experience in Spain (2007: 123-124)

[6] See also Orwell's 'Notes on nationalism' (1945) where he distinguishes between the dangers of nationalism when compared to patriotism, blaming nationalism for the use of scapegoating and Hitler's death camps. Alternatively, he argues, patriotism provides a form of inoculation against such nationalistic extremes. See also Tim Crook's reference to Melvyn New's description of Winston Smith who, like a Jew, is condemned to live as a victim in a totalitarian state which is portrayed as a concentration camp designed to destroy its citizens (2021: 249)

[7] Dorian Lynskey also misses this point with his comment: 'Goldstein's book insists that there is no racial discrimination in Oceania because the Party is united by ideology, not blood' (2019: 133)

[8] Interestingly, Glenn Burgess refers to the Goldstein book but fails to explain why he only cites two of the three slogans of the Party, omitting the slogan 'Freedom is Slavery' (see 2023: 248)

[9] Scholars tend to refer to it as 'The book within the book', with Gottlieb identifying six in all within the novel (1992: 282)

[10] Burnham highlighted the part played by Roosevelt's 'technocracy' or 'New Dealism', and argued that the US's involvement in the war would hasten its managerial development (2021 [1941]: 181, 255)

[11] Alok Rai identifies a fourth region which Goldstein calls a 'rough quadrilateral' of 'cheap labour', which he calls 'slaves', over which the superpowers are 'constantly struggling' (1988: 164)

[12] One wonders if Arendt had Orwell's words in mind ('war is peace') when she wrote: 'Peace is the continuation of war by other means' (2023 [1970]: 7)

[13] See his two main works: *The Prince* and *Discourses on Livy*, both published posthumously

[14] Alok Rai argues that Orwell was also critical of American capitalist consumerism and the deteriorating conditions in post-war London, both of which made them vulnerable to totalitarianism (1988: 119-122).

[15] A theological term based on the saying of Jesus: 'I and the Father are one' (John 10: 30)

[16] I have argued in a previous essay, O'Brien in *Nineteen Eighty-Four:* A new interpretation (2021]) that O'Brien is a genuine member of the secret Brotherhood; that because the telescreen cannot be turned off in the Ministry of Love as it was in his apartment, he must equivocate when he criticises the Party

[17] See also Philip Bounds's essay (2015) on the importance of Orwell's *Road to Wigan Pier* for the development of post-war socialism in Britain

[18] Burgess identifies Orwell's *Lion and the Unicorn: Socialism and the English Genius* as an important source for the development of his socialist views

[19] In light of the Appendix (as this paper has argued), caution should be used when Alok Rai concludes that at the end of Orwell's life there was a 'final despair' (1988: 164)

[20] Of particular interest is Orwell's 'Notes on nationalism', where he criticises the English intelligentsia for not seeing through the lies of the socialist movement as perpetrated particularly by Stalin

[21] Orwell coined this phrase in 'You and the atom bomb', *Tribune*, 19 October 1945. Bernard Crick reminds us that *Nineteen Eighty-Four* was not Orwell's 'last will and testament'; neither was it 'a repudiation of his democratic socialism' nor 'a culminating work' (2007: 146, especially 158 endnote 1)

[22] Gottlieb argues (1992: 279) the Appendix is the third book in a trilogy: the betrayal of the Revolution (*Animal Farm*); the aftermath of the betrayed Revolution (*Nineteen Eighty-Four*); and the total elimination of free thinking (Newspeak, 2050)

[23] I argue this in 'O'Brien in *Nineteen Eighty-Four:* A new interpretation' (2021: 62-75)

[24] See his review (2024) of Mark Fisher's book *Capitalist Realism: Is There No Alternative?* (2008)

[25] The phrase is taken from a verse Orwell included in his essay 'The prevention of literature' (1946)

## REFERENCES

Arendt, Hannah (2023 [1970]) *On Violence*, London: Penguin Random House

Atwood, Margaret (2005) *Curious Pursuits: Occasional Writing*, London: Virago

Bloom, Ian (2023) The ever-present antisemitism of George Orwell, *Jewish Chronicle*, 22 June. Available online at https://www.thejc.com/lets-talk/the-ever-present-antisemitism-of-george-orwell-mk2pu7e9

Bounds, Philip (2009) *Orwell & Marxism: The Political and Cultural Thinking of George Orwell*, London: Bloomsbury

Bounds, Philip (2015) Sectarians on Wigan Pier: George Orwell and the anti-austerity left in Britain, Keeble, Richard Lance (ed.) *George Orwell Now!*, New York: Peter Lang Publishing, Inc pp 129-144

Bowker, Gordon (2040 [2003]) *George Orwell*, London: Abacus

Burgess, Glenn (2023) *George Orwell's Perverse Humanity*, New York: Bloomsbury Academic

Burnham, James (2021 [1941]) *The Managerial Revolution: What is Happening in the World*, London: Lume Books

Crankshaw, Edward (1971) Orwell and communism, Gross, Miriam (ed.) *The World of George Orwell*, New York: Simon and Schuster

Crick, Bernard (2007) *Nineteen Eighty-Four*: Context and controversy, Rodden, John (ed.) *The Cambridge Companion to George Orwell*, Cambridge: Cambridge University Press pp 146-159

Crook, Tim (2021) Antisemitism: Moving beyond upbringing and perceptions, Keeble, Richard Lance (ed.), *Orwell's Moustache*, Bury St Edmunds: Abramis Academic Publishing pp 243-258

*CWGO* (1998) *Complete Works of George Orwell, XX Vols*, Davison, Peter (ed.) London: Secker & Warburg

Denning, G. Alexander (2021) O'Brien in *Nineteen Eighty-Four*: A new interpretation, *George Orwell Studies*, Vol. 5, No. 2 pp 62-75

Gottlieb, Erika (1992) *The Orwell Conundrum: A Cry of Despair or Faith in the Spirit of Man?* Ottawa, Canada: Carleton University Press

Ho, Janice (2020) Europe, refugees, and *Nineteen Eighty-Four*, Waddell, Nathan (ed.) *The Cambridge Companion to* Nineteen Eighty-Four, Cambridge: Cambridge University Press pp 141-154

Homes, Patrick (2024) Can we truly rebel?, Orwell Society website, 4 August. Available online at https://orwellsociety.com/can-we-truly-rebel/

## G. ALEXANDER DENNING

Keeble, Richard Lance (2020) *George Orwell, The Secret State and the Making of Nineteen Eighty-Four*, Bury St Edmunds: Abramis Academic Publishing

Keeble, Richard Lance (2021) *Orwell's Moustache*, Bury St Edmunds: Abramis Academic Publishing

Lynskey, Dorian (2019) *The Ministry of Truth: A Biography of George Orwell's 1984*, London: Picador

Marx, Karl and Engels, Friedrich (1999 [1848]) *The Communist Manifesto*, Boston: Bedford/St Martin's

Newsinger, John (2007) Orwell, antisemitism and the Holocaust, Rodden, John (ed.) *The Cambridge Companion to George Orwell*, Cambridge: Cambridge University Press pp 112-125

Newsinger, John (2018) *Hope Lies in the Proles*, London: Pluto Press

Orwell, George (1989 [1949]) *Nineteen Eighty-Four*, London: Penguin

Rai, Alok (1988) *Orwell and the Politics of Despair*, Cambridge: Cambridge University Press

Taylor, D.J. (2003) *Orwell: The Life*, London: Chatto & Windus

Trotsky, Leon (2015 [1936]) *The Revolution Betrayed*, London: Wellred Books

### NOTE ON THE CONTRIBUTOR

G. Alexander Denning trained as an ordained Baptist minister, having attained a degree in theological studies at Whitley College, Melbourne. Since leaving the ministry he had been involved in a number of entrepreneurial businesses before his retirement. For many years he has been interested in writing poetry and novels, all of which are unpublished. His interest in George Orwell was aroused in the late 1990s when a friend gave him a copy of *Nineteen Eighty-Four*. Being fascinated by the character of O'Brien, he wrote a paper which lay dormant in his bottom drawer for twenty years until its publication in *George Orwell Studies* with some revisions. This aroused his interest in other aspects of the novel.

PAPER

# Echoes from the 'Beasts of England': Orwell's 1947 BBC Radio Adaptation of *Animal Farm*

PETER MARKS
SIMON J. POTTER

*Many critics consider* Animal Farm *a simple, beguiling text that primarily offers Orwell's beautifully rendered take on the Russian Revolution. There has been little attention paid, however, to Orwell's adaptation of the text for the BBC Third Programme, broadcast in 1947. This paper concentrates on the surviving script to tease out how that performance offers new perspectives on the novel itself. It also deals with Orwell's own complex relationship with the BBC. Particular attention is paid to neglected characters, particularly Clover and Benjamin, and to largely-ignored elements such as the song 'Beasts of England'. The paper encourages critics and readers to return to the novel in search of hidden or neglected resonances.*

Key words: *Animal Farm*, the Russian Revolution, BBC Radio adaptation, 'Beasts of England', Clover and Benjamin

INTRODUCTION

George Orwell famously dismissed his time working in the Eastern Section of the BBC from 1941 to 1943 as 'two wasted years' (*CWGO* XVI: 22). One argument supporting that assessment is that, freed from the BBC's shackles, he quickly completed *Animal Farm*. As is well known, there was a lag of more than a year between the completion of the manuscript in February 1944 and its publication in August 1945, the result of repeated rejections by publishers and then printing delays due to wartime paper restrictions. *Animal Farm* would not be published in the United States until August 1946. A 1954 CIA-backed cartoon later adulterated the text to suit American Cold War prerogatives (Shaw: 91-114). But *Animal Farm* had an earlier Cold War incarnation. In a December 1946 letter, Orwell told *Partisan Review*'s Dwight Macdonald that he was adapting the novel for the BBC: 'I am at present struggling with a radio version of the book, which is a ghastly difficult job and will take a long time' (*CWGO* XVIII: 507).

In fact, he completed the adaptation relatively quickly, submitting the script that month; it was broadcast twice on the Third Programme in January 1947 and as a recording the following month (*CWGO* XIX: 15-18). Orwell inventively deployed the radio medium, incorporating a narrator, established actors playing characters, sound effects including animal noises and church bells, original music and renditions of 'Beasts of England' that fuse music and the voices of 'sixteen members of the BBC Variety Chorus' (ibid: 18). No recordings of these broadcasts survive and the adaptation itself has attracted little critical attention. But examination of the script included as Appendix III to *Animal Farm* in the *Complete Works of George Orwell* (*CWGO* VIII: 115-195) reveals how Orwell utilised radio to cultivate aspects of the book often ignored by literary critics focused primarily on Russian Revolution parallels.

Orwell himself argued for a broader conception of the novel, telling Macdonald that:

> Of course, I intended it primarily as a satire on the Russian revolution. But I did mean it to have a wider application in so much that I meant that *that kind* of revolution … can only lead to a change of masters. What I was trying to say was 'You can't have a revolution unless you make it for yourself' (*CWGO* XVIII: 507).

This wider application explains why critical aspects of *Animal Farm* do not fit the Russian Revolution template. The overthrowing of Jones, for example, is only ever called 'the Rebellion', creating associations beyond Russia. Not that Orwell was averse to the word 'revolution', titling Part Three of *The Lion and the Unicorn*, written two years earlier, 'The English Revolution' (*CWGO* XII: 418-432). Earlier in that polemic he argues that it is 'only through revolution that the native genius of the English people can be set free' (ibid: 415). Later, he suggests that 'a specifically *English* [sic] Socialist movement' has 'never existed before', one mark of that non-existence being that the 'movement has never produced a song with a catchy tune' (ibid: 426-427). *Animal Farm*'s 'Beasts of England' is that tune, featuring repeatedly in the novel. In the radio adaptation, its emotional and ideological impact is heightened by listeners hearing it accompanied by music and the BBC Chorus. Critically, after the narrator intones the final words that between pigs and men 'it was impossible to say which was which', Orwell adds the direction: '*"Beasts of England"* to conclude' (*CWGO* VIII: 194). Listeners must register again the song's symbolic and political significance. The radio version also substantially enhances the roles of Clover and Benjamin, making them astute commentators on events. Neither has a specific Russian Revolution parallel, further decoupling the adaptation from such associations. These and other aspects of the radio version encourage a return to the novel to discover hidden or neglected resonances.

## ORWELL AND THE BBC

Orwell worked for the BBC Eastern Service as talks producer from 1941-1943. Peter Davison, the editor of the *Complete Works*, usefully summarises his work on 'newsletters, news reviews and news commentaries' (*CWGO* XIII: 82-92), D.J. Taylor explaining that Orwell prepared:

> … three series of commentaries on the daily news in English for transmission to India, Malaya and Indonesia … there were further separate series translated into vernacular languages … together with programmes on educational, political and cultural issues (Taylor 2023: 407).

Setting up such programmes allowed Orwell to build up a network of influential contacts, from colleagues such as literary critic William Empson to writers such as T.S. Eliot, Mulk Raj Anand, Stevie Smith and H.G. Wells, alongside intellectuals including Herbert Read, J.D. Bernal and Joseph Needham. Orwell established *Voice*, a radio series devoted to poetry, and in 1943 alone adapted Ignazio Silone's 'The Fox', H.G. Wells' 'A slip under the microscope', *Macbeth* and Hans Christian Andersen's 'The emperor's new clothes' for radio. Tim Crook sees Orwell as 'fully professionalised and immersed in a creative public broadcasting institution', acknowledging his 'significance as a radio dramatizer, sound playwright and critic of the genre' (Crook 2015: 194). His radio work frustrated Orwell's urge to write extended fiction, but these years were scarcely wasted.

There were recognisable downsides for Orwell working at the BBC at this time. As Simon Potter explains, during the war 'the BBC was a key tool of British cultural diplomacy and propaganda. Its services for overseas listeners helped further Britain's global and imperial interests' (Potter 2022: 71). Yet Potter adds that as a corporation, not a government department, the BBC's appearance of:

> … autonomy was valuable and recognized as such. It allowed the BBC to continue to speak with many voices and offer a range of viewpoints. This marked it out from some of its rival broadcasters in allied, neutral, and enemy countries, which were clearly the mouthpiece of their respective government (ibid: 72).

Orwell was clear-eyed about the compromises involved in working for the BBC, explaining to George Woodcock: 'For heaven's sake don't think I don't see that they are using me,' while adding 'that one

**PETER MARKS**
**SIMON J. POTTER**

can't effectively remain outside the war and by working inside an institution like the BBC one can perhaps deodorise it to some small extent' (*CWGO* XIV: 214). In his resignation letter, he emphasised that 'on no occasion have I been compelled to say anything on air that I would not have said as a private individual' (*CWGO* XVI: 251). This relatively positive view of the BBC informs his 1945 essay 'Poetry and the microphone', on radio's potential to transmit poetry to a mass audience (*CWGO* XVII: 74-80). While no longer a BBC employee, Orwell continued to contribute, Peter Davison observing that in 1946 he was more active in 'radio work than at any time since leaving the BBC's Eastern Service in 1943', adapting *The Voyage of the Beagle* and 'Little Red Riding Hood' (*CWGO* VIII: 115). Orwell's BBC experience fed into his February 1946 *Tribune* piece, 'The cost of radio programmes' where he discusses the financial limitations on radio dramas. Unlike stage plays, he notes, they usually were performed only once, placing crushing economic and creative limitations on writers, producers and performers. Truly experimental radio drama required that 'commercial considerations are ignored. This means, after all, setting aside one wavelength for uncompromisingly "highbrow" programmes' (*CWGO* XVIII: 88). Six months later the BBC introduced the Third Programme for just this purpose. A year after 'The cost of radio programmes', Orwell's adaptation of *Animal Farm* appeared on that network.

### THE THIRD PROGRAMME

The Third Programme was one of a series of BBC networks. Simon Potter explains that while the Home Service, established in September 1939, provided 'a daily mixture of material aimed at the "ordinary listener",' and the Light Programme, begun in July 1945, was for those looking for 'relaxation and amusement', the Third Programme, launched in September 1946, was:

> … dedicated to the arts, high culture, and academic discussion. … It sought to serve the 'serious listener' and broadcast 'without regard to length or difficulty, the masterpieces of music, art, and letters which lend themselves to transmission in sound'. It never attracted more than a tiny minority of listeners (Potter 2022: 114-115).

Orwell knew Third Programme producer Rayner Heppenstall, the two having shared accommodation in the 1930s and, despite fighting, maintained contact. Heppenstall produced *The Voyage of the Beagle*, and 'discussed the possibility of Orwell adapting Maupassant's *Boule de Suif* and making contributions to a series of imaginary conversations' (*CWGO* VIII: 116). When the Maupassant project collapsed, the BBC's director of features was instructed to adapt *Animal Farm*, with Heppenstall as producer.

The latter wrote to Orwell in October 1946 commissioning the adaptation. A length of ninety minutes was suggested, but if Orwell felt this was too restricting he could propose a modification. Orwell did, telephoning Heppenstall and suggesting that the adaptation be split into two parts each lasting one hour with a short interval between them (ibid: 117-118). In December, Orwell submitted his script, but his suggestion for splitting the adaptation was not taken up, Heppenstall editing the piece to the roughly 90 minutes allotted. In more ways than one, then, the broadcast adapted the novel.

While Peter Davison reveals that Orwell's original script does not survive, the one included in the *Complete Works* was used by Frank Atkinson, who played Jones and sundry animals in the production (ibid: 122). The exact number of lines Heppenstall excised is uncertain, Davison guessing that 'some 490 lines are known to be cut of which 253 were spoken by the narrator'. From an initial script of some 2,260 to 2,290 lines about 1,710 lines were broadcast (ibid: 120). These cuts illustrate Heppenstall's concern to reduce narration, which he thought impeded the play's dramatic energy. Orwell disagreed, tetchily replying to Heppenstall after the first broadcast: 'People are always yearning to get rid of the narrator, but it seems to me that unless certain problems have been overcome you only get rid of the narrator at the expense of having to play a lot of stupid tricks in order to let people know what is happening' (ibid: 121). Orwell's resistance came not just from being *Animal Farm*'s author as from his considerable experience adapting literary texts. As Crook indicates, Orwell was no novice, having a sophisticated feel for what worked dramatically on air (Crook 2015: 198-206). For all the cuts Heppenstall made, though, the broadcast version primarily presents Orwell's adaptation of *Animal Farm*.

As for the Third Programme itself, David Hendy sees it as reflecting the 'desire in the corridors of Broadcasting House to see post-war Britain reconnect once more with the best of world culture' (Hendy 2022: 356), while Edward Stourton more sourly describes the network as 'a by-word for cultural elitism' (Stourton 2018: 312). Simon Potter explains that the BBC's director general, William Haley, believed that:

> … the British listening public formed a pyramid of taste, with a broad-based popular audience served by the Light, a narrower but still substantial middle group served by the Home, and a cultivated elite by the Third. The BBC would … encourage individual listeners to climb the pyramid over time, thus gradually raising the cultural level of the entire structure (Potter 2022: 115).

PETER MARKS
SIMON J.
POTTER

*Animal Farm* may be seen as exercise in encouragement. Broadcast at 9.15pm on 14 January 1947, four months after the network's opening, it was preceded by the Henry Wood Promenade Concerts (more colloquially, 'the Proms') conducted by Sir Adrian Boult, and followed by songs by Bach and Mozart (*Radio Times* 1947). Children clearly were not the target audience, but the book's bestseller status made it likely to attract a broader audience than the Proms or Bach. Quality was guaranteed by stalwarts such as the show's narrator, Ronald Simpson (who had played the patrician Soames Forsyte in the 1945 radio adaptation of John Galsworthy's *The Forsyte Saga*), and pianist and composer Antony Hopkins, who wrote and conducted the music provided by flute, piccolo, trumpet, percussion and tubular bells. The BBC Variety Chorus provided vocal accompaniment.

THE IMPORTANCE OF CLOVER AND BENJAMIN

The first sounds heard in the production, as befits a radio drama, are effects: '*Heavy boots clumping over flagstones and then dying away. An owl hoots twice.*' While the narrator then notes Jones going to bed and the creatures gathering in the barn, the sounds of that gathering precede the narrator introducing Major and other important characters in a truncation of the novel's opening scene. The adaptation immediately adds new material that foregrounds characters regularly ignored in interpretations focused on the Russian Revolution. In the novel, Major gives his speech while the other animals remain mute. In the adaptation, when he asks, 'What is the worst enemy that we animals have to contend with?,' Benjamin responds sarcastically: 'Fleas!' (*CWGO* VIII: 128) prompting general laughter. When Major dismisses Benjamin with 'There are things worse than fleas, believe me,' Clover suggests 'The whip'. To this, Major replies: 'That is nearer the mark. I will answer my own question, comrades. *Man* is our enemy' (ibid: 129, italics in the original). Orwell's added responses identify Benjamin and Clover from the outset as knowing creatures, with insight and potential agency.

Clover is dismissed by many literary critics as the stalwart mate of the heroic workhorse, Boxer. But she functions regularly in the radio version as a quizzical observer, a repository of the farm's oral history and as the animals' collective conscience. One of Orwell's more radical moves in the radio version occurs near the conclusion, after the narrator announces that 'Three years went by' (ibid: 177). Clover tells a new horse: 'We shall have to start teaching you the rules of the farm and the history of the Rebellion,' before launching into a lengthy flashback that begins with her assessment of Snowball – 'a clever pig, but he turned traitor'(ibid: 177) – and ends with her giving an extended account of Boxer's death. This incorporates short contributions from Benjamin, Squealer and others (ibid: 183), but for seven pages in the radio script Clover's is the primary voice and point of view. We may see this as Orwell transmitting information via another source than the narrator, but Clover's importance in the radio version has parallels in the novel. In its final chapter, for example, new horses 'accepted everything that they had been told about the Rebellion and the principles of Animalism, especially from Clover' (ibid: 86). It is Clover who first sees Squealer walking on hind legs (ibid: 89) and it is Clover who, though she cannot read fluently, asks Benjamin to confirm what she suspects: 'Are the Seven Commandments the same as they used to be, Benjamin?' (ibid: 90). By this point they have been replaced by ALL ANIMALS ARE EQUAL BUT SOME ANIMALS ARE MORE EQUAL THAN OTHERS. Clover leads the animals up to the house where the pigs and men have their final meeting, and it is from her perspective that readers first glimpse the grotesque transformation of the pigs:

> What was it that had altered in the faces of the pigs? Clover's old dim eyes flitted from one face to another. ... But what was it that seemed to be melting and changing? (ibid: 94).

More important still is something readers are told earlier in the final chapter of *Animal Farm*: that the animals had not given up hope and that 'Even the tune of "Beasts of England" was perhaps hummed secretly here and there: at any rate it was a fact that every animal on the farm knew it, though no one would have dared to sing it aloud' (ibid: 88). The creature most associated with singing the song is Clover.

The adaptation illuminates how the novel repeatedly advertises Clover's prominence, most obviously after the slaughter of the supposed traitors. As the animals 'huddled about Clover' and 'her eyes filled with tears', Orwell presents her thoughts in one sustained insight over almost a page:

> If she could have spoken her thoughts, it would have been to say that this was not what they had aimed at when they had set themselves years ago to work for the overthrow of the human race. ... If she herself had any picture of the future, it had been of a society of animals set free from hunger and the whip, all equal, each working according to his capacity, the strong protecting the weak. Instead – she did not know why – they had come to a time when no one dared speak his mind, when fierce, growling dogs roamed everywhere. ... Whatever happened she would remain faithful, work hard ... and accept the leadership of Napoleon. But still, it was not for this that she and all the other animals had hoped and toiled (ibid: 58-59).

PETER MARKS
SIMON J.
POTTER

Clover's perceptive, emotionally charged assessment is easily the novel's most sustained exploration of a character's thoughts. More importantly, Orwell presents her as the spokesperson for collective understanding. This section ends: 'Such were her thoughts, though she lacked the words to express them' (ibid: 59). Instead, she begins to sing 'Beasts of England'. So often celebratory, in this harrowing moment Clover refashions it as a lament for lost ideals, a critique of conditions on Animal Farm and a plaintive call for solidarity. The impact of her action is immediate, the other animals taking it up, singing 'it three times over – very tunefully, but slowly and mournfully, in a way they had never sung it before'. Immediately, Squealer arrives to announce: 'From now onwards it was forbidden to sing it' (ibid: 59). While the final chapter never explicitly links the song's survival to Clover, her intimate association with it, her part in transmitting the Rebellion's history and her central role in noticing critical changes in the Commandments and the pigs all register her as far more significant than most critics assume.

Clover's importance is repeatedly foregrounded in the adaptation. It is she who asks Benjamin: 'Have you noticed that the sheep always break into [four legs good, two legs bad] when Snowball is speaking, never when Napoleon is speaking?', to which Benjamin replies sardonically: 'Quite a coincidence, is it not?' (ibid: 156). Clover registers that the pigs have commandeered the milk and the apples, and she tells Boxer that 'The pigs have moved into the farmhouse and are living there' (ibid: 161). She observes the pigs 'have also taken to sleeping in the beds' (ibid: 162) and realises the pigs have 'discovered some barrels of beer. ... and now I hear every pig gets a ration of a pint of beer a day' (ibid: 165). When the supposed traitors are slaughtered Clover provides sober commentary: 'It is the first time that blood has been shed. In the old days, in Jones's time, these slaughters used to happen; but now they are happening among ourselves. Since Jones left, until today, no animal has killed another animal' (ibid: 174). In the novel, these insights are presented as thoughts Clover 'could have spoken', but Orwell uses radio's power to personalise characters by broadcasting her voice, substantially intensifying the emotional resonance of her insight. She immediately launches into 'Beasts of England', the symbolic power of which is enhanced by its literally being heard with music.

Like Clover, Benjamin does not easily fit the Russian Revolution interpretation of *Animal Farm*. Consequently, he, too, is largely ignored, written off as a cynic whose only redeeming feature is devotion to Boxer. His other distinguishing characteristic is intellectually level with the pigs, being able to read fluently. But Benjamin's sardonic view that 'no one has ever seen a dead donkey' causes him to stand aside from events.

This aloofness is exposed as morally bankrupt, especially his failure to alert his fellow comrades to the gradual adulteration of the Seven Commandments by the pigs. He pays a terrible price, of course, when Boxer is taken away to the knacker's. Where the other animals believe the pigs' lies that their sick companion is being taken to the vet for treatment, Benjamin's literacy alerts him to the truth: 'Fools! Don't you see what is written on the side of the van?' (ibid: 81). Of course they can *see* what is written, but only Benjamin can read fluently enough to understand the reality. In one of the book's most wrenching scenes, his failure to employ his literacy socially dooms his beloved friend. As Crook argues: 'Benjamin might live a long time, but his conscience will be forever troubled. Knowing without action is the delusion of the fool. Politically, *Animal Farm* is about a society that cannot control its own language ... Benjamin understands, but raises the issue so late his intelligence only serves to write his own epitaph' (2016: 69). In the adaptation, Clover retrospectively recalls Boxer's death:

> ... we saw Benjamin come galloping towards us, braying at the top of his voice. It was the first time anyone had seen Benjamin excited – in fact, it was the first time we had even seen him gallop.
>
> EFFECTS: (*braying fading in from 'field'*)
>
> BENJAMIN: Quick, quick! Come at once! The van's here! They're taking Boxer away! (ibid: 180).

As with Clover's despair after the slaughter of the traitors, radio's capacity to render speech and thought in emotionally compelling ways deepens the pathos of this critical scene, especially given Benjamin's previous mordant tone. His terrifying cry: 'They are taking Boxer to the knacker's!' activates a despairing cry from a cock, Muriel, a goat, and Mollie, a white horse, for Boxer to get out of the van, after which we hear:

> HORSE: (*Distant whinnying. Fade*) (ibid).

Benjamin's braying and Boxer's whinnying are racking in themselves, but the instruction to '*Fade*' carries an immense emotional weight that radio can provide.

In the novel's final chapter, we read that 'old Benjamin was much the same as ever, except for being a little greyer about the muzzle, and since Boxer's death, more morose and taciturn than ever' (ibid: 85). Yet he necessarily is the one Clover turns to in order to confirm what she has only faintly perceived, the final change from the original Seven Commandments to one.

As many commentators note, Orwell's contempt for intellectuals (recognising, of course, that he comfortably fitted the definition)

PETER MARKS
SIMON J.
POTTER

bordered on the obsessive (Collini 2006: 350-374). They are written off as dangerously power hungry (controlling the Inner Party in *Nineteen Eighty-Four*), politically naïve (blithely supporting the Soviet Union) or buffoonish (fruit juice drinkers and sandal wearers). We may see it as part of Orwell's revenge on intellectuals generally that he requires Benjamin to read aloud one of political fiction's most infamous statements that some animals are more equal than others; he is not mentioned again in the novel. He does, however, appear in the finale to the adaptation, initially with other animals who notice Clover's alarm at the pigs walking on their hind legs (*CWGO* VIII: 186). Clover, so often the most perceptive of the animals, asks well before the others register the change in the pigs: 'What's happening? Something's happening to their faces.' Other animals admire how the pigs play cards like humans, but Benjamin whispers dejectedly: 'Come away. They don't want us. We're not wanted here' (ibid: 193). This dark insight does not take place in the novel. In this moment, Benjamin is less sardonic outsider than despondent insider, recognising himself among the underclass discarded in the new hierarchy. His insight is telling not only for what is said, but that he says it aloud; radio accentuates insight in this instance literally by giving it voice. After the men and pigs quarrel over cards, the narrator details how, as the animals' eyes shift back and forth, something 'seemed to be melting and changing in the faces of the pigs', to the point where it becomes impossible to distinguish them from the men, to 'say which was which'. But this is not how the adaptation ends, the last words spoken being an interchange between Clover and Benjamin:

CLOVER (*whispering*): It started to happen when he said 'Manor Farm'. Tell me, Benjamin, is it really happening? Or is it only because my eyes are growing so dim?

BENJAMIN (*whispering*): No, Clover, there is nothing wrong with your eyes. It is happening (ibid: 194).

This final interchange boldly conveys the importance Orwell gives to Clover and Benjamin as insightful creatures, aware of and broadcasting the horrid new reality. The adaptation encourages critics to return to the novel to consider the significance of those characters who have little or no place in the Russian Revolution interpretation of *Animal Farm*. The radio version suggests that they and other such elements warrant critical attention.

Clover and Benjamin are important as the last characters to speak, but equally important is how they speak. Accent is critical in the adaptation to characterisation and to more general questions of class. Betty Hardy (see https://www.imdb.com/name/nm0362589), who voiced Clover, would later play cleaner Clara Midgley in *Coronation Street*, while Bryan Powley (Benjamin) had appeared in films as middle-class figures such as Dr Gribble in *A Night of Terror* (1937) (see https://www.imdb.com/name/nm0668021). Benjamin was likely, therefore, to speak with a middle-class accent that sets him apart from the other oppressed animals. One might imagine his cynical indifference being amplified by his 'superior' accent. By contrast, Frank Atkinson, who played Jones, would later voice Euphan Todd's comic rural scarecrow, Worzel Gummidge. Jones, given the broken dialogue Orwell assigns him and other farmers, would have had a decidedly 'rural' accent. Norman Shelley, who played Napoleon, voiced upper middle class characters such as Colonel Danby in the radio soap opera *The Archers*, while Raf De La Torre (Major) was the decidedly middle class 'Mr Quelch' in the television series *Billy Bunter of Greyfriars Hall*. The strict social hierarchy encoded in the respective accents reinforces divisions between the intellectual pigs and the other animals, while accentuating the rustic background of the farmers. The radio audience literally hears class distinctions from the outset that are less distinguishable in the novel: Major, the other pigs and Benjamin are middle class intellectuals; the animals remain undeniably working class; the farmers are 'rural'. The narrator, too, is middle class, a subtle index of narrative (and perhaps, political) control.

As Orwell would have foreseen, all the accents in the adaptation were impeccably English; none came with Russian cadences. He had admitted to Dwight Macdonald that he had meant *Animal Farm* to have a 'wider application' than the Russian Revolution, and that he was trying to say: 'You can't have a revolution unless you make it for yourself.' *The Lion and the Unicorn* had been his 1941 case for revolution, one that had not come to pass. Orwell admitted that the idea for *Animal Farm* had first come to him after his return from fighting on the Republican side during the Spanish Civil War in 1937. He understood that a novel written during World War Two and published at the start of the Cold War would now be broadcast to a British audience in early 1947. Orwell was always attentive to his readers, noting in 'Why I write', written in the same year he adapted *Animal Farm*, that his motivation was 'because there is some lie that I want to expose, some fact to which I want to draw attention, and my initial concern is to get a hearing' (*CWGO* XVIII: 319). His time at the BBC showed him equally attentive to radio audiences. In an 'As I Please' *Tribune* column written in December 1946 (the same month he was adapting *Animal Farm*) he noted that Britain might just be beginning 'an uncomfortable reconstruction period which may last for years' (*CWGO* XVIII: 514). A parallel in *Animal Farm* might be the grim period following the destruction of the windmill. Orwell knew that the BBC adaptation would only play to a British audience. This may explain why it finishes not

PETER MARKS
SIMON J. POTTER

with the novel's mordant fusing of pigs and men, nor even with the dialogue between Clover and Benjamin, but with something perfectly attuned to a British radio audience entering a period of struggle: 'Beasts of England'.

THE IMPORTANCE OF 'BEASTS OF ENGLAND'

Critics wedded to the Russian Revolution reading of *Animal Farm* often assume that 'Beasts of England' is a parody of Eugène Pottier's proletarian anthem 'The Internationale' (Meyers 1991: 190; Armstrong 1985: 20). Leaving aside that the song was written neither for, nor about that revolution but by a French socialist in 1871, the 'parody' reading ignores Major's revelation in his final speech, that 'Beasts of England' came to him 'in a dream of the earth as it will be when Man has vanished'(*CWGO* XIII: 6) and that the words of the song 'I am certain ... were sung by the animals long ago and have been lost to memory for generations' (ibid: 7). It is not a proletarian call to arms, but a totemic song that taps into fundamental emotions and communal awareness buried deep in the history of animal consciousness. As noted, Orwell had argued in *The Lion and the Unicorn* that the English socialist movement had never produced a song 'with a catchy tune – nothing like *La Marseillaise* or La Cucuracha' [sic] (ibid: 426-427). *Animal Farm* describes 'Beasts of England' in strikingly similar terms, as 'a stirring tune, something between "Clementine" and "La Cucuracha"' [sic] (*CWGO* VIII: 7). It is Orwell's catchy tune for English socialists. Although the song references 'Beasts of England/ Beasts of Ireland/ Beasts of every land and clime', the primacy of England there connects to the *Lion and the Unicorn*'s appeal for the English to make a revolution 'for yourself'. As a potent statement of solidarity and aspiration, able to revive consciousness of long-held hopes and new possibilities, the song embodies factors acutely pertinent to a British audience in early 1947. Sung by Major and later Clover, both accompanied by professional singers with musical accompaniment, 'Beasts of England' repeatedly creates opportunities for that audience to experience moments of solidarity and hope.

The radio version deftly insinuates 'Beasts of England' into its soundscape. In the opening scene it is sung all the way through by the animals to Hopkins's musical score. Major is heard 'declaiming' two verses accompanied by the BBC singers (cit: 132), who then perform the song's chorus on their own. While Jones's gunshot quietens the singing, a musical instruction indicates ('"*Beasts of England" in solemn minor*') (ibid: 133). From the outset, the vitality and communality intrinsic in the song are paramount, words and music combining to celebrate the animals' long-lost aspirations and their rejection of human rule. When Jones is driven out, the animals sing it as a triumphant coda. Its power to represent the new assertiveness of the animals beyond Animal Farm is registered aurally soon after when the song of a blackbird, heard behind the voices of farmers discussing the Rebellion in the Red Lion, is subtly added to by a cock '*Humming "Beasts of England" off mike*' (ibid: 148). Sound effects accentuate the tension: (*Crack of a whip. Squawk. Humming stops. Blackbird continues.*) As the farmers discuss changes on Animal Farm, listeners hear rebellious undertones:

> MUSIC: (*The whistling of the blackbird changes into the whistling of 'Beasts of England'.*)
>
> FARMER 2: 'Ere. Give us a stone. Get off, you devil, you!
>
> EFFECTS: (*Flutter of wings. Whistling stops.*)
>
> FARMER 1: It's all over the place, that tune is (ibid: 148).

Another musical element is introduced: (*Church bells begin playing faintly in the distance and continue behind the men's voices*). Moments later, the bells are '*now ringing somewhat louder*'. After the farmers decide to attend church, the bells sound louder still, before: '*Suddenly it changes to "Beasts of England", plays a few bars and fades under*' (ibid: 149). The adaptation highlights the song's centrality to the spread and potency of the animals' new perspective.

As in the novel, the song functions differently after the slaughter of the traitors. As noted above, the thoughts Clover 'could have spoken' *are* spoken in the adaptation, the point about the shedding of blood extending to a personal statement that sums up the communal sense of horror, confusion and fear:

> CLOVER: I do not understand. This is not what we looked forward to on the night when Major first put the idea of rebellion into our heads. The farm is our own. As far as the eye can see, every inch of it is ours. And yet .... [sic] No one dares speak his mind because huge dogs are prowling everywhere, and you have to watch your comrades confess to huge crimes and then be torn to pieces. That was not what we expected.
>
> MUSIC (*CHORUS holding sustained chords, with hint of melody of refrain.*)
>
> I do not wish to rebel or disobey. I know the pigs are cleverer than we are. I will work hard, I will do whatever Napoleon tells me. But, no! This is not what we intended. I think – I don't know what to think –
>
> (CLOVER *sings very slowly and tunefully.*)
>
> Soon or late the day is coming,
>
> Tyrant man shall be o'erthrown,

And the fruitful fields of England

Shall be trod by beasts alone.

CHORUS: Beasts of England, beasts of Ireland,

Beasts of every land and clime,

Hearken to my joyful tidings,

Of the golden future time.

CLOVER (*declaiming over CHORUS*)

Rings shall vanish from our noses

And the harness from our back,

Bit and spur shall rust –

(Breaking off as – )

SQUEALER: Comrades! Silence if you please! (ibid: 175-176).

Clover understands the new reality all too well, but desperately clings to the ideals celebrated in the song. The musical introduction is followed by her solitary voice, the introduction of the Chorus masterfully fusing keen political insight and emotional intensity in fewer than 90 seconds of airtime. Where 'Beasts of England' hitherto has been joyous and inspirational, here it is despairing, combining recuperated hopes with an awareness of present terror, amplified by the confluence of music and voice, both individual and collective.

Squealer's subsequent call for silence is politically and thematically significant, his dictat that 'Beasts of England' is now forbidden literally muting the most powerful expression of solidarity and potential dissent the animals have enjoyed. In the novel's final chapter, 'Beasts of England' is still secretly hummed, something that does not occur in the adaptation. But the song still resonates, perhaps more powerfully, the broadcast as a whole ending with Orwell's instruction: '"*Beasts of England*" to conclude' (ibid: 194). It is unclear how much is sung, by whom or whether there is musical accompaniment. But we might imagine a stirring, extended rendition harking back to the song's initial inspirational communality. Another possibility would accentuate hopes and ideals smothered but not entirely killed off. That no recording survives frustrates any conclusive assessment. But given that Orwell repeatedly deploys the song's dramatic and political importance, making it the last thing the audience hears accentuates its thematic, emotional and political significance. The final words spoken by Clover and Benjamin speak to their recognition of the transformation of the pigs into men.

The coda reintroducing 'Beasts of England' reminds listeners of hopes betrayed. Yet the song's ability to tap into ancient ideals while prophesying future triumph also celebrates hopes still unfulfilled, a poignant and potent message for a BBC audience in 1947.

## CONCLUSION

The song's return in the adaptation invites readers to reassess its importance in the novel. As noted above, in the final chapter 'Beasts of England' is hummed secretly, and every animal knows it. This crucial element is usually disregarded in readings that emphasise Russian Revolution parallels, but it speaks to a neglected aspect of the novel itself: that the song, lost to the animals before Major's speech, and transformative in their political awareness, is still known universally. That it is suppressed is an index of repression, but the novel ends not with a return to the *status quo ante*, for all the animals retain the song that celebrates freedom from tyranny. Its rebellious potential resides on the renamed Manor Farm. By having the adaptation finishing on that song, Orwell literally and metaphorically commemorates that resilient rebellious power.

In his 1947 preface to the Ukrainian edition of *Animal Farm*, he noted that while critics and readers assumed that the novel ended with 'the complete reconciliation of the pigs and humans; on the contrary, I meant it to end on a loud note of discord' (ibid: 113-114). Similarly, critics and readers often accept that the novel ends with the crushing of the Rebellion and the animals' return to servility. But the radio version indicates a mournful ending that is not without hope. The final interplay between Clover and Benjamin shows them aware of new realities, while the finale reminded listeners in 1947 of communal ideals and desires as they struggled to rebuild Britain. Orwell's adaptation spoke to a BBC audience in new circumstances, one less focused on the Russian Revolution and more on reconstructing a battered nation. More broadly, the radio version emphasises the ancient aspirations embodied in 'Beasts of England'. The centrality of the song and the elevation of characters such as Clover and Benjamin asked its first listeners to think beyond Russian Revolution readings; it asks readers to do so today.

- This paper incorporates ideas and research developed collaboratively by the authors while Professor Marks was a Benjamin Meaker Distinguished Visiting Professor at the University of Bristol in 2023.

## REFERENCES

Armstrong, Jean (1985) *Orwell: Animal Farm*, London: Macmillan

Collini, Stefan (2006) *Absent Minds: Intellectuals in Britain*, Oxford: Oxford University Press

Crook, Tim (2015) George Orwell and the Radio imagination, *George Orwell Now!*, Keeble, Richard Lance (ed.) New York: Peter Lang pp 193-208. Available online at https://kulturapress.com/2024/03/29/orwell-and-the-radio-imagination/, accessed on 25 January 2025

Crook, Tim (2016) Only donkeys survive tyranny and dictatorship: Was Benjamin George Orwell's alter ego in *Animal Farm*? *George Orwell Studies*, Vol. 1, No. 1 pp 56-72

Hendy, David (2022) *The BBC: A People's History*, London: Profile Books

Meyers, Valerie (1991) *George Orwell*, London: Macmillan

Orwell, George (1998) *The Complete Works* (*CWGO*) XX Vols, Davison, Peter (ed.) London: Secker & Warburg

Potter, Simon J. (2022) *This Is the BBC: Entertaining the Nation, Speaking for Britain, 1922-2022*, Oxford: Oxford University Press

*Radio Times* (1947) Available online at https://genome.ch.bbc.co.uk/page/41ce44460675474cb34f188acbfed129, accessed on 15 November 2024

Shaw, Tony (2001) *British Cinema and the Cold War: The State, Propaganda and Consequences*, London: I.B. Tauris

Stourton, Edward (2018) *Auntie's War: The BBC during the Second World War*, London: Transworld

Taylor, D.J. (2023) *Orwell: The New Life*, London: Constable

## NOTES ON THE CONTRIBUTORS

Peter Marks is Emeritus Professor of English at the University of Sydney. He is the author of numerous articles and chapters on George Orwell, surveillance, utopias and dystopias, and the essay form. He has published four monographs, including *George Orwell the Essayist: Literature, Politics and the Periodical Culture* (2011) and *British Literature of the 1990s: Endings and Beginnings* (2018) and is one of the editors of *The Palgrave Handbook of Utopian and Dystopian Literatures* (2022).

Simon J. Potter is Professor of Modern History at the University of Bristol, UK. His published works include *Broadcasting Empire: The BBC and the British World, 1922-1970* (Oxford University Press, 2012); *Wireless Internationalism and Distant Listening: Britain, Propaganda, and the Invention of Global Radio, 1920-1939* (Oxford University Press, 2020); *This is the BBC: Entertaining the Nation, Speaking for Britain?* (Oxford University Press, 2022) and, as lead author of a co-written book, *The Wireless World: Global Histories of International Radio Broadcasting* (Oxford University Press, 2022).

PAPER

# Orwell and Fisher: Rebellion and Realism

PATRICK HOMES

*Mark Fisher (1968-2017) was a Marxist philosopher at Goldsmiths, University of London. His 2008 book* Capitalist Realism: Is There No Alternative? *suggested an analytical framework to help explain why capitalism, once a transitory ideology like any other, has become the only imaginable reality. Likewise, one of the great strengths of* Nineteen Eighty-Four *is how it portrays the futility of resistance. I propose that by applying Fisher's analysis to Orwell's novel a more comprehensive understanding of the book can be created, in particular a more thorough analysis of Goldstein's dissident 'The theory and practice of oligarchical collectivism', a somewhat understudied component of the text.*

Key words: Mark Fisher, capitalist realism, *Nineteen Eighty-Four*, Emmanuel Goldstein, 'The theory and practice of oligarchical collectivism'

## CAPITALIST REALISM

Before I begin applying Fisher's analysis to Orwell, some explanation of Fisher's thesis is required. Fisher's capitalist realism is essentially the process by which 'capitalism seamlessly occupies the horizons of the thinkable' (Fisher 2008: 12), that is to say when capitalism, by near universal consensus, becomes the only practical political and economic ideology. Fisher, writing during the 2008 global financial crisis, is perplexed by how, at the time of its greatest trial, capitalism is reaffirmed, as well as how absolutely futile the actions of the anti-capitalist opposition were. For example, the 'Occupy America' movement, a supposedly radical opposition to capitalism, had little real policy impact. Fisher suggested that these protests, lacking any sophisticated or realistic 'alternative political-economic model', became 'a kind of carnivalesque background noise to capitalist realism' (ibid: 16), full of sound and fury but achieving nothing. Indeed, Fisher usefully points out the numerous similarities between this round of protests and the earlier Live 8 concerts in 2005 (which aimed to highlight global poverty). Both are filled with 'exorbitant demands' (ibid: 16) that, in their hearts, the protesters know can never be fulfilled and are, therefore, free to be expressed. It is this kind of 'senseless hope' (ibid: 9) that has real applications to Orwell's *Nineteen Eighty-Four*. Throughout the novel, the purportedly revelatory dissidence that Winston undertakes, whether it be reading Goldstein's book or renting Mr Charrington's room, prove futile in the face of the Party. Yet the true genius of Orwell is to show not just Winston's ultimate defeat but the echoes of this defeat embedded throughout the text that make it an inevitability. By applying Fisher's analysis, I will seek to uncover these echoes and illustrate how they work to frustrate Winston's dissidence and result in his final failure.

### 'THE THEORY AND PRACTICE OF OLIGARCHICAL COLLECTIVISM'

Unique within the novel 'The theory and practice of oligarchical collectivism' is the one section that is not told from Winston Smith's perspective. Instead, it is a book within a book, purportedly written by the dissident Emmanuel Goldstein. It seemingly lays bare the true, hideous reality of Ingsoc and the Party. It openly reveals that Oceania is alternately at war with Eurasia and Eastasia, 'for in spite of the re-grouping which occurs every few years, it is always the same war' (Orwell 2018 [1949]: 189). It contains revelation after revelation, that the war which so dominated life in Oceania is designed – as explicitly recognised by the Inner Party – only to 'use up the products of the machine without raising the general standing of living' (ibid: 191). Moreover, there is a kind of global conspiracy between the seemingly cut-throat rivals, for they are not fighting against each other but against their own subjects (ibid: 201). In essence it exposes every category of lie ever told by the Party. This supposedly revelatory character is somewhat reflected in its physical appearance, 'the pages were worn at the edges … as though the book had passed through many hands' (ibid: 186), as if many had been astounded by its knowledge and as if Winston were joining a long line of intellectual dissidents. This is even reflected in Winston's reaction for he knows he 'will ultimately read and re-read every word' (ibid: 187).

Indeed, one of the great successes in the construction of the novel is to give this hope and intellectual clarity in a world of Newspeak and obfuscation and then to dash it upon the rocks. But more than that, to suggest that it never existed in the first place. In properly understanding the place of Goldstein's book within the novel, I argue that Fisher's analytical framework is particularly useful. Fisher describes 'settled', 'alternative' or 'independent' cultural zones 'which endlessly repeat older gestures of rebellion … as if for the first time' (Fisher 2008: 13). I would suggest that the most helpful way of viewing Goldstein's book is as one of these zones, because, for all its anti-establishment character, the core of its worldview is not too dissimilar from the underlying ideology of Ingsoc.

Indeed, it begins, in a likely allusion to the opening of the first Chapter of the *Communist Manifesto*: 'The history of all hitherto existing society is the history of class struggles' (Marx 1848): 'Throughout recorded time ... there have been three kinds of people in the world, the High, the Middle, and the Low' (Orwell 2018 [1949]: 187). It is this view of the world as eternally hierarchical, specifically of the Low never being 'even temporarily successful in achieving their aims' (ibid: 204), that bears some striking similarities with O'Brien's school of thought. O'Brien's dismissal of the proles: 'They are helpless, like the animals' (ibid: 271) and of their ultimate impotence is not so different from Goldstein's certainty that they can never win. Likewise, although Goldstein's view of the world as eternally hierarchical is nuanced, since he also claims that, due to technological advancement, 'human equality had become technically possible' (ibid: 205) by outsourcing the escaping of the cycle to an essentially uncontrollable process, Goldstein inculcates the kind of learned helplessness which Fisher emphasises as the basis of capitalist realism. Likewise, the entirety of Goldstein's work is pure analysis; nowhere is a serious, achievable, political alternative presented. Indeed, the work is without any kind of moral force, of right or wrong. Such an amoral view of history and society, of power as the ultimate force, undoubtedly serves as the core of O'Brien's, and Ingsoc's, worship of power 'Power is not a means, it is an end' (ibid: 265), a view which Winston eventually correctly internalises as 'GOD IS POWER' (ibid: 280, capital letters in the original). This ultimate cynicism also presents itself as the ultimate truth, as the final stripping away of illusion. In this way Orwell predicts a great deal of Fisher's and, indeed, Slavoj Žižek's, thinking. Žižek declares that 'today's society must appear post ideological: the prevailing ideology is that of cynicism' (Žižek 2008 [1989]: 41). Similarly O'Brien presents Ingsoc as the final and complete exposition of the eternal truth of human societies: that power is all.

Furthermore, these similarities can also be seen in the language of the Party propaganda and Goldstein's book itself. Again, they are superficially opposed, one being filled with Newspeak and lies, and the other with purportedly clear language. However, the language of both can be seen as propagandistic in the way that Orwell describes in 'Politics and the English language'.(1946). For example, the Inner Party orator resembles very closely the contemporaneous politicians Orwell describes. The orator's 'endless catalogue of atrocities' (Orwell 2018 [1949]: 183) accords fairly closely with the 'bestial atrocities ... blood-stained tyranny' Orwell describes as the stock-terms of the politicians of his own day (Orwell 1946). And the end result is the same, for in the essay Orwell notes that this kind of slavish language results in a 'reduced state of consciousness ...

**PAPER**

favourable to political conformity' (ibid) while in *Nineteen Eighty-Four*, the orator is able to make the greatest leap of *doublethink*: 'Nothing altered in his voice or manner, or in the content of what he was saying, but suddenly the names were different' (Orwell 2018 [1949]: 184). In essence, the language has been reduced to such a stock form that no thought in the delivery of the speech is needed.

Studies, such as Harris (1959), have correctly identified the above link between the novel and Orwell's essays, but such a consideration of the language of Goldstein's book is not so prominent. Indeed, the faux-academic style in Goldstein's book is riddled with the language Orwell deplores. In fact, one Latinate term which Orwell specifically deplores, namely 'historic' (Orwell 1946), can be found within the book '… no historic change has ever meant much more than a change in the name of their masters' (Orwell 2018 [1949]: 204). Indeed, the 'ready-made phrases … arranged as to be more or less euphonious' (Orwell 1946) can be seen in the above quotation, with its euphonious alliterations of 'm's and 'n's particularly in the somewhat stock formulation 'much more'. Thus, although the language of Goldstein's book appears precise and academic, it suffers from the same lack of original thought that defines propaganda.

Of course, all these similarities are not hugely surprising; it is, after all, O'Brien who gives Goldstein's book to Winston. As I have illustrated, the opposition provided by Goldstein's book is entirely superficial in its hopelessness; indeed, in its own language, it is not a true act of rebellion. In this way, Goldstein's book accords with Fisher's account of realism, since 'alternative and independent don't designate something outside mainstream culture' (Fisher 2008: 13). For Goldstein is not outside the Party but an essential working component of its intellectual framework, he provides a superficial opposition whilst, at the core, affirming the basic assumptions of Ingsoc's underlying ideology.

### MR CHARRINGTON'S SHOP

Another 'cultural zone' is Mr Charrington's antique shop which provides a false safe haven for Winston and Julia. The importance of the shop becomes clear in the portrait of the glass and coral knick-knack Winston purchases: 'What appealed to him about it was not so much its beauty as the air it seemed to possess of belonging to an age quite different from the present one' (Orwell 2018 [1949]: 95).

It is, then, a remnant of the world before the Revolution, where there was 'no telescreen!' (ibid: 97). And in a world where history is deliberately erased, the ability to awaken 'a sort of ancestral memory' (ibid: 96) is valuable beyond estimation. Again, like Goldstein's book, the shop appears to be a revelatory space where Winston can escape the oppression of the Party. Yet, like the book, this proves to be entirely illusory.

In order to illustrate this, examining the nursery rhyme Mr Charrington teaches Winston is instructive. First, in the exhumation of long-forgotten buildings, as a remembering of history the Party erased, the recitation of the rhyme is a rebellious act. For example, the line 'You owe me three farthings, say the bells of St Martin's' (ibid: 98) uncovers the truth that the Victory Museum used to be a church. In this way, the architecture of old London is revealed. However, the same fatalism, the same lack of a true alternative ideology, is embedded in the rhyme, since the last line '… here comes a chopper to chop off your head' tells of the same ultimate failure. It is mentioned for the first time by Mr Charrington (ibid) and then, somewhat miraculously, Julia repeats the line uncoached, as she was taught the rhyme by her purged grandfather (ibid: 148). Here, the fatalistic sense predominates, as these 'older gestures of rebellion and contestation [are repeated] as if for the first time' (Fisher 2008: 13) and always have the same ending, foreshadowed in the purging of the grandfather. Indeed, in the novel, it does have the same ending as in all the other instances of dissidence in Oceania; for at the moment of Winston and Julia's arrest, in their small room above the shop, O'Brien also repeats that same line '… here comes a chopper to chop off your head' (ibid: 224).

Furthermore, when they are arrested, Orwell foregrounds the small coral antique. Winston reflects upon this beautiful object, described in a poetic simile 'pink like a sugar rose-bud from a cake' (ibid: 225) – this kind of colourful language being alien to the drab world of the Party – and thinks to himself: 'How small … how small it always was!' (ibid). Here the coral object, just as it was a symbol for his hope of dissidence earlier on, has remained his hope, small and insignificant in the face of the Party.

## WINSTON'S CHARACTER

It is small wonder, then, since so much fatalistic pessimism is present through all the avenues of dissidence, that Winston himself does not truly believe in the ability to resist the Party. Throughout the novel, Winston constantly believes 'The end was contained in the beginning' (ibid: 161), that he will always fail in the end. His one hope is that, echoing Goldstein's book, 'Out of those mighty loins [of the proles] a race of conscious beings must one day come' (ibid: 223). Yet, it is interesting how Goldstein's book influences this belief: the idea that technological progress would create consciousness in the lower class and that they would then 'sweep away' (ibid: 192) the ruling class. Yet with the effective delaying of technological and material progress on account of the 'continuous war' (ibid: 193) that Goldstein describes, this becomes a 'senseless hope' (Fisher 2008: 9), one that cannot realistically come to pass. Thus, as with anti-capitalist movements which deliberately pose demands that can never be fulfilled, the one alternative, imaginable future is also one that cannot be fulfilled. In such an intellectual environment it is no surprise that Winston always envisages his rebellion as futile.

Furthermore, as Sperber postulates, Winston himself might be 'partly their [the Thought Police's] creation' (Sperber 1980: 215), a heretic, an internal enemy, over which the Party can continually, and most importantly, always, triumph. In such a way, Winston himself becomes part of the system of Ingsoc realism, a component of the machine designed to create enfeebled opposition to continue the Party's eternal rule. Indeed, the Appendix 'On the principles of Newspeak' has been interpreted as supporting this view. Scholarly opinions differ, but one such view, Lee's (1969) is that the Appendix is a confirmation of the 'loss of consciousness' that is the ultimate evil in the novel. Indeed, as has been demonstrated, the climax of the novel, particularly in its final line 'He had won the victory over himself. He loved Big Brother' (Orwell 2018 [1949]: 300), is towards one of defeat for Winston and of vindication for the Party.

ORWELL AND FISHER: CONCLUSION

By applying Fisher's analysis to *Nineteen Eighty-Four*, I have illustrated how a kind of Ingsoc realism is constructed in the book, how controlled opposition, in addition to the most studied control of language and erasure of history, contributed to make the end of the world more imaginable than the end of the Party. Additionally, in pointing out these similarities between Fisher and Orwell, I hope to have also shown how Orwell pre-empted a great deal of Fisher's work.

REFERENCES

Fisher, Mark (2008) *Capitalist Realism: Is There No Alternative?*, London: John Hunt Publishing Ltd

Harris, Harold (1959) Orwell's essays and *1984*, *Twentieth Century Literature*, Vol. 4, No. 4 pp 154-161

Orwell, George (2018 [1949]) *Nineteen Eighty-Four*, London: Penguin English Library

Orwell, George (1946) Politics and the English language. Available online at https://www.orwellfoundation.com/the-orwell-foundation/orwell/essays-and-other-works/politics-and-the-english-language/, accessed on 22 February 2025

Sperber, Murray (1980) Gazing into the glass paperweight: The structure and psychology of Orwell's *1984*, *Modern Fiction Studies*, Vol. 26, No. 2 pp 213-226

Žižek, Slavoj (2009 [1989]) *The Sublime Object of Ideology*, London: Verso

NOTE ON THE CONTRIBUTOR

Patrick Homes is a BA student majoring in Classics at the University of Melbourne.

He has previously written for *Antigone* on the value of Latin in secondary education and a paper on political analyses of the Late Roman Republic is forthcoming. In addition to his Classical background, he has a passion for English literature, particularly the works of Orwell and their interface with political philosophy, as well as the works of the *fin-de-siècle* period including Oscar Wilde and G.K. Chesterton.

# PAPER

PAPER

# High Praise and Critique: Tom Hopkinson's Early Assessment of George Orwell

## TIM CROOK

*Before there was any standalone book study or biography of George Orwell, the legendary editor of* Picture Post, *Tom Hopkinson, wrote the first – a forty-page pamphlet published by Longmans, Green & Co. for the British Council and National Book League in 1953. It became the first detailed introduction and guide to the life and writings of George Orwell for English-speaking people all over the world and remained in print for many decades. Hopkinson did not hold back in striking at Orwell's failures and inadequacies as a writer.* The Road to Wigan Pier *was condemned as his worst book and even* Nineteen Eighty-Four *was analysed as deeply flawed, though he regarded* Animal Farm *as a work of genius. This paper investigates and explores Hopkinson on Orwell and how and why such a powerful figure in the journalism establishment, whom Orwell labelled as a 'crypto communist' in his notorious 'little list' to the Information Research Department in 1949, produced such a critical, robust and short assessment which undoubtedly advanced Orwell's reputation in the immediate years after his death..*

Key words: Hopkinson, British Council, Orwell pamphlet, *Writers and their Work*, *World Review*, Edward Hulton

INTRODUCTION

There are five major threads of connection between the legendary editor of *Picture Post*, Sir Tom Hopkinson (1905-1990) and George Orwell (1903-1950): writing fiction, journalism, socialist politics, middle class bourgeois background and resisting censorship. Orwell was a brilliant novelist and writer of short essays, though some of his essays could be classified as short stories when the creative element dominates the style of documentary journalism. Hopkinson was also a published novelist and short story writer though not a successful one.

Orwell acknowledged that the contents of his notorious 'little list' of crypto-communists he handed over to the newly-formed secret propaganda outfit, the Information Research Department, in 1949, should be 'strictly confidential' (National Archives) because his observations might well have been libellous. This is certainly possible since Hopkinson would have known the novelist and journalist Arthur Calder-Marshall whom Orwell summarised as 'Previously close fellow-traveller. Has changed, but not reliably. Insincere person' (National Archives FO 1110/89). The industrial correspondent for the *Manchester Guardian*, John Anderson, was, according to Orwell, a 'Good Reporter' but also 'Stupid' (ibid).

Orwell had clearly read Hopkinson's fourth novel *Down the Long Slide* (1949), published by Hogarth Press, as it is included in his reading for November 1949 though he did not review it (*CWGO* XX: 222). Hopkinson's fictional output included short stories written and published in periodicals and compendia such as *New Writing, Folios of New Writing, Penguin New Writing, Penguin Parade, Chamber's Journal* and *English Story* between 1935 and 1947 (Hopkinson 1948: vii). Nine of them were published by Horizon under the title *The Transitory Venus* and *Bookseller* magazine ran an advertisement for it describing Hopkinson as 'an increasingly important writer. Recommended by the Book Society' (*Bookseller* 1948: 1220).

Hopkinson's second collection of short stories was published in 1958 under the title *The Lady and the Cut-Throat* and was described by reviewer Margaret Willy for the *Birmingham Post and Gazette* as providing 'a decided taste for the unexpected situation and a keen sense of absurdity' (Willy 1958: 3).

Hopkinson's first novel, *A Wise Man Foolish*, had been published in 1930 by Chapman & Hall, three years before Orwell's debut as a novelist and writer. It did not have the same impact as Orwell's *Down and Out in Paris and London*, but one review in the weekly *Southwark and Bermondsey Recorder* was most favourable:

> The author tells how there comes to a village in the Dales country a young parson full of energy and ideals. His flock, however, are a bitter, superstitious crew, and the countryside is dominated by a mysterious legend about a pedlar who had passed that way thirty years ago. The men had hounded him out of the village because of the tremendous hold he had over women. The women were certain that he would return. Meantime he had left them a secret. In a turn on the hill grew a weed which enabled its possessors to read the secrets of all hearts. Out of the ensuing conflict between superstition and incredulity springs a strong moving story, touched by the light of romance at every turn (*Southwark and Bermondsey Recorder* 1930: 6).

# TIM CROOK

At the beginning of World War Two, Hopkinson's novels began to be published by Hogarth Press and his second, *The Man Below*, was described by the *Daily Herald* as 'a kind of Pilgrim's Progress in modern dress, the story of a boy who, during his growth to manhood, exercises his natural cowardice by extravagant self-assertion. It is written quietly and rather more than competently and it holds the attention. The best part of the book is a really thrilling account of a leaky sailing-boat's flight with a storm during a madcap trip from Liverpool to Ireland' (*Daily Herald* 1939: 8).

Hopkinson's third novel, *Mist in the Tagus*, published by Hogarth in 1946, was favourably received by the critics. An Edinburgh evening newspaper said the publishers had brought out a story 'with a refreshing difference in setting and denouement' with the author wisely developing a main young English woman character (*Edinburgh Evening Press* 1946: 3). The novel was enthusiastically received by the novelist L.P. Hartley in *The Sketch* who said Hopkinson had introduced 'a rather seedy offshoot of that now almost legendary community, the international smart set' (Hartley 1946: 338). The heroine, Caroline Page, attempts to help two Germans dodging military service in Portugal, the war is approaching and 'no country seems to want them'. But things do not turn out as she planned (ibid). Hartley said Hopkinson was 'a very interesting writer, at times curiously naïf, yet subtle, penetrating, uncompromising, sincere. His local colour is not only rich, but essential to his general design, which always takes into account the contrast, in way of life and habit of mind, between the rich and the poor, the tourists and the *indigenæ*' (ibid).

Hopkinson was a journalist motivated by the politics of the world and how they impacted on human society and individuals. While his obituary in *The Times* in 1990 did not mention any of his fiction, it did highlight the fact that his self-styled book of political satire, *A Strong Hand at the Helm*, was published by Victor Gollancz in 1933, the same year and publisher of Orwell's first book *Down and Out in Paris and London*. The obituary further noted that Hopkinson's writing was 'an astringent photograph-and-caption-and-quotation commentary on the incoherence of Ramsay Macdonald and his national government' (*Times* 1990: 14). There the similarities end. Hopkinson's book was polemical journalism with picture story-telling. Orwell's rather blended fiction with iconoclastic documentary writing.

However, Hopkinson's fourth novel, *Down the Long Slide*, had an immediate appeal to Orwell because it was clearly political fiction in which, to quote the words of *Yorkshire Post* reviewer Lettice Cooper: 'Ruritania is now a totalitarian State' (Cooper 1949: 2). Hopkinson's novel came out in 1949, the same year as *Nineteen Eighty-Four*, and Cooper observed: 'Arthur Koestler's *Darkness at Noon* was the tragedy of revolution. *Down the Long Slide* is the comedy, a comedy with a bitter twist, but admirably told in quick clean prose, a good story with a moral for the Christmas stocking' (ibid).

Moreover, the publisher's blurb indicated an exploration of the Orwellian theme of totalitarianism: '*Down the Long Slide* is a novel of suspense, the story of an escape. An old-guard Communist, the head of the State Publishing House in a Central European country, finds himself in danger of denunciation' (*Bookseller* 1949: 958).

However, there the coincidences and similarities end. Notice the opening sentences of the respective novels. In *Nineteen Eighty-Four* there is a gripping intensity of foreboding:

> It was a bright cold day in April, and the clocks were striking thirteen. Winston Smith, his chin nuzzled into his breast in an effort to escape the vile wind, slipped quickly through the glass doors of Victory Mansions, though not quickly enough to prevent a swirl of gritty dust from entering along with him.
>
> The hallway smelt of boiled cabbage and old rag mats. At one end of it a coloured poster, too large for indoor display, had been tacked to the wall. It depicted simply an enormous face, more than a metre wide: the face of a man of about forty-five, with a heavy black moustache and ruggedly handsome features (*CWGO* IX: 3).

The dystopian mystery of the clock striking thirteen is immediate. The suffering and persecuted identity of the central character, Winston, is as striking as the incongruous setting of dislocated time.

In *Down the Long Slide* Hopkinson gives his first chapter the uninspiring heading 'A battle in committee' and opens with:

> Something was going wrong with the conference. Brusilov, an immense landslide of a man commanding the long table from its centre, shifted uneasily inside his clothes, conscious that his shirt beneath his arms was soaked with sweat.
>
> 'As Director of the State Publishing House,' he declared, 'I am fully entitled to know why one of my best assistants has been treated in this way. His union card was withdrawn without any warning and he came home to find his wife and children, with all their belongings, turned out into the street' (Hopkinson 1949: 9).

It could be argued that Hopkinson has written what Orwell once described as 'a good-bad-book' (Schimanski 1950: 17). As the Hogarth Press advertisement in *Bookseller* says, Hopkinson may have written a 'gripping narrative ... which for sheer excitement it would be hard to beat' (*Bookseller* 1949: 958). But Orwell's prose has the edge and pulse of a much more experienced novelist. Hopkinson's prose feels as though it is the first draft of a long caption for his weekly magazine *Picture Post* and has not been edited by himself nor anyone else. That is not to say *Down the Long Slide* was not well received. *The Times Literary Supplement*' reviewer remarked: 'Mr Hopkinson's new book is short, packed, dialectically brilliant and organised ... Mr Hopkinson's most sustained piece of writing so far' (1949: 821).

Orwell and Hopkinson certainly shared a sense of political vision. Significantly, Canon William Loveless wrote to *The Times* in response to Hopkinson's obituary to emphasise that the late editor of *Picture Post* and South African campaigning anti-apartheid magazine *Drum* deserved to be recognised for his tremendous and courageous 'forward thinking' (Loveless 1990: 12). He recalled: 'In early 1941, when our country was wondering whether it would survive, never mind win the war, *Picture Post* devoted a whole issue to a "New Britain", anticipating what was later to be called the Welfare State' (ibid). It could be argued that Orwell paralleled Hopkinson's visionary journalism of documentary photograph and caption in his essay *The Lion and the Unicorn: Socialism and the English Genius* also published in 1941.

## HOPKINSON AND THE ORWELL BIOGRAPHIES

Tom Hopkinson is rarely mentioned in the leading biographies and studies of George Orwell published between 1967 and 2023. There is no mention in Peter Stansky and William Abrahams' *The Unknown Orwell* (1974) and *Orwell, The Transformation* (1984), nor in Jeffrey Meyers' *Orwell: Wintry Conscience of a Generation* (2000), nor in D.J. Taylor's *Orwell: The Life* (2003) and *Orwell: The New Life* (2023). Gordon Bowker, in *Inside George Orwell: A Biography* (2003), simply mentions Hopkinson as being included in Orwell's list of over a hundred names of possible 'cryptos' (Bowker 2003: 468).

George Woodcock's *The Crystal Spirit*, first published in hardback by Jonathan Cape in 1967 and more widely read in the Penguin version published in 1970, refers to Hopkinson describing *The Road To Wigan Pier* as Orwell's worst (Woodcock 1970 [1967]: 125), that he thought Orwell only took to writing novels because it was the form which 'everyone was writing in the 1930s' (ibid 269) and cited Hopkinson's 1953 study of Orwell as one of those worthy of bibliographical citation (ibid: 280).

He is considered important enough to be explored in one of the seminal works on Orwell's impact on literature and culture by John Rodden. In *George Orwell: The Politics of Literary Reputation* (2002), Rodden describes Hopkinson as one of Orwell's acquaintances who praised his writing in *The World Review* of June 1950 (Rodden 2002: 46), recognised that Hopkinson 'wrote the first critical study of Orwell' and 'made the much-quoted statement that *Wigan Pier* was Orwell's "worst book"' (ibid: 109). Rodden emphasises that Hopkinson, as a writer about Orwell, ranked among the subject's 'slight acquaintances' such as his Eton contemporary and later Conservative MP Christopher Hollis (ibid: 147).

Bernard Crick's *A Life* (1980) recognised how Hopkinson appreciated the importance of the first betrayal of revolution in *Animal Farm* when the pigs justify hoarding the milk and apples for themselves through Snowball's speech: '"Comrades," he cried. "You do not imagine, I hope, that we pigs are doing this in a spirit of selfishness and privilege? Many of us actually dislike milk and apples"' (ibid: 490). He said Hopkinson gave the passage 'pride of place in a famous assessment of *Animal Farm*, just after Orwell's death, in which he said: "I know only two present-day works of fiction before which the critic abdicates: one is Arthur Koestler's *Darkness at Noon*, the other Orwell's *Animal Farm*"' (ibid).

Hopkinson receives only eleven citations in Peter Davison's twenty-volume *The Complete Works of George Orwell* (*CWGO* XX: 429): nothing to compare to the number of references given to Orwell's close friends Tosco Fyvel, David Astor or Richard Rees. In a footnote to Orwell's wartime diary for 28 August 1940, Davison says: 'Tom Hopkinson, one of the founders of the unofficial Home Guard Training School at Osterley Park, tells how a Brigadier Whitehead attempted to have the school stopped in the autumn of 1940 because it did not have a licence, see *Of This Our Time* (1982)' (*CWGO* XII: 241).

There are five references in Vol. XVIII: *Smothered Under Journalism 1946* because Davison covers the time Hopkinson lunched with Orwell in London. Orwell wrote about it to Arthur Koestler on 2 January 1946: 'I have arranged to have lunch with Tom Hopkinson and Barbara Ward about a week hence' to talk about a plan Koestler and he had to develop a 'Rights of Man' body 'to counter the decline in democratic feeling throughout the world' (*CWGO* XVIII: 7). Orwell had drafted a new charter. In a footnote, Davison provides a short biography of Hopkinson and stresses: 'Of his two autobiographies, *Of This Our Time* (1982) … is concerned with the period in which Orwell was working' (ibid). In a letter to Arthur Koestler on 10 January 1946, Orwell writes:

> I saw Barbara Ward and Tom Hopkinson today and told them about our project. They were both a little timid, chiefly I think because they realise that an organisation of this type would in practice be anti-Russian, or would be compelled to become anti-Russian, and they are going through an acute phase of

anti-Americanism. However, they are anxious to hear more and are not hostile to the idea. ... I have no doubt these two would help to the extent of passing our ideas on to others, but at some stage it might be more useful to contact Hulton [proprietor of *Picture Post*] personally, which I could do (ibid: 28).

Davison also credits Tom Hopkinson for donating to the George Orwell archive, set up at University College London in 1960, the manuscript of his British Council-censored pamphlet on English cooking. This had been commissioned and written in 1946. An editor called Sykes thought Orwell's writing was 'excellent but that it would be unwise to publish it for a continental reader at this time' (ibid: 201).

In 2019, the British Council publicly apologised for the blunder of turning down Orwell's thoughts on English cuisine (Flood 2019) and Davison records: 'Sykes concluded: "I hope you will understand how sorry (and angry!) I am about this, and that you will write for us in the future – starting off on the right foot!" Orwell did not write for the British Council again' (*CWGO* XVIII: 201). But Hopkinson wrote about Orwell for the British Council's *Writers and their Work* series, published by Longmans three years after his death.

In Orwell's 'As I Please' *Tribune* column for 4 April 1947, he analysed the work of the Royal Commission on the Press: 'Recently I was talking to the editor of a newspaper with a very large circulation, who told me that it was now quite easy for his paper to live on its sales alone' (*CWGO* XIX: 117). Even though technically *Picture Post* was not a newspaper, Davison speculates that Orwell was referring to Hopkinson and his views in this column (ibid: 119).

## *WORLD REVIEW* TO BRITISH COUNCIL PAMPHLET

Hopkinson was further connected and involved in the first two significant printed publications analysing and celebrating the life of George Orwell and his writings following his untimely death at University College Hospital on 21 January 1950. Hopkinson's proprietor, the Conservative Party-supporting Edward Hulton, also published *World Review*. The journalist employed on *World Review* by Hulton, Stefan Schimanski, proposed that the June 1950 edition should focus on George Orwell. Schimanski asked Hopkinson to contribute a critique on *Animal Farm*.

Richard Lance Keeble, in analysing the significance of this edition of *World Review*, comments: 'Interestingly, it mixed both celebration and critique. Orwell's personality as much as his writings clearly fascinated many – and this is reflected in the articles here' (Keeble 2017). He concludes that 'the various articles provide a fascinating if rather idiosyncratic insight into the early reception of Orwell' (ibid).

In discussing Hopkinson's glowing analysis of *Animal Farm*, Keeble contextualises the *Picture Post* editor's contribution in this way:

> Actually, his stint at *Picture Post* was soon to be ended abruptly after Hulton objected to his publication in October 1950 of reports by James Cameron and photojournalist Bert Hardy of UN atrocities in the Korean War – and promptly sacked him. In his article, Hopkinson provides a precis of the novel, ending in glowing terms: 'Orwell's knowledge of farming helps to maintain the necessary faint illusion of reality. Nothing is shirked – even the relations of "Animal Farm" with its human neighbours. Everything is treated with combined lightness and assurance that suspend disbelief. ... *Animal Farm* is a work of genius in the lofty tradition of English humorous writing' (ibid).

The Hopkinson review of *Animal Farm*, running to almost four full pages, was the longest analysis of one of Orwell's books in the periodical. *World Review*'s other intrinsic value was in publishing for the first time an edited form of Orwell's World War Two diary covering the Blitz in London during 1940 and 1941 and continuing through 1942 when he was working at the BBC. Schimanski observed 'the records as he left them in his notebooks have, indeed, the value of a document that brings to life a forgotten and short-lived period of high expectation' (Schimanski 1950: 4). Orwell's sociological and documentary style of writing about London and its people during the fall of France and the Blitz would be echoed by Hopkinson's introduction to John Neville's *The Blitz: London Then & Now* published in 1990, the last year of his life.

Both men shared a compassion for their fellow citizens struggling to survive. Hopkinson, for instance, wrote of the 'families who had at first camped out in the Anderson, joined the nightly trek into the underground, where at least there was warmth and company as well as security' (Hopkinson 1990: 26). Orwell, for his part, wrote of the 'Nondescript people wandering about, having been evacuated from their houses because of delayed-action bombs. Yesterday two girls stopping me filthily dirty: "Please, sir, can you tell us where we are?"' (Orwell *Notebook* 21 September 1940 in Schimanski 1950: 34).

Schimanski made it clear at the end of his *World Review* editorial: 'ANNOUNCEMENT: *The next issue, July, will be the last under the present editorship. S.S.*' (ibid: 4). As Hopkinson explained in his first autobiography: 'Schimanski told me that Hulton disapproved of his efforts to make *World Review* into a serious literary magazine and was dispensing with his services. Knowing Schimanski to be a competent reporter and journalist in addition to his literary interests, I at once offered him a job on *Picture Post*. In view of my own precarious situation at the time, this can be considered as either quixotic or idiotic, or possibly both' (Hopkinson 1982: 279). Schimanski began reporting the Korean War with the photographer Haywood Magee, but Schimanski was killed when an American plane flying him back to Korea from Tokyo exploded over the sea (Hopkinson 1982: 280-1 & see https://picturestoriesfilm.com/haywood-mageewar-again). Hopkinson would hire foreign correspondent James Cameron, recently recruited from the *Daily Express*, and photographer Bert Hardy to continue reporting the worsening conflict and his support for them would cost him his editorship (ibid 282-97 & see https://spartacus-educational.com/Jhopkinson.htm).

## HOPKINSON ON ORWELL

In his second autobiography, *Under the Tropic* (1984), Hopkinson charted his life after leaving *Picture Post*: 'I wrote ... a short book or pamphlet on George Orwell, commissioned by the British Council for their series *Writers and their Work*. This came out in the summer of 1953 and received, according to the British Council report, "more critical notice than any in the series, the overwhelming majority being favourable"' (Hopkinson 1984: 15-16).

Hopkinson's 40-page booklet included Vernon Richards's best photographic portrait of Orwell with white carnation button-hole,

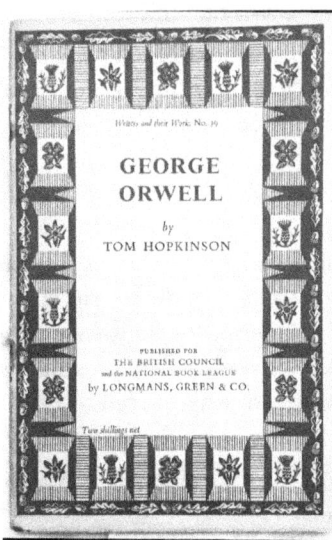

Cover of *George Orwell* by Tom Hopkinson published by Longmans Green & Co. for the British Council and the National Book League in 1953

looking down at his cigarette next to a cup of tea on the side table. It also contained drawings of the *Animal Farm* characters, Squealer, Napoleon, Old Major, Boxer and Benjamin by John Helas and Joy Batchelor from the cartoon film version of the book which would be released the following year, partly funded by the US Central Intelligence Agency (CIA) (Leab 2007).

The British Council, in conjunction with the National Book League and the publisher Longmans, was also projecting British 'soft power' through their concise, highly readable celebrations of British literary culture. Orwell was in a collection of 60 *Writers and their Work* which included Charles Dickens, Daniel Defoe, Rudyard Kipling, Jane Austen, Virginia Woolf, H.G. Wells, Shakespeare and Somerset Maugham.

Photograph of George Orwell by Vernon Richards on page 2 of *George Orwell*, by Tom Hopkinson. By kind permission of Vernon Richards' estate

The two shilling (10 pence in post-1970 currency) booklet had the most up-to-date and extensive bibliography of Orwell's publications and index of essays hitherto published and understandably would remain in print well into the 1970s. The British Council was correct when assessing the strength of the critical reception which recognised that Hopkinson was not engaged in untrammelled hagiography. The *Belfast Newsletter* observed: 'Hopkinson's judgements seem harsh at times – he had little imagination, little understanding of human relationships, little sympathy with individual human beings, was a somewhat didactic talker, was without historical perspective, all his novels are alike, concentrates on himself, and so on. But, on the whole, the picture is a fair, objective one. The author of *Animal Farm* deserved his place in this series' (*Belfast Newsletter* 1953: 3).

Maurice Cranston, in *Truth*, was inspired by the Hopkinson study to turn his review into a lengthy essay comparing Orwell with Kipling and justified this by arguing Orwell's story 'told by Tom Hopkinson in this excellent British Council monograph, is a curious one. Not the least curious is the resemblance between Orwell's early life and that of Rudyard Kipling, who was born 50 years before him and who might seem to have been the very antithesis of the kind of man that Orwell was' (Cranston 1953: 918).

*The Times Literary Supplement* said Hopkinson had given 'a well-balanced and most readable survey of George Orwell's life and writings. He shows clear sympathy for Orwell, without being blind to his failings: a point which he stresses is Orwell's inclination, in common with other satirists, to sympathise with humanity *en masse* but to keep remote from, or even to be repulsed by, its individual members. Orwell had the very real and fine generosity of

Illustration of Boxer and Benjamin by John Halas and Joy Batchelor from the cartoon version of *Animal Farm* published on page 40 of *George Orwell* by Tom Hopkinson. By kind permission of Vivien Halas and The Halas & Batchelor Collection Limited

the liberal, but as for so many liberal humanists 'charity, for him, tended to begin abroad' (*TLS* 1953: 418).

Hopkinson's study inevitably drew upon much of Tosco Fyvel's biographical section in the 1950 *World Review*. The 1950s was the decade when the first and longest of individual studies of Orwell's writings were published. There is evidence Hopkinson certainly informed and may well have inspired the authors of three book-length analyses of Orwell as a writer: John Atkins in *George Orwell: A Literary Study* in 1954, Laurence Brander, in *George Orwell* also in 1954, and Christopher Hollis, in *A Study of George Orwell: The Man and his Works* in 1956. Hopkinson started some important discussions about Orwell's works. Atkins, for example, said:

> Everyone who has written on Orwell has noticed the constant mortification to which he subjected himself and has tried to explain it. Tom Hopkinson attributes it to Orwell's lack of historic sense, by which only the present seems significant to him. The future (about which Orwell never stopped worrying) was simply the projection of the present; the past, with the sense of perspective that it gives, hardly existed for him (Atkins 1954: 108).

Brander, the representative of British intelligence who worked alongside Orwell while he was producing programmes for the BBC's Eastern Service (1941-1943), references Hopkinson five times. He credited him for 'his interesting speculation about Orwell's preference for painting things darkly (Brander 1954: 6). According to Brander, there may have been in Orwell as 'Mr Hopkinson says, an element of relief in feather-bedding himself at the very bottom of society without any responsibilities. But it was done with courage and integrity' (ibid: 69). Brander also engages strongly with Hopkinson in his chapter on *Animal Farm*:

> Mr Tom Hopkinson remembers a war-time lunch in Soho in 1943, at which there were loud praises of Russia. Orwell who was there, listened for a while and then asked: 'What explanation do you give for the imprisonment of Russian writers?' No one answered; one did not criticise Russia. For the same reason, four publishers rejected *Animal Farm* (ibid: 170).

Christopher Hollis challenges Hopkinson's view that *The Road to Wigan Pier* is Orwell's worst book:

> Mr Hopkinson's criticism is not to my mind wholly fair nor indeed his analysis of it wholly accurate. The last thing that Orwell calls for in this book is what Mr Hopkinson asserts – 'an immediate resolution of all class differences'. On the contrary, his plea is exactly the opposite. It is that it is an

insincere folly for members of the bourgeoisie to pretend that they have not got snobbish habits (Hollis 1956: 77).

*Down and Out*, Hopkinson says, 'is a remarkable and fascinating work, somewhat scrappy ... did not sell well, but it received high praise ... was noticed and praised by leading critics' (Hopkinson 1953: 18).

*Down and Out* was, indeed, lauded by J.B. Priestley in the *Manchester Evening News*. Under the headline 'J.B. Priestley finds AN EPIC of the underworld', Priestley writes: 'This book is not and does not pretend to be a contribution to literature, but it is uncommonly good reading and a social document of some value. It is, indeed, the best book of its kind I have read for a long time' (Priestley 1933: 6).

The *Times Literary Supplement* reviewer comments: 'It is a vivid picture of an apparently mad world that Mr Orwell paints in his book, a world were unfortunate men are preyed upon by parasites, both insect and human, where a straight line of demarcation is drawn above which no man can hope to rise once he has fallen below its level' (*TLS* 1933: 22). Indeed, Hopkinson argues Orwell 'could endure the company of a down-and-out in the next hospital bed by conscious effort, but the moment the conscious effort was relaxed, other human beings appeared odious and detestable – the more odious and detestable, the closer their relation to himself' (Hopkinson 1953: 10).

Hopkinson's study gives pre-eminence and critical recognition for literature which could deploy 'in Swiftian satire against mankind, or in the recording of frustrating personal experience. ... Orwell, besides novels and essays, wrote two admirable records of misfortune, *Down and Out in Paris and London* and *Homage to Catalonia* (his picture of the Spanish War), as well as one satire, his masterpiece *Animal Farm*' (ibid 11). But he does not consider *Nineteen Eighty-Four* a masterpiece:

> The weakness of *Nineteen Eighty-Four* is a double one. Orwell, sick and dispirited, has imagined nothing new. His world of 1984 is the war-time world of 1944, but dirtier and more cruel – and with all the endurance and nobility which distinguished mankind in that upheaval, mysteriously drained away. Everyone by 1984 is to be a coward, a spy, and a betrayer. ... Even technically, the book shows little imagination. ...
>
> The book's second weakness is another aspect of the first. By amputating all courage and self-sacrifice from his human beings, Orwell has removed any real tension from his story (ibid: 35).

This judgement is in contrast to the full-page *Times Literary Supplement* review of the novel by Julian Symons in 1949. Symons concludes: '...the last word about this book must be one of thanks, rather than of criticism: thanks for a writer who deals with the problems of the world rather than the ingrowing pains of individuals, and who is able to speak seriously and with originality of the nature of reality and the terrors of power' (Symons 1949: 380). But Symons does agree with Hopkinson's criticism's of Orwell's style: 'The sobriety and subtlety of Mr Orwell's argument, however, is marred by a schoolboyish sensationalism of approach' (ibid).

## HOPKINSON'S ORWELLIAN LEGACY

Tom Hopkinson wrote the best and shortest combination of biography and literary study of George Orwell it is possible to find. Forty pages, one photograph, four illustrations for two shillings written and published only three years after the subject's death was, and arguably remains, the best value introduction to one of the world's most famous English authors.

Orwell, were he alive, would surely pay tribute to an acquaintance whose short pamphlet accelerated and elevated his reputation and significance. What better resource for students of all levels wishing to study Orwell's writing whether in Britain or abroad. By the late 1950s, Orwell's *Nineteen Eighty-Four*, *Animal Farm* and essays were already being taught to school sixth forms, adult classes and training college students (Bott 1958: vii).

Orwell and Hopkinson were kindred spirits in their stress on fairness and human dignity which is where their socialism coalesced. Their writing was also crystal clear and humanitarian. In different ways, they experienced the injustice and frustration of censorship. But both men were rightly angry about the unjust denial of human rights for others less fortunate than themselves.

## REFERENCES

Atkins, John (1954) *George Orwell: A Literary Study*, London: John Calder

*Belfast News Letter* (1953) Among the new books: Miscellaneous, Belfast, 10 October p. 3

*Bookseller* (1948) Horizon Books, 20 November p. 1220

*Bookseller* (1949) As exciting as any thriller! *Down the Long Slide*, 22 October p. 958

Bott, George (ed.) (1958) *George Orwell: Selected Writings*, London: Heinemann Educational Books Ltd

Bowker, Gordon (2003) *Inside George Orwell: A Biography*, London: Little, Brown

Brander, Laurence (1954) *George Orwell*, London: Longmans, Green and Co.

Cooper, Lettice (1949) Three new novels, *Yorkshire Post and Leeds Mercury*, 2 December p. 2

Cowan, Evelyn E. et al. (1939) Recommended new novels, *Coming Up For Air*, *Times Literary Supplement*, No. 1954, 15 July p. 428

Cranston, Maurice (1953) George Orwell: The Etonian who dwelt in doss houses, *Truth*, 24 July p. 918

Crick, Bernard (1980) *George Orwell: A Life*, Harmondsworth, Middlesex: Penguin

CWGO (1998) *The Complete Works of George Orwell, XX Vols*, Peter Davison (ed.) London: Secker & Warburg

*Daily Herald* (1939) Negro fact and fiction, 2 March p. 8

Dunton, Mark (2019) George Orwell: Surveillance and the state, National Archives, 6 June. Available online at https://blog.nationalarchives.gov.uk/george-orwell-surveillance-and-the-state/, accessed on 10 February 2025

*Edinburgh Evening News* (1946) Among the new books, 30 November p. 3

Flood, Alison (2019) George Orwell: British Council apologises for rejecting food essay, *Guardian*, 7 February, Available online at https://www.theguardian.com/books/2019/feb/07/george-orwell-british-council-apologises-for-rejecting-food-essay, accessed on 15 February 2025

Fyvel, Tosco (1982) *George Orwell: A Personal Memoir*, New York: Weidenfeld & Nicolson

Hartley, L.P. (1946) The literary lounger, *Sketch*, 11 December 1946 p. 338

Harvey, G.E. (1935) New novels: Burmese Days, *Times Literary Supplement*, No. 1746, 18 July p. 462

Hollis, Christopher (1956) *A Study of George Orwell: The Man and his Works*, London: Hollis and Carter

Hopkinson, Tom (1930) *A Wise Man Foolish*, London: Jonathan Cape

Hopkinson, Tom (1933) *A Strong Hand at the Helm*, London: Gollancz

Hopkinson, Tom (1939) *The Man Below*, London: Hogarth Press

Hopkinson, Tom (1946) *Mist in the Tagus*, London: Hogarth Press

Hopkinson, Tom (1949) *Down the Long Slide*, London: Hogarth Press

Hopkinson, Tom (1950) Animal Farm, in Schimanski, Stefan (ed.) *World Review*, June, New Series 16, London: Edward Hulton pp 54-57

Hopkinson, Tom (1953) *George Orwell*, London: Longmans, Green & Co. for the British Council and the National Book League

Hopkinson, Tom (1958) *The Lady and the Cut-Throat*, London: Jonathan Cape

Hopkinson, Tom (1982) *Of This Our Time*, London: Hutchinson & Co.

Hopkinson, Tom (1984) *Under the Tropic*, London: Hutchinson & Co.

Hopkinson, Tom (1990) Introduction, Neville, John, *The Blitz: London; Then & Now*, London: Hodder & Stoughton

Keeble, Richard Lance (2017) Orwell appreciated: Just months after he died, Orwell Society website, 17 January. Available online at https://orwellsociety.com/orwell-appreciated-just-months-after-he-died/, accessed on 14 August 2024

Keeble, Richard Lance (2021) The pleasure and politics of food, in *Orwell's Moustache: Addressing More Orwellian Matters*, Bury St Edmunds: Abramis pp 117-138

Leab, Daniel J. (2007) *Orwell Subverted: The CIA and the Filming of* Animal Farm, Pennsylvania: Penn State University Press

Loveless, Canon William (1990) Sir Tom Hopkinson, *Times*, 29 June p. 12

Meyers, Jeffrey (2000) *Orwell: Wintry Conscience of a Generation*, New York: W.W. Norton & Co.

# TIM CROOK

National Archives (1948) IRD material: possible use of material in Middle East, central and South American press, Foreign Office and Foreign and Commonwealth Office: Information Research Department: General Correspondence, catalogue reference FO 1110/89, National Archives, Kew, Richmond, Surrey TW9 4DU

Orwell, George (1938) Letters, *Homage to Catalonia*, *Times Literary Supplement*, No. 1895, 28 May 1938 p. 370

Priestley, J.B. (1933) Men, women and books, *Manchester Evening News*, 12 January p. 6

Rodden, John (2002) *George Orwell: The Politics of Literary Reputation*, New Brunswick and London: Transaction Publishers

Ross, Alan (1949) Behind the headlines, *Down the Long Slide*, *Times Literary Supplement*, No. 2498, 16 December p. 821

Schimanski, Stefan (ed.) (1950) *World Review*, June, London: Edward Hulton

*Southwark and Bermondsey Recorder* (1930) A wise man foolish, 20 June p. 6

Stansky, Peter and Abrahams, William (1974) *The Unknown Orwell*, London: Constable and Co.

Stansky, Peter and Abrahams, William (1980) *Orwell, The Transformation*, London: Constable and Co.

Symons, Julian (1949) Power and corruption, *Times Literary Supplement*, No. 2471, 10 June p. 380

Taylor, D.J. (2003) *Orwell: The Life*, London: Chatto & Windus

Taylor, D.J. (2023) *Orwell: The New Life*, London: Constable

*Times* (1990) Obituary: Sir Tom Hopkinson, 22 June p. 14

TLS (1940) Sociological critic: Mr Orwell on Dickens, *Times Literary Supplement*, No. 1994, 20 April p. 192

TLS (1953) Books received: Hopkinson, Tom, *George Orwell*, The Times Literary Supplement, No. 2682, 26 June p. 418

Willy, Margaret (1958) Short stories, *Birmingham Post and Gazette*, 22 July p. 3

Woodcock, George (1970 [1967]) *The Crystal Spirit: A Study of George Orwell*, Harmondsworth, England: Penguin Books

## NOTE ON THE CONTRIBUTOR

Tim Crook is Emeritus Professor at Goldsmiths, University of London and is a longstanding journalist, author and academic. He has written extensively on George Orwell, is currently researching and writing a study of *Orwell on the Radio* for Ashgate – and with Richard Lance Keeble editing the 320,000-word *Routledge Orwell Companion*.

# Wyndham Lewis Reading (and Misreading?) George Orwell

**NATHAN WADDELL**

*This paper investigates the attention paid to George Orwell by the modernist painter and writer Wyndham Lewis (1882-1957) who made his name as an intellectual provocateur. It focuses on Lewis's late book* The Writer and the Absolute *(1952), which culminates with a forty-page analysis of Orwell's life and work. Orwell and Lewis were highly dissimilar: the first an internationally celebrated journalist, essayist and novelist associated with the political left; the second a less well-known, though still very significant, modernist painter, writer and critic associated with the political right. Despite these differences, they were drawn to each other's writing and ideas, and* The Writer and the Absolute *remains a key early response to Orwell's work and an idiosyncratic chapter in his literary-historical reception.* The Writer and the Absolute *also shows how strategically Lewis tended to interpret the activities of his literary contemporaries, who often act in his criticism as a foil against which he polemically outlines and defends his own principles. Having traced certain connections and points of difference between Orwell and Lewis, the paper examines the response of M.W. Freer to Lewis's criticisms of Orwell – and concludes by suggesting that* The Writer and the Absolute*'s value lies less in what it tells us about Orwell and more in what it reveals about Lewis's tendency to subject his peers to contempt.*

Key words: Orwell, Wyndham Lewis, *The Writer and the Absolute*, M.W. Freer

Writing to Brenda Salkeld in September 1932, George Orwell remarked:

I see Wyndham Lewis (*not* D.B. Wyndham Lewis, a stinking RC) has just brought out a book called Snooty Baronet, apparently a novel of sorts. It might be interesting. All I've ever read of his was a queer periodical called The Enemy, & odd articles, but he's evidently got some kick in him – whether at all a sound thinker or not, I can't be sure without further acquaintance. The copy of The Enemy I read was all a ferocious attack, about the length of an average novel, on Gertrude Stein – rather wasted energy, one would say (1998: 268).[1]

# NATHAN WADDELL

Regularly mistaken, then and now, for the journalist and humourist Dominic Bevan Wyndham Lewis (1891-1969), author of *François Villon* (1928) and co-editor of *The Stuffed Owl: An Anthology of Bad Verse* (1930), the Wyndham Lewis Orwell had in mind is the modernist painter and writer who was born in 1882 and who died in 1957. This Lewis, born Percy Wyndham Lewis but dropping the 'Percy' in adulthood, made his name as an artist, novelist, cultural critic, political analyst and philosopher – and as a contrarian and controversialist. Author of *Snooty Baronet* (1932), a satire on the world of inter-war publishing, Lewis wrote many other novels, including *Tarr* (1918), which concerns the lives of artists in pre-war bohemian Paris; *The Apes of God* (1930), an existential send-up of Bloomsbury and its artistic hangers-on, and *The Human Age* trilogy (1928-1955), a near-unclassifiable work of theological science fiction. Lewis also edited several journals, starting with *BLAST* (1914-1915) and continuing with *The Tyro* (1920-1921) and *The Enemy* (1927-1929). He was a magnificent draughtsman, oil painter and watercolourist, creating technically unsurpassed artworks throughout his career until his sight began to fail him in the late 1940s. The boldness Orwell detected in Lewis was not due to deep or sustained familiarity, as he admitted. But it was an accurate trait to have noticed. One thing Lewis did not lack was 'kick'.

Nearly a decade after Orwell wrote to Salkeld, Lewis asked his publisher to send copies of his new novel *The Vulgar Streak* (1941) to three authors: Naomi Mitchison, H.G. Wells and a 'Mr. Orwell', whose first name Lewis could not remember (1963: 307). Lewis did not explain in the letter why he wanted his publisher to send Orwell the book, though he indicated that he knew his *The Lion and the Unicorn*, which had appeared in February of that year. Clearly, Lewis thought that Orwell would find *The Vulgar Streak* interesting, given its focus on class politics and on the Munich conference of 1938. We know that Orwell read the novel because in *The English People* (1947) he notes that the 'English working class, as Mr. Wyndham Lewis has put it, are "branded on the tongue"' (2001b: 202-203). This near-quotation alludes to a moment in *The Vulgar Streak* when its protagonist emphasises that he grew up in England's 'poisonous air' of 'class-discrimination: of the superstition of *class* like a great halter round one's neck – in which [his] very tongue was branded as if [he] were a despised property' (1985: 38, italics in the original). Orwell's allusion indicates the slim outline of a connection between two figures who in many respects were highly dissimilar: one an internationally celebrated journalist, essayist and novelist associated with the political left; the other a less well-known, though still very significant, modernist painter, writer and critic associated with the political right.

The slimness of the connection is one of the most interesting aspects of it: a near-miss of personalities who may, under different circumstances, have enjoyed some kind of friendly rivalry. There is no surviving evidence to show that Orwell and Lewis corresponded. They neither knew each other socially nor met in person. Yet evidently they knew *of* each other. Orwell had access to at least one copy of *The Enemy* because the journal was stocked in the Hampstead bookshop, Booklovers' Corner (1998: 386), where he worked from 1934-1936.[2] Although in *Keep the Aspidistra Flying* (1936) Gordon Comstock dismisses Lewis, along with T.S. Eliot, Ezra Pound, W.H. Auden, Roy Campbell, Cecil Day-Lewis and Stephen Spender as a damp squib, 'Inside the whale' (1940), his essay on Henry Miller which takes in a critical overview of the literature of the 1920s and 1930s, suggests that Orwell had read and understood Lewis's novel *Tarr* and that he regarded him as an important contemporary. We know Orwell read Lewis's study of English national character, *The Mysterious Mr Bull* (1938), because he reviewed it alongside the English translation of Ignazio Silone's *The School for Dictators* (1939) in the *New English Weekly* in June 1939 (2000: 353-355). However, Orwell never wrote a major essay on Lewis – there's no assessment in the mould of his pieces on Charles Dickens, T.S. Eliot, Rudyard Kipling or Jonathan Swift.[3] Rayner Heppenstall recalled Orwell 'inveighing' against Lewis, along with Scottish nationalists, bishops, civil servants, Roman Catholics, well-to-do Bohemians, psychiatrists and 'most socialists', including John Middleton Murry (1988: 42). This attitude seems to have led Orwell to trust in rumour. As he wrote in 1946: 'Wyndham Lewis, I am credibly informed, has become a Communist or at least a strong sympathiser, and is writing a book in praise of Stalin to balance his previous books in favour of Hitler' (2001d: 287). Politically, Lewis was nowhere near communism in 1946, and the idea that he was writing a sympathetic book on Stalin to balance out his ill-judged book *Hitler* (1931) and its anti-fascist, though still controversial, follow-up, *The Hitler Cult* (1939), is a near-groundless fantasy.[4]

It's a compelling fantasy, all the same. Lewis later dismissed it as 'utter nonsense' (1984b: 84), not least because he thought it came close to libel. Yet Orwell's claim remains interesting because of how it prompted Lewis to show his hand. Shortly after learning about Orwell's 'credibly informed' allegations, he wrote a letter to the American author and journal editor, Dwight Macdonald, in which he described Orwell as a 'silly billy' who lacked a 'serious mind': 'He's full of political tittletattle – but he gets it all wrong. He thinks people are always falling in love with political Stars' (1963: 403). Six months later, in an August 1947 letter sent from London to the young Canadian writer David Kahma, Lewis renewed the offensive:

**NATHAN WADDELL**

Mr. Orwell (as they call him here 'bore-well') is an excitable idiot, who spends his time affixing political labels to people. There is no foundation whatever for the rumour you mention that I become a politician. I impartially dislike all factions: and I am not susceptible as is silly Mr. Orwell, to the fascination of political Stars (nor ever have been). I have always been inclined to keep a stupid old bitch known as Brittania (sic) out of dog-fights, that is all (1963: 411).

Indulging here in some obvious self-revisionism, Lewis underplayed his drift into appeasement politics in the mid 1930s and also conveniently forgot that he was highly susceptible to the 'fascination of political Stars', Mussolini and Hitler among them, in the late 1920s and early 1930s.[5] As ever with Lewis, the thought that someone had slighted him impelled him to entertaining mockery. The same spirit emerged in his autobiography *Rude Assignment* (1950): 'As to the meaning of [Orwell's] personal attack upon me, it was again, I suppose, the sporting instinct. The Sahib imagined himself in the jungles of Burma, doing a bit of rogue-elephant hunting! – I have not, however, proved myself a very savage animal. I have contented myself with shaking him off. I have not eaten him alive!' (1984b: 86). This is typical Lewisian excess, only barely concealing a grudging esteem. Having dismissed Orwell in 1947 as 'an excitable idiot', by 1950 Lewis was willing to concede, in the most backhanded of indirect compliments, that Orwell was 'not by any means a brainless person' (ibid).

The most substantial reference to Orwell in Lewis's writing appears in his late book *The Writer and the Absolute* (1952), written when he had gone blind. It fixes on a career-long theme: what Lewis calls the 'dragooning' of 'the man of letters' to a particular, and usually political, cause (1952: 3). The end of this book, which on the way considers the work of Jean-Paul Sartre, André Malraux, Albert Camus and Martin Heidegger among others, contains a surprise, its closing forty pages being devoted to a long commentary on 'Orwell, or two and two make four'. This part of *The Writer and the Absolute* begins with Lewis's claim that his 'subject, George Orwell, is of the English war and post-war writers, not alone the one most worthy of attention, but … the only one' (ibid: 153). Typically idiosyncratic in their style and characteristically sardonic in their tone, Lewis's remarks about Orwell offer an insight into what a leading modernist made of the most famous political writer in England at the time. Lewis concludes his observations by stating that Orwell 'possessed a very vigorous mind', and that 'he went much farther on the road to an ultimate political realism than any of his contemporaries' (ibid: 193). Yet Lewis's comments in *The Writer and the Absolute* come very close, at times, to the kind of 'savage' analysis he decried in *Rude Assignment*. They also show just how strategically Lewis tended to interpret the work of his literary contemporaries, who often act in his criticism as a foil against which he polemically outlines and defends his own principles. Although Lewis evidently deemed Orwell a major figure, he never quite shook the thought that he made a career out of 'misdirected energy' (ibid).

My concern in this paper lies with Lewis's responses to Orwell, rather than with Orwell's responses to Lewis.[6] Writing about these connections, Alan Munton has insisted that any discussion of Orwell and Lewis 'must be about their differences' (2025: 587).[7] Much of what I have to say in what follows proceeds in this line, pointing out the dissimilarities between the two figures and concentrating especially on how Lewis reads and arguably misreads Orwell in *The Writer and the Absolute*. Yet I also want to address their points of overlap, remembering Kristin Bluemel's insight that 'the middle years of the twentieth century' are characterised by a 'web of sometimes subtle, sometimes obvious associations between … writers, institutions and cultural forms' (2009: 1-2). Lewis and Orwell are hardly two peas in a pod, and it's difficult to think of two writers with such different literary styles. There are parallels in their thought, however, and these point to several intriguing 'associations'. To quote Julian Symons, who knew both men:

> Like Orwell [Lewis] maintained intellectual independence in a time favourable to one or another sort of conformity; like Orwell had an itch for politics; like Orwell was ignored, because of his ideas, by some people in important positions; like Orwell was utterly informal, without a trace of literary or social affectation. Yet although he was so easy to talk to Lewis was inhuman, in a way that Orwell was not; he was a man devoured by a passion for ideas, which he wished to put to the service of art (1957: 53).

Having traced some of these overlaps and discussed Lewis's response to Orwell in *The Writer and the Absolute*, I conclude by suggesting that the value of Lewis's account lies less in what it tells us about Orwell and more in what it reveals about Lewis's tendency, or need, to subject his peers to contempt.

DIFFERENT TEMPERAMENTS, ILLUMINATING CONNECTIONS

A central figure in London's avant-garde scene in the early to mid-1910s, during which he founded the art movement Vorticism, Lewis has been described as Orwell's 'arch-enemy' (see Loewenstein, 1996).[8] Part of this reputation comes from the shape of Lewis's political sympathies, which were consistently inflected by authoritarian thinking even as they moved from a kind of anarchism at the start of his career to an ill-judged sequence of

NATHAN WADDELL

brushes with fascism and other kinds of undemocratic thought in the 1920s and then appeasement rhetoric in the 1930s; and finally to an ambivalent commitment to social democracy in the 1940s and 1950s (see Munton 2006). Orwell's politics were similarly complicated and full of transitions, though broadly speaking he was aligned throughout most of his working life with the political left. In many other respects these two figures led extremely different lives. Lewis was educated at the Slade School of Fine Art, in London, before travelling through central Europe for much of the early 1900s. Having returned to London he co-launched the Rebel Art Centre in 1914, and it was here that he incubated Vorticism (a rival to Cubism and Italian Futurism). Lewis fought in the First World War as an Artillery Officer before returning to London, where he lived until the Second World War when he moved to the US and Canada. His final decade was spent back in London and blighted by ill health and deteriorating eyesight.

Lewis and Orwell had very different temperaments, yet there are similarities in their lives and careers.[9] This begins with their birthplaces, which in both cases were out and away from England: Orwell in India and Lewis in Canada (by legend on his father's yacht off the coast of Nova Scotia), and these respective origin points may explain some of their 'outsider' status in so much of what they did in their lives.[10] Like Orwell, who went to Eton from 1917-1921, Lewis had a public school education, attending Rugby from 1897 to 1898. Both men spent time in Paris in their mid-twenties and wrote books informed by their experiences there: Lewis's *Tarr* and Orwell's *Down and Out in Paris and London* (1933). Lewis's combat experience in France in 1916 and 1917 was matched by Orwell's time in Spain precisely two decades later in 1936 and 1937. Both men wrote books about Spain, too: *The Revenge for Love* (1937), a novel written by Lewis in 1934 and 1935 which deals with pre-Civil War political fellow-travelling; and *Homage to Catalonia* (1938), Orwell's account of his time fighting in the Civil War with the POUM. Both men were 'traumatised' figures, carrying the impact of their time in war, as so many combatant-writers do, into everything they did thereafter. Both were widely read in European literature. Both were committed defenders of free speech and the public sphere, and staunch critics of political and economic threats to writers' liberties throughout the inter-war and post-war periods. Both were innovators in the nascent field of what later became known as Cultural Studies. And while neither figure thought of himself as a prophet, many of their ideas turned out, in the end, to be prophetic.

There are some uncanny foreshadowings of Orwell's ideas in Lewis's books, too, many of them anticipating the issues taken up in *Nineteen Eighty-Four* (1949). The title of Lewis's most polemical book of political theory, *The Art of Being Ruled* (1926), evokes the need to live adeptly under totalitarianism experienced by Winston Smith.[11] Lewis argues in the book that the 'physical part of power', violence, is less important than 'the effective way' of reducing a person to nothing and 'making him yours': i.e. education, with which rulers can 'get inside a person's mind and change his very personality' (1989a: 94).[12] His worries about a 'hymn of hate' directed against intelligent individuals resonates with the Two Minutes Hate of *Nineteen Eighty-Four*, which is also directed at an enemy intellect, just as Lewis's remarks about the 'functionaries' likely to emerge under collectivism ('veritable *omniarchs* – that is to say, despots to a degree and on a scale of which humanity has up till now had no experience') look ahead to O'Brien, Winston Smith's torturer in *Nineteen Eighty-Four*, and possibly to Big Brother, too (ibid: 235, 303). Lewis even refers in the book, albeit in a different context, to the idea of 'two and two make four' (ibid: 85).[13] A decade later, in *Left Wings Over Europe* (1936), Lewis disparages the *Alice in Wonderland*-style logic of 'contemporary political jargon – where "Peace" means War, "Neutrality" means Intervention, and "Independence" means Economic Servitude' (1972: 204), thereby anticipating Ingsoc's three great slogans. There are even unlikely connections to *Nineteen Eighty-Four* in Lewis's idiosyncratic study of Englishness, *The Mysterious Mr Bull* (1938), which pays attention to systems of 'masterly camouflage, by means of which all the *ukases* [decrees] of oligarchical government can be made to masquerade as spontaneous outbursts of the will of the Sovereign People' (1938: 91).

When Lewis returned to Orwell in *Rude Assignment*, he praised, in language directly reminiscent of *Nineteen Eighty-Four*, the now-dead writer's ability to grasp the transitions of 'a society where all the [political] labels have been changed overnight'. In this scenario of 'inevitable vertigo', Lewis claimed that all previous standards had been inverted: 'For *good* now read *bad*, for *black* read *white*' (1984b: 92). Yet the broader position of *Rude Assignment* is that Orwell was not as accomplished as his developing reputation in the 1940s and early 1950s was beginning to suggest, even though he was 'one of England's best highbrows' and 'not … a rank and file intellectual' (ibid: 86) – an ambivalent perspective that aligns with the double-sided examination provided by Lewis in *The Writer and the Absolute*. In the later book, Lewis often gives with one hand what he takes away with the other: Orwell is 'the only good writer of a decade or more', a 'genuine', 'honest' man with a literary career of 'very great interest', but he is also uninterested in the aesthetic possibilities of language, 'impregnated with Victorian class-snobbery' and committed to a naïve socialism (1952: 153, 160, 159, 155, 159). Orwell is important enough to have a long section of a book devoted to his life and work, yet sufficiently problematic not to be given a free pass. Geoffrey Wagner rightly describes Lewis's account of Orwell as 'acrimonious' (1957: 66) though I also think its rancour counterintuitively indicates how genuinely and favourably Lewis viewed Orwell – just as Orwell viewed Lewis – as a major player in the landscape of post-war letters. With Lewis, hostility very often entailed respect, concealed or otherwise (though it was frequently just antagonism plain and simple). In Orwell's case, Lewis's goal was to analyse Orwell's literary style and to uncover the value systems it encompassed.

By the time he turned in a sustained way to Orwell's work, Lewis had already lost his sight. He started to have trouble with his eyes in the late 1940s and had gone fully blind by 1951, a predicament with radical implications for how he engaged with the literary culture of his time. Because he could no longer see to read, everything had to be read to him.

> [The musician] Agnes Bedford remembered reading George Orwell novels aloud so that he could pass judgement on them in Part IV of *The Writer and the Absolute* …. She recalled his extraordinary powers of absorbing and retaining what was read to him and that he rarely asked her to make note of a particular point, ever confident that he would remember what he heard (O'Keeffe 2000: 569).

Lewis's achievement in *The Writer and the Absolute* is remarkable given that he produced it in such circumstances. And there were further practical constraints on his capacities. He could not obtain a copy of Orwell's *A Clergyman's Daughter* (1935), which consequently plays no part in his analysis; the text's absence shows how hard it could be to provide a comprehensive response to Orwell's legacy so soon after his death. Another problem is that there was no standard biography on which Lewis could draw, leading him to assemble at least some of his knowledge about Orwell's life and career from the inconsistently trustworthy information given in *Down and Out in Paris and London*, *The Road to Wigan Pier* (1937) *Homage to Catalonia* and, more awkwardly, from certain fictional passages in *Coming Up For Air* (1939) and *Keep the Aspidistra Flying*.

The central charge against Orwell in *The Writer and the Absolute* is that throughout his writing, but above all in *Animal Farm* (1945) and *Nineteen Eighty-Four*, he did not sufficiently detach the fictional from the political. This was a familiar theme for Lewis just as it was for Orwell, who long held to the view that, while it was possible for writers to detach themselves to some extent from their political commitments, 'no book is genuinely free from political bias' (2001d: 318). Yet 'Inside the whale' (1940) emphasises that 'a writer does well to keep out of politics', a view Orwell located in the literary history of the 1930s: 'For any writer who accepts or partially accepts the discipline of a political party is sooner or later faced with the alternative: toe the line, or shut up' (2002: 105).[14] Central to Orwell's position was the claim that an 'atmosphere of orthodoxy is always damaging to prose, and above all it is completely ruinous to the novel, the most anarchical of all forms of literature' (ibid), which helps to explain why *Animal Farm* and *Nineteen Eighty-Four* are pitched against the orthodoxy of what Orwell called the 'Russian *mythos*' (2001c: 373). Neither work accepts the Soviet 'line', even if they both articulate fragile socialist visions of changed societies. Orwell's goal in so much of what he wrote from the mid-1940s onwards was to provide a positive account of socialism that did not ignore socialism's 'totalitarian possibilities' (2001a: 270). Lewis, by contrast, claimed that Orwell's fiction in some reductive sense 'expressed' his politics, 'a quite literal ... declaration of love for the working-class' (Lewis 1952: 163). Tellingly, Lewis did not offer any fine-grained attention to how Orwell's novels frequently investigate their author's political attitudes (see Gąsiorek 2005). Here lies one of Lewis's giveaway tactics: his tendency strategically to misrepresent, or selectively to represent, a fellow writer's position in order to make it easier to outline his own.

Lewis has nothing to say in *The Writer and the Absolute* about 'Inside the whale', an absence attributable to the fact that he was not working from the collection *Inside the Whale and Other Essays*, published by Gollancz in 1940, but from *Critical Essays* (1946) and *Shooting an Elephant and Other Essays* (1950), neither of which contained the 1940 piece. The absence of commentary is unfortunate given that among the central planks of Lewis's intellectual and critical project is a distinction between '*political* revolution' and 'all thought and activity that is certainly revolutionary, and so disturbing to the comfortable average, but not committed to any particular *political* doctrine – that is to say to any practical programme of change' (1931: 134, italics in the original).[15] This point of difference, between working to achieve political ends, on the one hand, and thinking politically without any commitment to a specific model or vision of political transformation, on the other, underpins the bulk of Lewis's response to the relationship between politics and literature (see Gąsiorek 2011). He conceded that in the 'politics-ridden' inter-war years writers experienced 'irresistible pressures, this way or that' (1952: 193), but he also insisted on the need, as he saw it (and in language that evokes the phrasing of Orwell's 'Inside the whale'), for detachment:

Every writer should keep himself free from party, clear of any group-pull: at least this is *my* view of truth. My truth is objective truth, in other words. In England the entire intellectual atmosphere is impregnated with liberalism, or rather what liberalism transforms itself into so as to become more-and-still-more liberal. With us the pressure to achieve conformity is very great. Whether in the matter of costume, or hair-cut, or intellectual fashion (ibid, italics in the original).

Orwell, so Lewis argued, did not (or could not) live up to this standard, though whether the ideal was realistic in the first place is a moot point.[16] In *Time and Western Man* (1927), Lewis defended 'the finest type of mind, which lifts the creative impulse into an absolute region free of Spenglerian "history" or politics' (2023: 13), and this led him to endorse artworks unimpeded by the 'group-pull' of particular political or ideological positions. He accepted that 'politics do invade and pollute spheres where the plain man is not taught to expect to find them', but he rejected any equivalence between good art and political proselytism: '... when [politics] are discovered operating in the creations of science or of art, it is invariably some inferior personality or thinker, you will find, who is responsible for that, rather than the material in which he works' (ibid: 104). Lewis attacked Oswald Spengler's cyclical view of history, in which cultures develop into civilisations and, in so doing, begin to decline, on the grounds that it reduced everything – '*all* manifestations of art, mathematics, biology, [and] physics' (ibid: 103) – to politics, instead prioritising what in *The Art of Being Ruled* he called the 'life of the intelligence', which amounted to 'the very incarnation of freedom' (1989a: 374): the absolute region free of Spenglerian 'history' or politics.[17] The 'absolute' of *The Writer and the Absolute*, by contrast, is precisely *the political*, which to Lewis's mind it is the writer's job to resist.

Orwell did not live to see *The Writer and the Absolute*. But had he been able to answer its charges, he may well have reiterated the points he made in 'Why I join the ILP' (1938): 'The impulse of every writer is to "keep out of politics". What he wants is to be left alone so that he can go on writing books in peace. But unfortunately it is becoming obvious that this ideal is no more practicable than that of the petty shopkeeper who hopes to preserve his independence in the teeth of the chain-stores' (2000: 167). Lewis regularly expressed similar opinions, articulating his annoyance at being drawn into commenting on political matters, while never abandoning his commitment to standing 'above the *mêlée*' and to functioning 'as an instrument of impartial truth' (1989b: 227). Those who were able to reply to *The Writer and the Absolute*, some of them Orwell's allies, took different shots at it. Neville Braybrooke described Lewis's comments on Sartre and George Orwell as 'among the silliest and shrewdest that have yet been published' (1952: 7). The position adopted in *The Listener* was that Lewis wrote against Sartre, Malraux, Camus and Orwell because, while they could 'detach themselves' from 'parties in power' or those 'striving for power', they still flirted with 'the possibilities of political affiliation' (Unsigned 1952a: 111). *The Times Literary Supplement* went further, pointing out that Lewis and Orwell had much in common:

> In his essay on Dickens, Orwell showed himself very alert to the dangers of political flirtation; and anyone who studies [*The Writer and the Absolute*] closely – having an eye to its characteristic turns of phrase, its half-humorous exaggerations, its almost morbid honesty – will probably come to the conclusion that there is more in common between Orwell and Mr. Lewis than between either and M. Sartre. They are, after all, in much the same tradition, though Orwell was for a time attracted by the continental version of Socialism, while Mr. Lewis wrote a book about Hitler. Both have expressed their belief that two and two make four, an old-fashioned assumption that 'the eighteen-year-olds in the Paris bars' – who are M. Sartre's real and acknowledged public – would find no difficulty in contradicting (Unsigned 1952b: 464).

Cyril Connolly, writing in *The Sunday Times*, came to a similar conclusion. He felt that Lewis 'snap[ped] the handcuffs' on Orwell, a 'literary giant', only to let him go with a slapped wrist because 'these two lonely, poor and truthful artists have too much in common' (1952: 5). The thought that he had *too much* in common with Orwell may help to explain why Lewis was so critical of him.

## LEWIS READING ORWELL

Lewis's analysis of Orwell's work begins by charting an evolution from *Down and Out in Paris and London* to *Coming Up For Air*, concentrating on Orwell's departure from Eton in 1921, his time in Burma between 1922 and 1927, and his return to England in 1927. Orwell's desire to go down and out, what Lewis calls his 'preoccupation with the under-dog', came from having had too much to do with 'young over-dogs in his schooldays' (1952: 160) at Eton and from the ensuing sentimental attachment to social justice – or '"pink" rash' (ibid: 168) – that Lewis claims he contracted there. On Orwell's novel *Burmese Days* (1934), based to a certain extent on his time as an Imperial Policeman in Burma, Lewis says it is 'juvenilely "enlightened"' because it dishes up 'all the stale anti-imperialism of liberal England … in its most conventional form' (ibid: 173). To Lewis, the better book of a comparable type was Norman Lewis's *Samara* (1949), for where *Samara* offers an 'acute understanding of the situation involved in Berber North Africa', *Burmese Days* rests on cliché: the depicting of 'an exotic colonial background … with the object of presenting the white interlopers in a detestable light' (ibid).[18]

The critique of *Burmese Days* that Lewis offers in *The Writer and the Absolute* is in the same line of analysis developed in two earlier critical texts: *Time and Western Man* and *Men Without Art* (1934). Running through both books is a desire – one that Orwell shared – to look behind surface appearances so that hidden meanings can be accessed: in *Time and Western Man*, the need to 'get behind morals' (2023: 23) and, in *Men Without Art*, 'the injunction to look *behind* everything, however trivial, in the art-field, as a matter of routine, and challenge all "face values"' (1987: 12-13, italics in the original). In mocking what he considers the unsophisticated politics of *Burmese Days*, Lewis indulges in one of his favourite hobbies: platitude hunting. His initial and in some ways reasonable objections to the novel are that it follows a conventional Victorian plot structure, making it timeworn; that it scores cheap points at the cost of the detestable Europeans who gather in the club in Kyauktada, their self-evident unpleasantness indicating Orwell's narrowness of satirical vision; and that it adheres to a naïve moral high ground that does not allow Orwell to get underneath the surface of the things he seems so eloquently to dissect. The fact that *Burmese Days* appears to be a straightforwardly autobiographical novel means that its unsophistication lies in the closeness between the club members and Orwell's experiences in Burma:

> This is no doubt a very understandable *cri de cœur* of an 'enlightened' Etonian, brutally translated from the delectable atmosphere of Eton to a nasty little hill-station in Burma, condemned indefinitely to enjoy the society of a small group of drunken businessmen. And all the book no doubt adds up to just this: but the same criticism of the English character could have been staged anywhere in England itself, in the saloon bar or the local golf club of any provincial centre, or for that matter in any city office (1952: 175).

For Lewis, the core weakness of *Burmese Days* is the fact that it takes the club members' dreadfulness so seriously. Lewis rejects the right of man to 'govern man', to 'have the power to order him about', to 'be his economic master', calling it 'wrong' and 'even disgusting' (ibid). But Orwell's inability or reluctance to situate his protagonist John Flory's experiences in a larger global context of colonial exploitation – including relations between the British and the revolutionary goals of Kwame Nkrumah in the African Gold Coast, now Ghana, and frictions between classes back in England – prompts Lewis to sarcasm:

All I would say is that just a little sense of these larger realities would prevent anybody from taking too high a moral tone about mild-mannered, if besotted, Anglo-Saxon intruders in parts of Asia. Such intrusion was so obviously a brief episode in the cosmic power-game. It is such considerations as these which make this performance boring and juvenile (ibid: 175-176).

Lewis's characterisation of the impact of 'Anglo-Saxon intruders' is debatable, but what stands out here, given his interest in the arc of Orwell's writing, is his description of *Burmese Days* as a 'performance'. As ever, Lewis's concern leads him into thinking about how this novel enacts or stages a particular political attitude.

*Burmese Days* was not only unconvincing at the level of plot, for Lewis, but also at the level of style. He extends this charge to *Keep the Aspidistra Flying*, which he describes, also with *Burmese Days* in mind, as a novel manifesting 'an even greater indifference to words and to the art of verbal expression' (ibid: 176), which as a criticism seems peculiarly wide of the mark.[19] Lewis is irked by Orwell's apparently 'carefree manner of slapping any old word down on the page that first comes into the jolly old head' (ibid). He is also annoyed by the novel's handling of the 'typical Orwell situation', namely the highlighting of an evil – money, in the case of *Keep the Aspidistra Flying* – of which neither Orwell nor his hero, Gordon Comstock, 'show any consciousness' (ibid). *Keep the Aspidistra Flying* is to be seen not as a penetrating satire on capitalism, but as a hackneyed treatment of an easy target. Lewis detects in the novel a childishness aligning it with *Burmese Days* and *Coming Up For Air*, the latter text being in Lewis's mind Orwell's worst published book before the Second World War. 'The principal figures in all his narrative books are insignificant, unattractive creatures,' Lewis claims, 'and usually colourless. But George Bowling, whose acquaintance we make here, possesses colour, but of so distasteful a kind as to make the reading of the book a peculiarly exasperating labour' (ibid: 178). Behind the figure of Bowling lie the characters of H.G. Wells, while behind the novel's plot lies G.K. Chesterton, neither influence helping it all that much. For Lewis, *Coming Up For Air* is a repetitive, artificial, shallow, incoherent mess, and he heartily sympathises 'with any future student of contemporary literature who has to read it' (ibid: 179).[20]

Lewis's responses to *Burmese Days*, *Keep the Aspidistra Flying* and *Coming Up For Air* lead him to remark, with characteristic acerbity, that Orwell's published work before 1939 has few 'openings for politeness' (ibid: 180). By contrast, the work of the 1940s has more to recommend it, and here Lewis settles on Orwell's essays, alongside *Animal Farm* and *Nineteen Eighty-Four*, as the evidence of 'a slender

**PAPER**

but valuable body of work, representing a writer who stood out among his contemporaries as one belonging to the main movement of European thought, or rather of Western thought' (ibid: 184). Lewis praises Orwell's commentaries on 'the shortcomings of the English' (ibid); reflects on the influence of Arthur Koestler's *Darkness at Noon* (1940) on *Nineteen Eighty-Four* (ibid: 185-186); and admires Orwell's remarks about 'the limitations of the English political writer when compared with the continental' (ibid: 187). Yet Lewis also doubles down on his argument that the creative writer should 'have no political affiliations' (ibid: 188). Orwell's remarks about revolutionary politics in his 1944 essay on Koestler indicate a desire, Lewis claims, 'to save socialism' (ibid: 187), and it is this desire that, in Lewis's opinion, limits his writerly faculties; not because socialism is wrong *per se*, but because 'every party is wrong for a philosopher or for an artist' (ibid: 188) – a strange charge to level at Orwell given his comments about 'the discipline of a political party' in 'Inside the whale'.[21] The thread running through Lewis's analysis of Orwell's work comes into the foreground here: Orwell's flaw, so Lewis thinks, is that he lets his politics get the better of his fiction.

*Animal Farm* marks another change. 'At last, in 1945,' Lewis states in his typically sardonic fashion, 'Orwell's literary ambition was realized. He wrote a good book' (ibid: 189). Within the terms of Lewis's analysis, the quality of *Animal Farm* lies not in its language, which he considers 'business-like and adequate', but in its 'feat of political lampooning' (ibid), which marks an admirable conscience: '[Orwell] showed the same courage in writing this as he had displayed as a "fighter for Freedom" in Spain (which subsequently he found was not Freedom after all, but slavery)' (ibid). Lewis goes on to attribute to Orwell's novella an even wider significance:

> *Animal Farm*, by reason of its success, made it respectable to think clearly or to write without humbug, if a young man was so disposed. It was in a sense an iron curtain that came down on the period of literary fellow-travelling, the work of an ex-fellow-traveller (ibid).

And yet Lewis suggests that *Animal Farm* did not enable Orwell to move beyond what he calls the 'silliness' (ibid: 191) of *The Road to Wigan Pier*, a silliness he locates in Orwell's remarks about the class myths he was peddled in his childhood: the assumption of 'an honest and gifted man fantastically engaged in the pursuit of a chimera, or of a person doing a rather comic penance for a bad smell he ought not to have smelled' (ibid: 169).[22]

Alongside these readings of the novels, Lewis reconstructs the evolution of Orwell's politics. Lewis considers Orwell's Scottish ancestry and addresses its implications for his choice of pseudonym.

He reflects on the significance of Orwell's education at Eton, finding in it a 'virulent type of snobbery' that the school 'injected' into him (ibid: 159). He thinks about how Orwell 'repudiated the British Colonial Empire', tracing this action back to the 'pink rash' (ibid: 168). Lewis praises Orwell's decision to fight in Spain: 'he was one of the few "left-wingers" who took left-wingery sufficiently seriously to risk his life' (ibid: 160; see also 180). Lewis sees in Orwell's desire to go 'down and out', communicated in *Down and Out in Paris and London*, *Keep the Aspidistra Flying* and *The Road to Wigan Pier*, a key problem for his socialism, which begins in the 'bourgeois romanticism' (ibid: 162) of slumming, or what we might now call 'poverty tourism'. Orwell's commitment in his socialism to what Lewis calls 'the brotherhood of man' is not sufficiently watertight to disentangle him from the snobbish paradox of treating the working class as 'of another clay', leading to the claim that Orwell 'might be described as the Honest Snob. He is genuinely desirous of curing himself of his snobbery, but he goes about it snobbishly' (ibid: 167). Lewis mocks Orwell's enthusiasm for being so taken with 'the hordes of the revolutionary working-class' (ibid: 169) in Spain. However, Orwell's attitude to the Civil War, which he understands in terms of economic upheaval, recommends itself. Discussing essays written by 'the Orwell of 1945', Lewis mentions that at first he thought Orwell had 'joined the ranks of the Trotskyites' (ibid: 181),[23] but then analyses Spain's impact on Orwell's politics and reasserts his claim that his socialism was only skin-deep just as his anti-imperialism amounted to little more than a 'boyish enthusiasm' (ibid: 183). Among the most startling claims in this part of Lewis's analysis is his incredible, unsubstantiated claim that had Orwell been German by nationality he would have joined the *Schutzstaffel* (SS), Hitler's paramilitary organisation.

Lewis's analysis of Orwell's political development is woefully unspecific, not to mention divisive. The running idea that Orwell's socialism was 'a species of sport, as obviously as his plunge into the underworld of tramps was the act of a sportsman, not that of a missionary' (ibid: 183-184), is mere assertion. Likewise, the inflammatory remark that Orwell's supposedly 'militant' sympathies would have led him to join the SS is not explained.[24] Munton correctly says that Lewis 'chooses to discuss Orwell reductively by attempting to dissolve his varied politics … and tries to remove politics altogether from any discussion of writing and thinking: intellectual liberty, for Orwell, meant "possessing the right to say that two and two make four", whilst to be truthful in this way "one must have no political affiliations", and instead – like a scientist – inhabit a strictly objective universe"' (2025: 577). Yet Lewis does perceive the major change in Orwell's politics, tracing the development of

**PAPER**

'the author of *Keep the Aspidistra Flying*' to 'the author of *Animal Farm*' (ibid: 181) back to Spain. The key experience for Orwell is the Soviet crackdown he witnessed in Barcelona on the POUM (the anti-Stalinist, neo-Trotskyist militia he joined in Spain): this made Orwell increasingly critical of Stalin, untrusting of how the Russian 'myth' influenced Britain's intellectuals and alert to what Lewis called the '"hook in the bait" of socialism' (ibid: 180). At the same time, and responding specifically to the essay on Arthur Koestler, in which Orwell claims that although '[a]ll revolutions are failures, … they are not the same failure' (2001b: 400), Lewis thinks that Orwell never abandons his socialist commitments. *Animal Farm* and *Nineteen Eighty-Four* come down hard on the idea of social revolution, but only on authoritarian revolution. Social revolution Orwell does not reject, Lewis suggests and this, for him, limits the scope and power of his political insight.

## M.W. FREER: ON LEWIS MISREADING ORWELL

One of the most intriguing and hitherto uninvestigated ripostes to Lewis came in the form of a letter sent to him by a certain M.W. Freer, dated hesitantly by the Division of Rare and Manuscript Collections at Cornell University Library, where the letter is now held, to July 1952. The correspondent in question remains unidentified, but Freer's knowledge of Orwell is evident.[25] Self-described as an 'Orwell fan', Freer subjects the final section of *The Writer and the Absolute* to substantial criticism over the letter's six pages, beginning with the contention that Lewis's 'interesting' analysis is 'rather perplexing': Lewis begins his analysis of Orwell by stating his admiration for the recently deceased author and then proceeds to attack him 'for the next forty pages, hardly saying any good word for the man or his works all that time' (Freer 1952: 1). According to Freer, Lewis's objective is twofold: first, to show that 'Orwell's politics changed considerably throughout his life' and, second, to claim 'that all his earlier works are failures and it is only Animal Farm and 1984 [*sic*] that are worth consideration – these two only having been written during his period of enlightenment' (ibid: 2). Lewis's apparent inability to read Orwell's earlier work with care amazed Freer, who saw in this a failure of critical professionalism on Lewis's part, and he encouraged him to try to use his influence 'with Messrs. Secker & Warburg' to get them to reprint *A Clergyman's Daughter*, *The Road to Wigan Pier*, and *Keep the Aspidistra Flying* in order to secure greater public understanding of Orwell's left-wing credentials.[26] As Freer puts it: 'I should hate to feel that some people merely wish Orwell to be remembered as an anti-Communist author' (ibid: 6).

Freer's surprise that Lewis's admiration for Orwell is conveyed mainly by 'attack' indicates how unfamiliar he was with Lewis's critical method. Had Freer known Lewis's assessments of Ezra Pound and James Joyce in *Time and Western Man*, for example, or the accounts of Ernest Hemingway, William Faulkner, T.S. Eliot, Henry James and Virginia Woolf in *Men Without Art*, he would have understood that Lewis attacks the figures he admires not to be contrarian for contrarianism's sake but because he desires to establish how, in their importance, such figures are 'politically and morally influential' (1987: 12). This is why Lewis describes Orwell as 'very much more than the only good writer of a decade or more': he claims that Orwell has a shaping presence in culture, a capacity to alter the views of his audience and to change the terms of reference in his reception. Although Lewis finds little 'interest in writing for its own sake' in Orwell – contrasting him in this respect with 'the literary competence' of D.H. Lawrence, 'the stylistic resourcefulness' of Joseph Conrad and 'the expository clarity' of H.G. Wells (ibid), all of whom Lewis admits Orwell admired – he nevertheless discovers in Orwell a 'system of conduct, and judgements to match' (1987: 12). It is this 'system' that Lewis wants to draw out from Orwell's work, in accordance with his stated 'principles of intellectual *detection*' (ibid: 12, italics in the original). Lewis finds Orwell fascinating because in some respects he 'rescued himself from a convention' (socialist fellow-travelling) 'and finished his literary life in a burst of clairvoyance' (1952: 155).

Lewis's account of *Animal Farm* and *Nineteen Eighty-Four* is barely mentioned by Freer, who concentrates on the thought that Orwell freed himself from conventionality. In response to the accusation that Orwell's 'left-wingery never ceased to be skin-deep' (ibid: 183), Freer contends that, although this may have been true, it does not follow that Orwell's loyalty to 'the fundamental concepts of "leftism" were merely superficial and something that would easily be cast aside' (1952: 2). This is perceptive. Freer correctly insists that Orwell's politics are rooted in shared systems of everyday value: 'Orwell was always more concerned with people than with policies and his conception of socialism was based on the fairly general ideas of decency, brotherhood and toleration' (ibid). A similar argument has more recently been advanced by David Dwan: '… for Orwell, … our ordinary moral intuitions – so regularly appealed to in his journalism and his fiction – provide both the conditions and limits of political thought' (2018: 6). Freer notes that Lewis does not engage at any length with *The Road to Wigan Pier*, which means that he misses Orwell's 'attitude to bourgeois fellow-travelling' (1952: 2) in that book. The Orwell envisaged by Freer, and the Orwell unable to be detected by Lewis, is the Orwell who could write:

> We have got to fight for justice and liberty, and Socialism does mean justice and liberty when the nonsense is stripped

off it. It is only the essentials that are worth remembering. To recoil from Socialism because so many individual Socialists are inferior people is as absurd as refusing to travel by train because you dislike the ticket-collector's face (2001e: 205).

Freer rejects Lewis's suggestion that his 'old school tie' background advantaged him in the kitchens of Paris and in the doss houses of London, and dismisses the idea that Orwell would have joined the *Schutzstaffel*. Next, Freer speaks on behalf of Orwell's earlier works, 'the debasement of which' appears so important to Lewis, quoting Compton Mackenzie's support of *Down and Out in Paris and London*, *Burmese Days*, and *A Clergyman's Daughter* from the *Daily Mail*: 'I have no hesitation in asserting that no "realistic" writer during the last five years has produced three volumes which can compare in directness, vigour, courage, and vitality with these three volumes from the pen of Mr. George Orwell' (1935: 5). Reflecting on the thought, only half-suggested by Lewis, that Orwell identified with the character of Verrall (a handsome military officer whom Elizabeth is encouraged to pursue by her mother) in *Burmese Days*, Freer points out that Orwell aligns more obviously with the novel's protagonist, Flory.[27] For Freer, this sense of closeness between social misfits can be traced to Orwell's schooldays during which, as he explains in 'Such, such were the joys' (his posthumously published essay – part fact, part fiction – about his years at St Cyprian's prep school), he evolved a significant 'sense of unhappiness, guilt and failure': 'One does not have to be a psychologist,' Freer continues, 'to realise that here was the source of Orwell's conflict of mind and preoccupation with the underdog, shown in "Burmese Days" and in "Keep the Aspidistra Flying" and "Coming Up For Air"' (1952: 4), the books that, in *The Writer and the Absolute*, Lewis repeatedly belittles. Whereas for Lewis these three texts evidence Orwell's inadequacies as a writer, for Freer they are the best signs of 'Orwell's genius': his knack of forcing his readers to *feel* the 'dejection' that figures such as Gordon Comstock and George Bowling experience in being hopelessly trapped by socio-economic 'tentacles' from which they have little hope of extricating themselves (ibid: 4-5, italics in the original).[28]

Curiously, Freer pays almost no attention to Lewis's readings of *Animal Farm* and *Nineteen Eighty-Four*, the latter being Orwell's 'best book' (1952: 154), to Lewis's mind, even though he insists it isn't without its problems:

> This remarkable piece of work is a prophetic Wellsian nightmare of events in the future. Again we have not persons but dummies. Miss 1984 – but the eternal feminine as well – meets Mr. X, a rebelliously inclined robot. They 'click'. It is not a boy and girl business altogether. Unfortunately Orwell

was at the time of writing about forty-five, so his last hero, though not so old as that, is nearing forty. There is, it is true, a further reason why he is obliged to be on the elderly side: it is his function to remember the good old days, when you could go to bed at night without the secret police snooping from their telesnooper on the wall of your flat, or betray a healthy sexual interest without incurring all kinds of penalties.

A little terror, but no compassion for the principal performers can be felt because they are merely convenient abstractions. If the scenario and the machinery are Wellsian, so are the personae. They are conventional properties, secondary to the menacing blueprint of a horrible world of only thirty years hence.

Of course, the leading actors would not possess personalities of such reality as to compete with the scenery and apparatus of the book, which is the big thing, or clog its expository function. At all events, such colour as they have is that drab conventional tint with which his earlier novels will have familiarized us (ibid: 154).

Lewis repeats the charge that *Nineteen Eighty-Four* is 'Wellsian in form, Wellsian in the style of its writing, Wellsian in the colourlessness and anonymity of the personae' later in his analysis, where he also suggests that the novel lacks 'electricity' and that O'Brien is an 'uninteresting business man' (ibid: 190).[29]

Lewis concedes that in *Nineteen Eighty-Four* Orwell puts to admirable use the insight into Stalinist authoritarianism he acquired in Spain. Lewis also emphasises that the 'hideous palaces of Truth and Love are first-rate political creations' (ibid). He finds the extracts from *The Theory and Practice of Oligarchical Collectivism* to be well written, clear and plausible. The Room 101 sequence is 'impressively chilly and logical' (ibid). Yet O'Brien's 'four fingers or five' is absurd: '… partly because an acute sense of the ridiculous is not Orwell's strong point', and partly because 'since the human beings involved are prefabricated and bloodless' the reader experiences no 'sympathetic pang' at their fates (ibid).[30] Lewis thinks that the 'book as a whole is a first-rate political document', and that Orwell's depictions of the 'old London' encircling the Party's 'floodlit bureaucratic centre' are persuasive, yet he cannot stomach Winston Smith's 'Orwellian enthusiasm' for the proles, which in his view imports into *Nineteen Eighty-Four* the 'silliness' of *The Road to Wigan Pier* (ibid: 190-191). Winston's idea, which Lewis interprets as *Orwell's* idea, that the proles will take back their freedom, destroying Ingsoc in the process, is 'a very stupid affectation' (ibid: 191), one that discloses Orwell's entrapment in a 'long-out-dated socialism' (ibid: 192) more akin to the medievalist socialism of William Morris than to the politics of the post-war years. Hence Lewis's opinion that the '"prole" business' should have been left out of the novel in favour of 'a more realistic treatment of the probable condition of the mass of the population' (ibid: 193). Lewis concludes his analysis with an equivocal panegyric to Orwell's importance: on the one hand, a writer of powerful prescience; on the other, a writer who could not escape his own sentimentality or 'party badge' (ibid: 186).

CONCLUSION

Lewis assessed Orwell as a literary dignitary to be admired and as a politically symptomatic figure to be dissected. He criticised him as a writer who did not separate his fiction from his socialism and argued that he 'should have taken up a position of absolute detachment, upon having his eyes so thoroughly opened as to enable him to write *Animal Farm*' (ibid: 188). Emphasising that he was not writing against socialism as such, but against any collapsing of the political into the literary, Lewis agreed with Orwell's insistence that 'personal liberty for the intellectual or really for anybody else' depends upon 'possessing the right to say that two and two make four' (ibid). However, Lewis bemoaned how *Nineteen Eighty-Four* connects this insight to the possibility of proletarian revolution. The extent of Lewis's dissatisfaction indicates the high degree of difference he saw between himself and Orwell, at least partially bearing out Loewenstein's suggestion, quoted above, that they were 'arch-enemies', as well as C.J. Fox's claim that Orwell was 'one of Lewis's main antagonists' (1982: 198, n. 25). It also counter-intuitively testifies to a form of respect. Orwell might have been wrong, Lewis thought, but the manner of his wrongness made him worth taking to task.

Lewis's readings of Orwell in *The Writer and the Absolute* are sometimes perceptive but more often debatable and frequently hard to take seriously; they entail misrepresentation, selective reading and accurate insight and criticism, all bundled together in a hotch-potch of hassled, often cavalier scrutiny.[31] Lewis is too quick to align Orwell with his narrators, for instance, and too willing to map Orwell's biography onto his novels. Because so many of Lewis's claims about Orwell in *The Writer and the Absolute* are hurried assertions, his argument is often unpersuasive even when its polemical clarity makes it narratively compelling. All that said, aspects of Lewis's account of *Nineteen Eighty-Four* are credible, given how closely they echo the arguments made by Raymond Williams and more recently by Elinor Taylor: 'Orwell's proles … are a moral force in the novel and the key to the survival of humanity, but both these aspects are constructed in a way that excludes in advance any possibility of political agency' (2020: 165). Lewis's proposition that Orwell was limited by his refusal to accept Koestler's position, namely that '*all* Revolutions are certain to be equally unsatisfactory, and, after a disgusting blood-bath to develop into a disgusting tyranny' (1952: 186), allows him to score familiar points against the latent politics of *Nineteen Eighty-Four*, even if his claim that Orwell was liable to 'click back' into 'stock' positions (ibid) seems ill-judged.

*Burmese Days*, on the other hand, appears to have prompted Lewis to what Anne Quéma calls, in a discussion of Lewis's reading of the character Verrall, a form of 'veiled self-analysis' (1999: 181). Quéma locates this self-directed assessment in the closeness between Verrall's hauteur and Lewis's brushes with the 'mesmerizing' attractiveness of 'the image of the aristocrat' (ibid), an image he tended to resist more successfully in his fiction than in, say, *The Art of Being Ruled*. Yet *Burmese Days* also enabled Lewis implicitly to self-analyse his own evolution as a writer and, through criticising Orwell, to affirm the stance of moral and political impartiality idealised from the first page of *The Writer and the Absolute* to its last. For Lewis, *Burmese Days* was not only an immature, naïve text. It was also a text gripped by a 'stale' (1952: 173) anti-imperial politics, and to this extent a novel compromised by the subordination of the literary to the political that in Lewis's mind characterised Orwell's writing more broadly. A problem with Lewis's analysis of Orwell's politics, however, is that he failed to differentiate carefully enough between the transitions in Orwell's attitude towards socialism, which move from the incredulity and distrust of *The Road to Wigan Pier* (a text Lewis problematically simplifies) to the anti-authoritarian and anti-totalitarian interventions of *Animal Farm* and *Nineteen Eighty-Four*.

Lewis used Orwell's writing as a case study with which to test the properties and the limits of his own intellectual position-taking. Indeed, Lewis never settled on most argumentative postures for long, preferring instead to move between viewpoints like a philosophical gadfly, testing, disrupting and complicating matters as he did so. His objective was to subject his own aesthetic and political commitments continually to scrutiny, not because he was merely inconsistent but because he recognised the contingency and the precarity of opinion. His contempt for Orwell's writing is in some ways a simple point of aesthetic difference: to an extent, Lewis just did not care all that much for Orwell's style. Yet it was also part of a larger project to establish how fiction as such should be written in an age of 'collectivity', and at a time when Lewis, along with many others, feared that 'the individual may not be allowed for very much longer to express himself in writing' (1952: 194).[32] The just-about-detectable esteem in Lewis's contempt derives from how

NATHAN
WADDELL

seriously he takes Orwell as a writer to whom it is worth giving time. That seriousness, in turn, tells us something about the intellectual space Lewis desired for the kind of culture critique in which he was so invested.

Lewis's readings of Orwell may, in so many ways, be wrong and even occasionally unkind, but as a form of hostility they signal Lewis's deeper commitment to the Republic of Letters that he and so many other writers of the period sought to defend. Even in his most uncaring moments, he hoped to secure for 'the small world of writers … that unimpeded latitude of expression' which in his view most writers knew 'to be a condition of the best work'. Lewis thought that one way to achieve this would be through providing 'some master prophylactic against obsessional contagions' (1952: 53), thereby keeping the writer detached from all exterior and superfluous political certitudes. As he put it at the end of *The Writer and the Absolute*:

> By maintaining the highest technical standards in his work, and even more by austerely refraining from all watering down, sweetening, or in other ways rendering more popularly palatable, and of course by never departing from the truth as it shows itself to him, a writer cannot receive more than the barest worldly reward. But the place of honour, as I have never failed to recognize, is *outside* (ibid: 195-196, italics in the original).

Orwell was similarly committed to 'unimpeded latitude of expression', but he was far less convinced by the possibility of critical or political disinterestedness. Where Lewis sought a form of expression that could be divorced from political allegiances, Orwell held to the view that 'art and propaganda are never quite separable, and that what are supposed to be purely aesthetic judgments are always corrupted to some extent by moral or political or religious loyalties' (2002: 491). Orwell hoped in his late work to make his fiction serve the broader political goal of a socialist transformation of capitalist modernity, but his encoding of that objective in *Animal Farm* and *Nineteen Eighty-Four* was not as one-sided nor as simplistic as Lewis claimed. Persuaded by the thought that 'it is not necessarily the business of a novelist, or a satirist, to make constructive suggestions' (2002: 22) about how the world should or should not be changed, Orwell nevertheless ended up being one of the most 'suggestive' writers of the twentieth century.

- My thanks to Richard Lance Keeble, Douglas Kerr, Darcy Moore, Alan Munton, D. J. Taylor and Tim Crook for commenting on various drafts and aspects of this paper. I am very grateful for financial support from the British Academy through its Mid-Career Fellowship scheme (project ID MCFSS22\220035) which enabled the wider programme of research on which the argument is based.

## NOTES

[1] Orwell does not italicise Lewis's titles in this letter

[2] The reference to Gertrude Stein indicates that Orwell had been reading the first issue of *The Enemy*, which was dated to January 1927

[3] Orwell's modernist of choice was James Joyce. There is no homage to Lewis in Orwell's novels in the Joycean guise of Chapter III, Part I of *A Clergyman's Daughter* (1935)

[4] I write 'near-groundless' because according to one of Lewis's confidants. [Hugh Gordon Porteus is a man.], the rumour that Lewis had become a communist came from a joke Lewis told to the poet Roy Campbell, who then passed it on unwittingly to Orwell – who, in turn, assumed there was more truth to the matter than was in fact the case (Meyers 1980: 297)

[5] See also Lewis (1984b: 69). For two highly accessible overviews of Lewis's political trajectory, see Gąsiorek (2004: 77-99) and Munton (2006). A longer account is given by Edwards (2000). Lewis writes in *Rude Assignment* that he was not subject to 'violent reversals of opinion' (1984b: 87), which underplays how vigorously he reversed his thinking about Hitler, and about the wider fascist project, in the late 1930s

[6] I intend to discuss Orwell's readings and misreadings of Lewis in a monograph on Lewis's politics, which as of February 2025 is still in process

[7] See also Munton (2015: 76-79)

[8] The 'archenemy' remark can be found on a non-consecutive page of notes appended to Loewenstein's chapter (1996: 212, n. 40)

[9] Something of this closeness is hinted at by the fact that the front cover to David Wykes's *A Preface to Orwell* (1987) is adorned by Lewis's oil painting *Abstract* (1932)

[10] Paul O'Keeffe adds the following caveats: 'This much is true: Wyndham Lewis's father owned a 28-ton sloop, *Wanda*, of Canadian registry (St John, New Brunswick). … It may have been that the child was told a swashbuckling version of his birth at the yarn-spinning father's knee. It may have been that the two facts, the father's ownership of a boat and the son's birth in Nova Scotia, became conflated into a single colourful family legend. Either way the story, unquestioned, became chronicled: that Wyndham Lewis was born on a yacht in the Bay of Fundy' (2000: 5)

[11] Jeffrey Meyers has suggested that *The Art of Being Ruled* would have been 'a brilliant title for Orwell's novel' (2010: 147)

[12] Anne Quéma makes the interesting, albeit unproveable, point that Lewis's remarks in *The Art of Being Ruled* about oppressed individuals reading Tolstoy's *War and Peace* on the quiet (see Lewis 1989a: 112) 'could have inspired some of the scenes of Orwell's *1984*' (Quéma 1999: 179) – a claim evoking Winston Smith's furtive reading of Emmanuel Goldstein's dissident *The Theory and Practice of Oligarchical Collectivism* in the room above Mr Charrington's shop

[13] In the passage in question, Lewis is discussing (with typical provocativeness) the politics of education. Note that the protagonist of Lewis's *Snooty Baronet* describes being 'visited by a brain-wave' and then wondering if 'perhaps it was merely putting two and two together after all and making them come to four' (1984a: 84)

[14] Orwell continues: 'No decade in the past hundred and fifty years has been so barren of imaginative prose as the nineteen-thirties. There have been good poems, good sociological works, brilliant pamphlets, but practically no fiction of any value at all' (2002: 105). Of Lewis's 1932 novel *Snooty Baronet*, Orwell wrote: 'Enough talent to set up dozens of ordinary writers have been poured into Wyndham Lewis's so-called novels, such as *Tarr* or *Snooty Baronet*. Yet it would be a very heavy labour to read one of these books right through. Some indefinable quality, a sort of literary vitamin, which exists even in a book like [A.S.M. Hutchinson's] *If Winter Comes*, is absent from them' (2001c: 349)

¹⁵ Here note Gąsiorek's description of Lewis's novel *The Revenge for Love* (1937) which, as he says, is 'deeply hostile to socialist politics in general and to revolutionary politics in particular. It is in part a protest against the hegemony of left-wing thought in cultural and artistic circles in 1930s Britain, a hegemony discussed in detail in "Inside the whale"' (2004: 91-2)

¹⁶ However laudable we may find appeals to objectivity and disinterestedness, we belong in complex, interleaved ways to particular communities and networks of interlocution, and there are always, as Habermas has it, unavoidable connections between knowledge and human interests' (2001: 45)

¹⁷ Lewis continues: 'Where it [i.e. the life of the intelligence] is dogmatic and harsh it is impure; where it is too political it is impure: its disciplines are less arbitrary and less *political* than those of religion: and it is the most inveterate enemy of unjust despotic power' (1989a: 374, italics in the original)

¹⁸ Part of Lewis's enthusiasm for *Samara* presumably comes from his travels in Morocco, as recorded in his travelogue *Filibusters in Barbary* (1932)

¹⁹ For Orwell's literary skill, see Mullen (2025) and Rae (2025)

²⁰ Lewis's suggestion that 'character only held a feeble interest' (1952: 154) for Orwell is plainly wrong, the main witness for the defence being precisely the novel that Lewis least admired, *Coming Up For Air*. Lewis loathed this book, but his aesthetic objections to it are not corroborated by the kind of close reading that would make the charge stick. Students who have studied *Coming Up For Air* with me at the University of Birmingham have often had a very different reaction to this novel, finding it to be one of Orwell's more accomplished texts

²¹ It may be that Lewis simply did not know the 1940 essay existed, or that he was uninclined to pursue an exhaustive investigation of Orwell's essays because his blindness made it too difficult to achieve. Either way, the lack of engagement with the essay was a lost opportunity

²² Here Lewis has in mind Orwell's remarks in *The Road to Wigan Pier* about the 'impassable barrier' of the 'four frightful words' that taught him, in his younger years, to fear people on low incomes: 'The words were: *The lower classes smell*' (2001e: 119) – a socio-economic claim, it should be added, that Orwell rejects

²³ For more on this aspect of Orwell's politics, see Goodway (2025)

²⁴ Richard J. Voorhees argues that Lewis's accusation 'seems a perfect illustration of the irresponsibility with which Orwell charged many British intellectuals. Orwell no more had the viciousness of the Nazi than he had the naiveté of the Boy Scout' (1961: 53)

²⁵ A helpful suggestion from the Orwell Foundation that M.W. Freer, who wrote to Lewis from Hampstead in North London, could have been related to the Conservative MP Mike Freer (parliamentary under-secretary of state for courts and legal services 2022-2024) came to nothing. Darcy Moore has suggested to me that Lewis's correspondent might be the Michael Wynn Freer (1930-2013) who married in Hampstead in 1954. M.W. Freer's letter to Lewis is signed from Tanza Road, Hampstead, NW3, which is just round the corner from Parliament Hill (where Orwell lived from March to August 1935). I have been unable definitively to identify M.W. Freer and will be glad to hear from anyone who can or who has already

²⁶ Like Lewis, Freer had been unable to procure a copy of *A Clergyman's Daughter*

²⁷ Lewis writes: 'It has been remarked … that Verrall is, in *Burmese Days*, the character of Orwell's preference. But anyone familiar with the book will well understand how that might be, for at least Verrall is not always drunk, and is apparently able to speak without cursing … . Verrall had a rabbit face, like many of his class, "but a martial rabbit". His are very pale blue eyes which quell the most alcoholic of the club members. He dances divinely, just as his horsemanship is superb: yes, I suppose Orwell *is* a little too much impressed with his young aristocrat. But what member of the middle-class, born before 1914, could be otherwise?' (1952: 159)

[28] Compare this with a point from *The Listener* review of Lewis's book: 'The people [Lewis] is attacking are altruists – people with a social conscience; and they engage in politics (often to the detriment of their creative writing) because they believe that economic conditions must be changed before there can be any vital culture' (Unsigned 1952: 111)

[29] I discuss the supposedly 'unelectrical' quality of the main characters in *Nineteen Eighty-Four* at greater length in Waddell (2024)

[30] Noreen Masud (2025) shows decisively that Orwell did, indeed, have 'an acute sense of the ridiculous'

[31] Marguerite D. Bloxom's comment on Lewis's account of Orwell, appended to the proceedings from the *George Orwell & Nineteen Eighty-Four: The Man and the Book* conference held at the Library of Congress in 1984, is admirably poised in its restrained exasperation: 'A biographical summary based on an uncritical reading of the autobiographical portions of Orwell's work is followed by less than reverent criticism of his novels and essays' (Anon 1985: 125)

[32] J.M. Cohen begins his review of *The Writer and the Absolute*, published in *The Spectator*, by acknowledging Lewis's claim that the 'contemporary artist pretends … that this is a *public* age and that he enjoys freedom of expression, whereas it is in fact an age in which it is impossible to be truthful except in private, and when the freedom to write at all may, as in the totalitarian countries, at any moment be withdrawn from him'. Cohen ends his account of the book by addressing the ironies in Lewis's position: 'The fact is that Wyndham Lewis has read too much into his own difficulties in finding an audience when his own thought has gone consistently against the fashionable currents. Nevertheless, no one has, in fact, prevented the publication of this lively, provocative, sincere and in parts, I believe, wrong-headed piece of pamphleteering' (1952: 194, italics in the original)

## REFERENCES

Anon. (1985) *George Orwell &* Nineteen Eighty-Four: *The Man and the Book*, Washington: Library of Congress

Bluemel, Kristin (ed.) (2009) *Intermodernism: Literary Culture in Mid-Twentieth-Century Britain*, Edinburgh: Edinburgh University Press

Braybrooke, Neville (1952) Wyndham Lewis as a novelist, *Yorkshire Observer*, 10 July p. 7

Cohen, J.M. (1952) Wyndham Lewis v. the rest, *Spectator*, 8 August p. 194

Connolly, Cyril (1952) Unkindly light, *Sunday Times*, 29 June p. 5

Dwan, David (2018) *Liberty, Equality and Humbug: Orwell's Political Ideals*, Oxford: Oxford University Press

Edwards, Paul (2000) *Wyndham Lewis: Writer and Painter*, New Haven and London: Yale University Press

Fox, C.J. (1982) Wyndham Lewis and the schoolmaster of manslaughter: The Machiavellian presence, Cianci, Giovanni (ed.) *Wyndham Lewis: Letteratura / Pittura*, Palermo: Sellerio editore pp 192-202

Freer, M.W. (1952 [?]) ALS to Wyndham Lewis, Division of Rare and Manuscript Collections, Cornell University Library, Wyndham Lewis Collection (4612), Box 105, Folder 39 (6 pages)

Gąsiorek, Andrzej (2001) 'Jujitsu for the governed'? Wyndham Lewis and the problem of power, *Wyndham Lewis Annual*, Vol. VIII pp 30-50

Gąsiorek, Andrzej (2004) *Wyndham Lewis and Modernism*, Tavistock: Northcote House

Gąsiorek, Andrzej (2005) The politics of antinomianism: Orwell, the everyday, and the dream of a common culture, Gomis, Annette and Onega, Susana (eds) *George Orwell: A Centenary Celebration*, Heidelberg: Universitatsverlag, winter pp 99-120

Gąsiorek, Andrzej (2011) Wyndham Lewis on art, culture and politics in the 1930s, Gąsiorek, Andrzej, Reeve-Tucker, Alice and Waddell, Nathan (eds) *Wyndham Lewis and the Cultures of Modernity*, Farnham, Surrey / Burlington, VT: Ashgate pp 201-222

Goodway, David (2025) Orwell and Trotskyism, Waddell, Nathan (ed.) *The Oxford Handbook of George Orwell*, Oxford: Oxford University Press pp 266-282

Heppenstall, Rayner (1988 [1960]) *Four Absentees*, London: Cardinal

Lewis, Wyndham (1931) *The Diabolical Principle and the Dithyrambic Spectator*, London: Chatto and Windus

Lewis, Wyndham (1952) *The Writer and the Absolute*, London: Methuen

Lewis, Wyndham (1938) *The Mysterious Mr Bull*, London: Robert Hale

Lewis, Wyndham (1963) *Letters*, Rose, W.K. (ed.) London: Methuen

Lewis, Wyndham (1972 [1936]) *Left Wings Over Europe: or, How to Make a War About Nothing*, New York: Gordon Press

Lewis, Wyndham (1984a) *Snooty Baronet*, Lafourcade, Bernard (ed.) Santa Barbara: Black Sparrow Press

Lewis, Wyndham (1984b [1950]) *Rude Assignment: An Intellectual Autobiography*, Foshay, Toby Avard (ed.) Santa Barbara: Black Sparrow Press

Lewis, Wyndham (1985 [1941]) *The Vulgar Streak*, Edwards, Paul (ed.) Santa Barbara: Black Sparrow Press

Lewis, Wyndham (1987 [1934]) *Men Without Art*, Cooney, Seamus (ed.) Santa Rosa: Black Sparrow Press

Lewis, Wyndham (1989a [1926]) *The Art of Being Ruled*, Dasenbrock, Reed Way (ed.) Santa Rosa: Black Sparrow Press

Lewis, Wyndham (1989b) *Creatures of Habit and Creatures of Change: Essays on Art, Literature and Society 1914-1956*, Edwards, Paul (ed.) Santa Rosa: Black Sparrow Press

Lewis, Wyndham (2023 [1927]) *Time and Western Man*, Edwards, Paul (ed.) Oxford: Oxford University Press

Loewenstein, Andrea Freud (1996) The protection of masculinity: Jews as projective pawns in the texts of William Gerhardi and George Orwell, Cheyette, Bryan (ed.) *Between 'Race' and Culture: Representations of 'the Jew' in English and American Literature*, Stanford, CA: Stanford University Press pp 145-164

Mackenzie, Compton (1935) Passionate truth-teller, *Daily Mail*, 4 July p. 5

Masud, Noreen (2025) Orwell and the absurd, Waddell, Nathan (ed.) *The Oxford Handbook of George Orwell*, Oxford: Oxford University Press pp 426-440

Meyers, Jeffrey (1980) *The Enemy: A Biography of Wyndham Lewis*, London: Routledge & Kegan Paul

Meyers, Jeffrey (2010) *Orwell: Life and Art*, Urbana: University of Illinois Press

Mullen, Lisa (2025) Orwell the stylist, Waddell, Nathan (ed.) *The Oxford Handbook of George Orwell*, Oxford: Oxford University Press pp 30-44

Munton, Alan (2006) Wyndham Lewis: From Proudhon to Hitler (and back): The strange political journey of Wyndham Lewis, *e-rea*, Vol. 4, No. 2. Available online at https://journals.openedition.org/erea/220, accessed on 26 February 2025

Munton, Alan (2015) Lewis and cultural criticism, Gąsiorek, Andrzej and Waddell, Nathan (eds) *Wyndham Lewis: A Critical Guide*, Edinburgh: Edinburgh University Press pp 64-81

Munton, Alan (2025) Orwell and Wyndham Lewis, Waddell, Nathan (ed.) *The Oxford Handbook of George Orwell*, Oxford: Oxford University Press pp 577-593

O'Keeffe, Paul (2000) *Some Sort of Genius: A Life of Wyndham Lewis*, London: Jonathan Cape

Orwell, George (1998) *The Complete Works of George Orwell: A Kind of Compulsion, 1903-1936, Vol. X*, Davison, Peter with Angus, Ian and Davison, Sheila (eds) London: Secker & Warburg

Orwell, George (2000) *The Complete Works of George Orwell: Facing Unpleasant Facts, 1937-1939, Vol. XI*, Davison, Peter with Angus, Ian and Davison, Sheila (eds) London: Secker & Warburg

Orwell, George (2001a) *The Complete Works of George Orwell: Two Wasted Years, 1943, Vol. XV*, Davison, Peter with Angus, Ian and Davison, Sheila (eds) London: Secker & Warburg, revised edition

Orwell, George (2001b) *The Complete Works of George Orwell: I Have Tried to Tell the Truth, 1943-1944, Vol. XVI*, Davison, Peter with Angus, Ian and Davison, Sheila (eds) London: Secker & Warburg, revised edition

Orwell, George (2001c) *The Complete Works of George Orwell: I Belong to the Left, 1945, Vol. XVII*, Davison, Peter with Angus, Ian and Davison, Sheila (eds) London: Secker & Warburg, revised edition

Orwell, George (2001d) *The Complete Works of George Orwell: Smothered Under Journalism, 1946, Vol. XVIII*, Davison, Peter with Angus, Ian and Davison, Sheila (eds) London: Secker & Warburg, revised edition

Orwell, George (2001e [1937]) *The Road to Wigan Pier*, Davison, Peter (ed.) London: Penguin

Orwell, George (2002) *The Complete Works of George Orwell: A Patriot After All, 1940-1941, Vol. XII*, Davison, Peter with Angus, Ian and Davison, Sheila (eds) London: Secker & Warburg, revised edition

Quéma, Anne (1999) *The Agon of Modernism: Wyndham Lewis's Allegories, Aesthetics, and Politics*, Lewisburg: Bucknell University Press / London: Associated University Presses

Rae, Patricia (2025) Orwell the innovator, Waddell, Nathan (ed.) *The Oxford Handbook of George Orwell*, Oxford: Oxford University Press pp 45-64

Symons, Julian (1957) Meeting Wyndham Lewis, *London Magazine*, Vol. 4, No. 10 pp 47-53

Taylor, Elinor (2020) The problem of hope: Orwell's workers, Waddell, Nathan (ed.) *The Cambridge Companion to* Nineteen Eighty-Four, Cambridge: Cambridge University Press pp 155-167

Unsigned (1952a) *The Listener*'s book chronicle: *The Writer and the Absolute* by Wyndham Lewis, *Listener*, 17 July p. 111

Unsigned (1952b) Flirting with politics, *Times Literary Supplement*, 18 July p. 464

Voorhees, Richard J. (1961) *The Paradox of George Orwell*, West Lafayette, Indiana: Purdue University Press

Waddell, Nathan (2024) George Orwell: Politics and power, Potter, Rachel and Taunton, Matthew (eds) *The British Novel of Ideas: George Eliot to Zadie Smith*, Cambridge: Cambridge University Press pp 259-273

Wagner, Geoffrey (1957) *Wyndham Lewis: A Portrait of the Artist as the Enemy*, New Haven: Yale University Press

**NATHAN WADDELL**

NOTE ON THE CONTRIBUTOR

Nathan Waddell is a Professor of Twentieth-Century Literature at the University of Birmingham. He is the editor of *The Cambridge Companion to* Nineteen Eighty-Four (2019), the 2021 Oxford World's Classics edition of Orwell's *A Clergyman's Daughter* and *The Oxford Handbook of George Orwell* (2025). His book, *A Bright Cold Day: The Wonder of George Orwell*, will be published by Oneworld in June 2025.

ARTICLE

# Dear Charoux: Revealed – Orwell's 13 Letters to his Artist Friend

## DARCY MOORE

*George Orwell wrote at least thirteen letters to Siegfried Charoux which appear to be unknown to Orwell scholars. Twelve of these were handwritten from beds in three different hospitals, and one typed, at Orwell's home on the Isle of Jura. Darcy Moore reflects on what these letters tell us about Orwell, including the writer's sentimental attachment to ancestral portraits.*

On 19 November 1948, Orwell wrote to his friend and patron, the editor of the *Observer*, David Astor, thanking him for his advice:

It's very kind of Charoux to help about restoring the picture. When I can get round to doing so I'll make a crate and send it to him direct. I never can remember his address but I expect I have a letter of his somewhere (Orwell 1998 [1947-1948]: 468).

Peter Davison, editor of *The Complete Works of George Orwell*, included a footnote explaining that Charoux was 'a picture-framer and restorer' and that 'his address is given in Orwell's address book as 65 Holland Park Road, London, W14' (ibid: 469). There are only two other very minor references to Charoux in the *Complete Works*. One, in another letter to Astor, where Orwell says:

Dear David,

I wonder how you are getting on. I was slightly dismayed to hear from Charoux that you were getting along 'as well as can be expected'. I had thought the operation you were having was something very minor. Let me know how you are when you get a chance to write (Orwell 1998 [1949-1950]: 147).

And another, in a letter Orwell wrote to *Adelphi* editor and life-long friend Richard Rees, himself an accomplished amateur painter:

I've just had back that picture that went to be restored. He's made a beautiful job of it, & it is almost like a new picture. Apparently they can lift a picture right off & stick it onto a new piece of canvas. I have another old picture which I thought was past praying for, as the canvas is sort of moth eaten, but perhaps this chap could do something with it. He also put the picture in a quite nice new frame, & only charged 12 guineas for the whole job (ibid: 169).

Davison included brief footnotes for each: 'Charoux was a picture-framer and restorer recommended to Orwell by Astor to repair one of Orwell's pictures damaged in the move to Jura' and 'Rees, as a painter, might be expected to be particularly interested in what Charoux had been able to do' (ibid: 148; 169). It is now apparent that Siegfried Charoux was not a 'picture restorer' but had a friend who was one! Charoux was a sculptor, painter and caricaturist!

Siegfried Joseph Charoux © National Portrait Gallery, London, NPG x86678. © The Estate of Siegfried Charoux

THE LETTERS[1]

The first six letters to Charoux are written from Hairmyres Hospital in East Kilbride, Lanarkshire, where Orwell was being treated for tuberculosis. He had been admitted in December 1947 and was a patient until the end of July 1948. These letters, often written in appreciation for the gifts of food prepared by Siegfried and Margarethe Charoux, who were excellent cooks, include insights into Orwell's attitudes about his medical condition, the drug streptomycin which he was taking for his TB, art, smoking and ill-health. His son, Richard Blair, is a regular topic of conversation and Orwell's ever-present interest in nature is a feature, even though his observations are made while gazing out of hospital windows. Summaries follow.

13.1.48

A brief note where Orwell thanks Charoux for the food he has sent, especially the delicious cakes. He mentions that his appetite is returning. Orwell relays the good news that an X-ray has revealed 'one bit of his lungs is beginning to mend' and that there is a 'new treatment' putting the 'lung out of action for a long time to give it a chance to heal'. Orwell mentions 'David and Karl'[2] and that he has not worked on his book (*Nineteen Eighty-Four*) in three months.

### 30.1.48

Often illegible, this letter opens with niceties about the jam Charoux has sent, noting he has not had 'Oxford marmalade' since 1939. He provides some details about his medical condition saying: 'I think I am getting better.' He reports that X-rays continue to show 'distinct improvement'. His attitude towards tobacco is enunciated very clearly: 'If I am ill I don't enjoy smoking' as it does not have the 'proper taste'. He asks Charoux to remember him to his wife.

### 2.3.48

Charoux has sent more food and Orwell thanks him for the cakes which he shared with 'David and Karl'. He reports that he has been taking streptomycin for about ten days: 'I think it is doing me good.' He says he feels better and is doing a 'little light work – ie book reviews'.

### 21.4.48

More food has arrived for Orwell who is concerned that Charoux really cannot spare it. He reports that he has generally been 'a lot better' but over the last fortnight has suffered from the 'secondary effects of streptomycin'. He is hoping to 'get out of hospital' for the summer believing that only returning for 'periodical treatment' is a distinct possibility. He is depressed by his invalid status but hopes to be allowed outside 'in a chair' shortly. He has not noticed the seasonal arrival of the swallows yet and makes some other commentary about nature and farming.

### 12.5.48

Orwell thanks Charoux for the tin of marmalade and other food. He reports 'six negative tests' and hopes to check out of hospital by August (it is now mid-May). Orwell's chief worry is the length of time he has spent away from Richard. He is 'afraid' that his son may forget him and is looking forward to seeing him in the grounds of the hospital soon (noting that children are not permitted inside). Orwell tells Charoux that he feels well enough to 'get back into serious work again' soon. He has not 'heard from David for some time' (Astor is formally editing *The Observer* from 1948) and wonders if he is out of the country. There is much reflection on the progress of his garden at Barnhill, the remote farmhouse on Jura. The usual sign-off about Mrs Charoux.

### 10.6.48

More appreciation is expressed for yet another parcel of food including more Oxford marmalade. Getting out of the hospital room for two hours a day is making Orwell feel much better. The doctors have stopped (illegible – but something about his treatment/lungs). He has been told it will not be necessary to be an outpatient on departure (illegible something about Edinburgh). Orwell mentions Avril is 'going to bring my little boy to see me at the end of the month'. The writing is quite illegible in parts but mentions that Richard has already had measles and whooping cough and that Orwell has concerns about his son contracting scarlet fever. It appears these diseases only slightly impacted on Richard; it was difficult to keep him in bed. The weather on Jura is good he has been told. On a nearby ward a patient has procured bagpipes, which he feels is a little odd considering everyone has tuberculosis.

26.11.48

Typed letter to Charoux from Barnhill:

```
                                              Barnhill
                                              Isle of Jura
                                              Argyllshire
                                              26.11.48




                    Dear Charoux,
                               David said you very kindly
     volunteered to find someone to restore a picture for me. I am
     sending it to you by rail, I trust safely, as it is in a crate
     which belonged to a much bigger picture, but I think I have packed
     it tightly enough.

          It is a small canvas, about 16" by 20", date about 1790, and
     though of no value I think quite a good painting. The canvas is
     very frail, and Pickfords in bringing it here managed to make a
     large slit, unfortunately on the face, as well as a chip or two
     elsewhere. I imagine what it wants is a piece of canvas stuck behind
     the slit and then some faking up with paint on the surface. Incid-
     entally it wants cleaning, but I don't know if one can do that if
     one is also repainting a patch on the picture. If you do know some-
     one who could do it, I should be very much obliged if you could pass
     it on to him.

          I came out of the hospital in July feeling very much better,
     but I have not felt so grand since about September, and I am con-
     templating going into a sanatorium for the worst of the winter, ie.
     January and February. But I have not definitely fixed anything yet.
     I am busy typing out the book I have just finished and which I have
     been messing about with for something like eighteen months, six of
     which were in hospital, however. The weather has been somewhat better
     in the autumn than it was in the summer. Richard is getting enormous,
     and is tremendously active and well. He loves working on the farm,
     fishing and so forth. Recently he took to smoking, I am sorry to
     say, but he almost immediately made himself so sick that he has never
     repeated it. Please remember me to your wife. I trust you will not
     put yourself out in any way about this picture. There is not any
     sort of hurry about it.

                              Yours
                              Geo. Orwell
```

*Published with the kind permission of Richard Blair*

After being discharged from Hairmyres Hospital, in South Lanarkshire, Scotland, in July 1948, Orwell made a herculean effort to complete *Nineteen Eighty-Four*. He departed Jura early in January 1949 and was admitted to Cranham Sanatorium in the Cotswolds. His remaining months were spent there and at University College Hospital, London. The following six letters were written during the final six months of Orwell's life; four when he was a patient at Cranham Lodge and two from University College Hospital. Even as late as the second half of 1949, Orwell believed he had a good chance of survival.

### 10.6.49
A brief letter enquiring if the portrait he wanted restored ever arrived.

### 12.8.49
Orwell explains that he now knows the portrait was sent to the wrong address. He describes the painting as 'a small canvas, 18" by 15", painted about 1800 representing a young girl'. There is a 'bad slit in the canvas' and he suspects there may be 'weak spots' but he 'supposes it is repairable'. Orwell explains it 'has sentimental value and is a nice picture'. He describes himself as 'still rather so-so but better on the whole'. Richard has been staying here during the summer but will return 'to Jura shortly to attend the village school'. Usual sign-off about remembering him to Mrs Charoux.

### 24.8.49
Orwell thanks Charoux for his letter and reassures him the twelve pounds (something/illegible) is not too much for restoring the painting, acknowledging how trying a job it would be for the restorer. Orwell says his 'health has ups & downs' and that he will be in a 'London hospital shortly' but no date has been set.

### NO DATE 1949
A longer letter thanking Charoux for sending 'the beautiful water colour of Tarbet' and 'the cakes'. He had not been aware that Charoux 'painted in water-colour' acknowledging 'it is terribly tricky stuff'. He had heard that Charoux 'had been at Tarbet, but didn't get as far as Barnhill'. Orwell mentions his health saying that the specialist thinks he is 'not doing so bad' and will 'probably recover' but 'will have to lay still and not work, possibly for as long as a year'. He says this 'is worthwhile if it means he can work again later'. Richard is staying nearby: '… he is now just 5' and attends 'kindergarten school in the mornings'. It appears that David Astor has suggested Charoux does a bust of Orwell who enquires about the expense of bronze.[3]

# DARCY MOORE

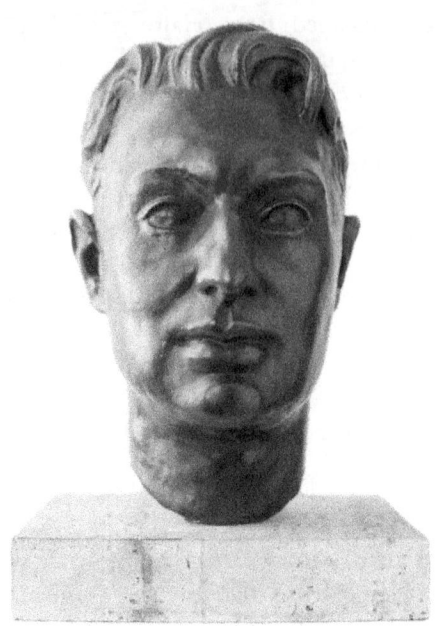

David Astor (1946). Bronze, height 29 cm, inventory number A0047
©The Estate of Siegfried Charoux, photograph by schultz+schultz

16.9.1949 (ROOM 65, PRIVATE WING UNIVERSITY COLLEGE HOSPITAL)
Orwell thanks Charoux for telling him that the picture has been restored successfully and plans to hang in his new hospital room. He is only allowed one visitor for twenty minutes a day and suggests Charoux phones him rather than making the 'expedition' to visit.

17.9.1949 (ROOM 65, PRIVATE WING UNIVERSITY COLLEGE HOSPITAL)
Charoux has sent more cakes and bananas. It is also clear that the restored painting has arrived and is 'almost like new'. Orwell mentions he has other paintings in need of restoration including a 'moth-eaten' canvas. The final letter in this sequence concludes with Orwell's news that he is going to wed Sonia Brownell:

> Did I tell you that I am going to get married again – though I don't quite know when, my health being what it is.

## SIEGFRIED CHAROUX (1896-1967)
Although born in Vienna and only emigrating to Great Britain when he was approaching forty years of age, Charoux has an entry in the *Oxford Dictionary of National Biography*.[4] Even this brief overview of his life indicates the sorts of traits which made David Astor and Orwell so well-disposed towards the Austrian émigré, naturalised a British citizen in 1946, the year he exhibited a bronze bust of Sir Stafford Cripps, chancellor of the exchequer in the Labour government 1947-1950, at the Royal Academy of Arts in London:

... a typical Austrian in appearance: fair-haired and blue-eyed, heroic in build, and with a magnificent head like a much more amiable version of Beethoven. Almost always he wore a faded old sculptor's smock, the rolled-up sleeves revealing a massive pair of forearms and hands. He seemed happy so long as he was making something – sculpture, pictures, pots, a new kiln, bread. (Jugged hare was one of his special culinary accomplishments.) He loved a good argument among friends and could be devastatingly funny, manipulating his enormous fingers to emphasize a point and wielding a shaky knowledge of English with wit and wisdom (Gross 2004).

Born Siegfried Joseph Buchta, he adopted his mother's maiden name 'Charous' in 1914 and formally changed it to Siegfried Charoux on marrying Margarethe Treibl, his life-long partner, in 1926 (Bockstefl and Veasey 2020: 2). A creative, intelligent and 'wilfully determined child' who much preferred roaming in the woods to the restrictive nature of formal academic studies, it is unclear whether Charoux immediately enlisted in the Austrian army at the outbreak of World War One or was conscripted in 1915 (Gross 2004; Veasey 2024: 6-7). Along with many of his generation who experienced the horror of mass mechanised slaughter, he grew resentful, disliking that he was fighting 'Russian peasants' for the 'Hapsburg monarchy' (Astor 1967). He was wounded twice and invalided out of the army in 1917.[5] A successful operation restored movement in his paralysed right arm (Gross 2004).

Charoux sought a traditional education at a prestigious Viennese art academy after the war – but never graduated. Struggling with the demotivating, conventional syllabus and professors derided as 'fire-extinguishers' (for their expertise in extinguishing self-expression), he left to establish a career as a professional sculptor in 1924 (Gross 2004; Veasey 2024: 7-9, 118). Always willing to challenge authority, a fervent supporter of democratic principles, left-leaning but no ideologue, Charoux was employed as a political caricaturist (1923-1928) for the *Arbeiter Zeitung* socialist newspaper (Groß 1997: 64; Gross 2004; Veasey 2024: 7-8, 118). His pseudonym, Chat Roux (Red Cat), clearly revealed his political sympathies as did his choice of satirical targets, which included the nazis as early as 1925 (Groß 1997: 64-217, 140; Veasey 2024: 7).

During the 1930s, Charoux exhibited works in several European countries, including Germany, accepting commissions for his sculptures to grace municipal buildings in Vienna (Gross 2004). In 1932, at the Viennese Art Exhibition, he exhibited busts of Stalin and Gandhi (Veasey 2024: 228). Charoux won a national competition to cast a memorial to one of his intellectual and artistic heroes, Gotthold Ephraim Lessing, the 18th century German

Enlightenment figure who had visited Vienna in 1775 (ibid: 15). In 1939, this bronze statue was removed by the nazis, who despised unconventional art from politicised artists such as Charoux, which they later melted down for armaments (ibid).

## DAVID ASTOR (1912-2001) AND CHAROUX

Considered a leading sculptor in 'Red Vienna', Charoux, whose wife was Jewish, was in the vanguard of European intellectuals and artists emigrating to London before the German annexation of Austria and invasion of Czechoslovakia, in March 1939. He and Margarethe were always adamant that they did not flee but had chosen 'self-exile' in 1935 after it became obvious that intellectual and artistic freedoms were curtailed in Austria (ibid: 18, 223).

On first arriving in London, having no studio, materials or patrons, Charoux thrived in 'gritty, uncompromising environments' where he connected with 'ordinary working men' – labourers and dock workers – whom he sketched (ibid: 31). Actively seeking patrons, he was fortunate to meet David Astor not long after arriving in the city. Cheekily, Charoux asked if Astor would consider sitting for a bust, not because he had an interesting head but because the wealthy aristocrat's status would assist with his career (ibid: 32, 166). Astor was vastly amused. The warm friendship which subsequently developed radiates from an unsigned obituary written over thirty years after that first meeting in late 1935:

> Siegfried Charoux was a man of many gifts and warm friendships. Sculpture and painting were his chief modes of expression, but he was also an inventor of technical devices in those arts, a memorable amateur cook and a powerful arguer.
>
> His political views were at the opposite pole from Adolf Hitler's. Journalism with him was not just an idea, but the conviction of a private soldier of the Hapsburg monarchy who had been made to fight Russian peasants against his will. During the chaotic times following World War I, he crossed many frontiers of Eastern Europe as a hobo, entering Russia illegally to see the revolutionary regime for himself.
>
> His voluntary exile to England in the thirties became a conversion. When he re-visited Vienna after the war, he felt homesick for London and its social tolerance. Yet his London home, with its piano, indoor plants, over-flowing book-shelves and rich compost of his own and other artists' work always exhaled a Continental atmosphere.
>
> He and his wife, who outlives him, were the most generous hosts. Even the austere Stafford Cripps used to unbend in their company. All their friends came to feel like relatives and

he will be greatly missed, although he will always survive for them in his lively and honest work (Astor 1967).

Charoux working on the clay model for the sculpture 'Mother and two children' for the Hugo-Breitner-Hof, 14th district, Vienna, in his studio at Holland Park Road, London, c. 1957, Langenzersdorf Museum, Austria, Charoux Archive,
Barratt's Photo Press Ltd., London
©The Estate of Siegfried Charoux

Astor supported Charoux and Margarethe financially, socially and artistically until their deaths. He was instrumental in having Charoux released from internment as enemy alien on the Isle of Man in 1941, as well as supporting their applications to become British citizens (Lewis 2017: 180; Veasey 2024: 223). Subsequently, they were employed by the BBC to broadcast propaganda (Veasey 2024: 40). Astor rented and then purchased a home for Charoux and his wife which became a haven for a circle of close friends, many of whom were British and European intellectuals and artists, well-known to Orwell.

PORTRAITS

There are several clues in letters, photographs and memoirs about the ancestral portraits George Orwell owned. The earliest of these clues, from 1936, when Eileen Blair (née O'Shaughnessy) noted while 'staying with the Blairs' how surprised she was that their 'very small' house was 'furnished almost entirely with paintings of ancestors' (Orwell 2013: 67). Anthony Powell wrote in *The Atlantic*:

**DARCY MOORE**

We dined with the Orwells at this house (in Kilburn, North London) one night, prior arrangements being made for sleeping there too, owing to the exigencies of wartime transport. The sitting room, with a general background of furniture dating from more prosperous generations of bygone Blairs, had two or three eighteenth-century family portraits hanging on the walls (Powell 1967: 65).

The house mentioned by Powell, 10 Mortimer Crescent, was 'blitzed' in mid-1944 resulting in Orwell moving to what would be his final London residence, 27 Canonbury Square, in Islington. Ancestral family portraits were hanging on these walls when Vernon Richards, the Anglo-Italian anarchist, photographed Orwell at home in this Islington flat. It is not possible to identify with certainty which Blair ancestors adorned this otherwise spartan abode but a portrait of Lady Mary Blair née Fane (c.1741-1813) was in the possession of his sister, Avril Blair (1908-1978), who had lived with him on Jura during the last years of his life (Stansky and Abrahams 1972: 8).[6] Indeed, if this were the case, many would consider it a peculiar choice of home decoration for the average socialist and possibly, perceiving such choices as bourgeois, may go a little way towards explaining Richards' lack of enthusiasm about Orwell and his work. Although these portraits cannot be identified from the photographs taken at this residence in 1946, it is possible to see there are several on the walls (Richards 1998: 8, 10, 14, 19-20, 29, 31, 34, 61, 71). Orwell must have inherited these paintings – his father dying in 1939 and his mother in 1943 – but what exactly was the small canvas, about 16 by 20 inches painted around 1790 that had sentimental value for Orwell (which he also described as 18 by 15 inches and painted about 1800) 'representing a young girl' so in need of restoration?

My research into Orwell's ancestors has identified family portraits by some of Britain's most illustrious artists and their protégés: Thomas Frye (1710-1762), Sir Joshua Reynolds (1723-1792), Thomas Gainsborough (1727-1788), Sir Nathaniel Dance-Holland (1734-1811), George Romney (1734-1802), Thomas Beach (1738-1806), Ozias Humphry (1742-1810), Sir Henry Raeburn (1745-1806), Philip Reinagle (1749-1833) and Sir Thomas Lawrence (1769-1830). These paintings, along with the gilded homes where they hung, were funded by a family of absentee landlords enriched from the sugar and rum produced on their plantations in Jamaica by enslaved people (Dresser 2013: 102; Hall 2014: 242-243; Moore 2020: 6-19; UCL 2020, 2024).

There is strong evidence the painting Orwell had restored was by Thomas Beach, who was a 'favourite pupil' of Sir Joshua Reynolds (Beach 1934). Beach, based in Dorset and often commissioned to paint the extended Blair family in the latter part of the 18th century, was an assured 'figure painter' and 'natural colourist' noted for his ability to 'capture a good likeness' (Graves 2009). Beach worked in Joshua Reynolds's studio in London (1760-1762) at the time when his master accepted the commission for a very large group portrait, which included Orwell's great-great-grandfather, Charles Blair (1743-1802) and his wife's brother, Henry Fane (Solnit 2022: 157-160; Baetjer 2010: 68-70). Lady Mary and Charles married in 1762, the same year that her father, Thomas Fane (1701-1771) became the 8th Earl of Westmoreland (ibid).

Beach's great-great-grand niece published a catalogue of his work in 1934, listing nine ancestral portraits in the 'Michel Collection' painted between 1777-1782:[7]

1. Portrait of a boy (Thomas Blair).

2. Portrait of a boy (Blair).

3. Portrait of a boy (Blair).

4. Portrait of a girl (Blair).

5. Portrait of a boy (Blair).

6. Charles and Henry Blair, two boys playing.

7. Charles Blair, 1777.

8. Charles Blair, 1782.

9. Colonel D.R. Michel.

10. Colonel D.R. Michel.

11. Mrs Michel.

12. Mary Michel.

13. Grace Michel (Beach 1934: 81).

'Blair. Portrait of a girl' is described as 19 inch by 15 inch and oval, very much the dimensions Orwell described to Charoux; the subject and period are also correct (ibid: 55). Listed on the same page is the painting of Henry Charles Blair (1775-1794) and Orwell's great-grandfather, Charles Blair (1776-1854) who were the sons of Lady Mary Blair, née Fane, and the elder Charles Blair (ibid). This painting, along with the portraits of Mary and Grace Michel, are the only works listed thus far located in auction records, suggesting they are possibly in the possession of Orwell's ancestors descended from his eldest sister, Marjorie Dakin, née Blair.

# DARCY MOORE

Thomas Beach (1738-1806) Portrait of the Masters Blair: Charles and Henry Blair, 1782 (Wikimedia Commons)

## REFLECTION

These letters to Charoux demonstrate Orwell cared deeply about the family portraits, carted from apartment to apartment and then to Jura, he had inherited. They also reveal he knew Charoux and his wife reasonably well and that more research is needed to understand their shared circles with other émigrés in Orwell and David Astor's milieu.

During the 1940s, Orwell's professional associates and friends expanded exponentially due to the popular and critical success of *Animal Farm* (1945), employment at the BBC and subsequent literary editorship of *Tribune*, along with his close relationship with Astor (Moore 2024b). Many of the most significant of these figures were Central European intellectuals, some of whom Astor referred to as 'the Professorate' when they were employed by the *Observer* and shaped the newspaper's post war policy directions (Ascherson 1999). Even a cursory overview of Charoux's life experiences and values suggests some common intellectual and political ground with Orwell, Tosco Fyvel, Isaac Deutscher, Sebastian Haffner and Arthur Koestler. Charoux can now be added to the social circles of these creative émigrés, escaping the anti-democratic regimes emanating from Russia, Austria and Germany, in Astor and Orwell's orbit.

Orwell's ability to write authoritatively about totalitarianism was mostly a result of his experiences in the Indian Imperial Police in Burma, as a militiaman during the Spanish Civil War and from a lifetime of wide reading. However, his circle of friends and associates included many who had experienced these regimes firsthand and must have been sources of information and insight. Another Austrian who had arrived in London during 1935, Franz Borkenau, wrote perceptively to Orwell in September 1949:

> The problem for all of us is of course that the horrors of the totalitarian regime are such that they defy both scholarly analysis and artistic creation.... Yours is the only book which seems to me to convey fully what a totalitarian regime means in terms of the individuals living under it (Orwell 1998 [1949-50]: 167).

There is some evidence that Orwell and his family provided imaginative inspiration for Charoux's own work. Based on conversations with David Astor, the present owners of Charoux's studio, Mark and Ruth Beedle, believe that George, Eileen and Richard Blair were the inspiration behind Charoux's monumental bas-relief for the Festival of Britain, *The Islanders* (Veasey 2024: 83).[8]

*The Islanders*, 1951 (demolished in 1952). Plaster, monumental bas-relief for the Festival of Britain, London; postcard 1951, Cardcraft Publishing Service, London
© The Estate of Siegfried Charouxx

- Special thanks to Dr Melanie Veasey for her extraordinary intellectual generosity in sharing knowledge and scholarship about Charoux. I have also greatly appreciated the support of Gregor-Anatol Bockstefl, manager of the Langenzersdorf Museum, Austria, and curator of the estate of Siegfried Charoux.

## NOTES

[1] Orwell's letters to Charoux are held in the Bodleian Libraries Special Collections, MS 15363/167

[2] Karl Schnetzler, a German electrical research engineer resident in England during the 1930s who had been interned (1939-1943) to later become a naturalised British subject in 1948. See *CWGO* 2893, as well as letters from Schnetzler to Ian Angus and Bernard Crick

[3] Charoux had finally completed a bust of Astor in 1946

[4] For detailed biographical information, I highly recommend Melanie Veasey's book, *Charoux's Sculptures*, which can be accessed online: https://www.lemu.at/wp-content/uploads/2024/09/Charouxs-Sculptures_Melanie-Veasey_LEMU_24-09-17.pdf and the less accessible but excellent German language book by Hans Kurt Groß, *Siegfried Charoux: die Wiener Jahre des Karikaturisten und Bildhauers* [*Siegfried Charoux: The Viennese Years of the Caricaturist and Sculptor*]. NB: The British Library is devoid of materials on Charoux

[5] Charoux claimed that he wandered through Russia as 'a hobo' immediately after being invalided out of the army where he grew increasingly interested in political ideologies, especially anarchism (Veasey 2024: 7-8)

[6] This portrait of Lady Mary, 'in terrible condition', was subsequently inherited by Henry Dakin (the son of Orwell's eldest sister) who had it restored. It is unknown if he carried out his plan to have Christies identify the artist and value it. Dakin thought it was painted c. 1780 (Dakin 1988). Contextually, considering the other Fane family portraits painted by Thomas Gainsborough (who rarely signed his work), it is not inconceivable that this painting is from his brush

[7] A paper on Orwell's Dorset ancestors, including the Fane and Michel families, is in preparation for a future edition of *GOS*. The tentative title: 'The ruling class'

[8] Dr Veasey kindly re-interviewed Mark and Ruth Beedle in February 2025 to confirm their recollections for this article

## REFERENCES

Astor, David (1967) Mr Siegfried Charoux, *Times*, 3 May

Ascherson, Neal (1999) Sebastian Haffner obituary, *Guardian*, 14 January

Baetjer, Katharine (2010) *British Paintings in the Metropolitan Museum of Art, 1575-1875*, Connecticut, Yale University Press

Beach, Elsie S. (1934) *Thomas Beach, a Dorset Portrait Painter: Favourite Pupil of Sir Joshua Reynolds*, London: John Bale, Sons & Danielsson

Bockstefl, Gregor-Anatol and Veasey, Melanie (2020) *Siegfried Charoux: Sculptor and Painter*, Langenzersdorf Museum

Dakin, Henry (1988) Letter, 3 April

Deutscher, Isaac (1955) *Heretics and Renegades and other Essays*, London: Hamish Hamilton

Dresser, Madge and Hann, Andrew (2013) *Slavery and the British Country House*, Swindon: Historic England

Graves, R.E., and Tomory, Peter (2009) Beach, Thomas (bap. 1737, d. 1806), portrait painter, *Oxford Dictionary of National Biography*, Oxford: Oxford University Press

Groß, Hans Kurt (1997) *Siegfried Charoux: die Wiener Jahre des Karikaturisten und Bildhauers* [*Siegfried Charoux: the Viennese Years of the Caricaturist and Sculptor*], Charoux-Museum, Langenzersdorf, Austria, Niederösterreichisches Pressehaus St. Pölten, NP-Buchver: Langenzersdorf, Verlag

Gross, Hans Kurt (2004) Charoux, Siegfried Joseph (1896-1967), sculptor, *Oxford Dictionary of National Biography*, 23 September, accessed on 20 October 2024

Hall, Catherine, Draper, Nicholas, McClelland, Keith, Donington, Katie and Lang, Rachel (2014) *Legacies of British Slave-Ownership: Colonial Slavery and the Formation of Victorian Britain*, Cambridge: Cambridge University Press, Kindle edition

Lewis, Jeremy (2017) *David Astor*, New York: Random Books: Kindle Edition

Moore, Darcy (2020) Orwell's Scottish ancestry and slavery, *George Orwell Studies*, Vol. 5, No. 1 pp 6-19

Moore, Darcy (2024a) Dear Charoux, *Darcy Moore's Blog*. Available online at https://www.darcymoore.net/2024/10/27/dear-charoux/

Moore, Darcy (2024b) Two letters: Orwell to Astor, *Darcy Moore's Blog*. Available online at https://www.darcymoore.net/2024/12/08/two-letters-orwell-to-astor/

Orwell, George (2013) *A Life in Letters*, Davison, Peter (ed.), London: Liveright

Orwell, George (1998 [1947-1948]) *The Complete Works of George Orwell: It Is What I Think, Vol. XIX*, Davison, Peter (ed.) London: Secker & Warburg

Orwell, George (1998 [1949-1950]) *The Complete Works of George Orwell: Our Job is to Make Life Worth Living, Vol. XX*, Davison, Peter (ed.) London: Secker & Warburg

Orwell, George (1948-1949) Letters from George Orwell to Siegfried Charoux (1942-1952), Bodleian Library, University of Oxford. Papers of George Orwell, MS 15363/167, Bodleian Library Special Collections

Powell, Anthony (1967) George Orwell: A memoir, *Atlantic Monthly*, Vol. 220, October pp 62-68

Richards, Vernon (1998) *George Orwell at Home (and Among the Anarchists): Essays and Photographs*, London: Freedom Press

Solnit, Rebecca (2022) *Orwell's Roses*, London: Granta Books

Stansky, Peter and Abrahams, William (1972) *The Unknown Orwell*, New York: Alfred A. Knopf

UCL Department of History (2020) Charles Blair senior, *Legacies of British Slave-Ownership Database*, Centre for the Study of the Legacies of British Slave-Ownership, University College London. Available online at https://www.ucl.ac.uk/lbs/person/view/2146636746, accessed on 6 September 2020

UCL Department of History (2024) Charles Blair junior, *Legacies of British Slave-Ownership Database*, Centre for the Study of the Legacies of British Slave-Ownership, University College London. Available online at https://www.ucl.ac.uk/lbs/person/view/2146630288

Veasey, Melanie (2024) *Charoux's Sculptures*, Langenzersdorf Museum

## NOTE ON THE CONTRIBUTOR

Darcy Moore is the recipient of the 2024 Peter Davison Award for his distinguished research into the life and writings of George Orwell. He is a deputy principal at a state secondary school in New South Wales. Darcy blogs at *darcymoore.net* and his X/Twitter handle is @Darcy1968. His Orwell Studies Library can be accessed at darcymoore.net/orwell-collection/. Darcy welcomes correspondence: dfjmoore@gmail.com.

ARTICLE

# Throwing Light on Darkness

**PAUL W.B. MARSDEN**

*Paul W.B. Marsden explains how he came to write his new novel which imagines George Orwell's stay with Arthur Koestler in Blaenau Ffestiniog around Christmas 1945.*

My new novel, *Darkness in 1984*, started out on Thursday 8 August 2024 when I was reading about the life and works of Arthur Koestler. I have acquired a habit of choosing an important writer, reading their biography and then systematically reading, in date order, their works. I 'did' Orwell the year before. That summer was my 'Koestler phase'. My socialist dad had met Koestler in Manchester in 1960 and mentioned to me that he was a famous writer who had written an important novel exposing the Stalin show trials. That novel, *Darkness at Noon*, made the Hungarian-born writer into an international celebrity. My dad died in 1985 one year after I had studied *Nineteen Eighty-Four* for my O Level (which to my intense embarrassment I failed from a brain freeze after dozens of other exams).

So back to reading Koestler – I came across a passing reference in Michael Scammell's 2009 biography to Koestler inviting the recently widowed George Orwell and his baby son, Richard, up to his remote cottage for Christmas 1945. It was the first peaceful Christmas for seven years and the first since Orwell's wife, Eileen, had died in March, earlier that year. It took some digging to figure out precisely the location of the cottage, Bwlch Ocyn (perhaps pronounced as Bork Okin in English), near Blaenau Ffestiniog – just over an hour from where I live. The significance was that it stirred memories of several childhood camping and crab fishing holidays with my mum, dad and older sister, at Porthmadog and touring around Snowdonia.

Whilst I continued reading about Koestler the brief details of what happened during Orwell's stay started to gnaw away at me. *Animal Farm* had just been published and was starting to sell well but at that Christmas Orwell was probably viewed more as a good journalist rather than a successful novelist. What did they discuss?

How did they celebrate Christmas? How did Koestler's *Darkness at Noon* influence Orwell's ideas for *Nineteen Eighty-Four*?

Koestler lived with his brilliant and attractive girlfriend, Mamaine Paget, and in a match-making move they also invited for Christmas Mamaine's twin sister, Celia Kirwan, who was recently separated from her alcoholic husband. There were a few more details gleaned from Mamaine's published letters on the layout of the cottage, a couple of photographs and tantalising details of Orwell's visit.

In red Moleskine notebooks I keep a journal and I wrote that there was a possible play lurking from this passing reference about the Christmas 1945 gathering. As I imagined the conversations between these colourful characters I began to make notes. I realised that at that time Bertrand Russell lived just a few minutes away and how Koestler and Orwell were working on bringing Russell on board to back a new League for the Freedom and Dignity of Man, (which was to eventually splutter and fizzle out but influenced other similar organisations.)

I could hear in my head the nightmares that both Orwell and Koestler suffered from their experiences in the Spanish Civil War and I could see their indomitable spirit in action as they both *did* things rather than just *talk* about them. My notes fleshed out a plot with their arguments, teasing, joking, deep political discussions and the influence the twins had on their lives during the stay. Koestler suffered deep depression and could be serious and abstract. Orwell was more phlegmatic and playful. Yet even as different characters, they were good friends for several years.

An idea of a play became my first novel and despite 82 (no that's not a typo) rejections by literary agents, I was honoured that the manuscript was awarded the *Eyelands Magazine* Winner for Historical Fiction for an unpublished novel last December. I went ahead and self-published it as a first dramatised novel about Orwell and Koestler.

What is fascinating is delving deep into the characters of real people and taking that knowledge to project what they might say in a certain situation and with another person. Connections and coincidences were thrown up: I realised that the twins' birthday was 7 September, Koestler's was 5 September and the birthday of Orwell's wife, Eileen was 25 September and how a throw-away joyful comment on 'September birthdays' by Koestler could cause angst in Orwell.

In the book's excerpt below, Orwell retells how he had been shot on the Republican frontline near Aragón and Koestler had for months thought he would be executed as a prisoner of Franco. An interesting coincidence comes to light as Orwell speaks:

ARTICLE

**PAUL W.B. MARSDEN**

'... It was Twentieth of May when I was hit and for two months I could only whisper. The doctors said I would never get my voice back, but I did, obviously.'

There was silence between them with only the raindrops clattering through the oak leaves.

Koestler said: 'Twentieth of May, '37?'

George nodded staring down into the waters below.

'They released me from Seville on the Thirteenth of May, '37. Small world.'

George looked at him. 'For months you thought you would get shot and were released. For months I'd got it into my head I couldn't get shot and I was. Small world.'

He paused and with a mischievous look at Koestler said: 'Although you were in the Comintern, and I was with the Trotskyite anarchists, POUM. If *your* lot got hold of me, they would have shot me.'

Koestler looked away and then down. 'I was wrong. Very wrong. I should have known much earlier.'

I also imagined how Koestler and Orwell taking long walks around the nearby mountains could have damaged Orwell's health (given his TB), if caught in a Welsh rainstorm. The dynamic of baby Richard in their midst provided opportunities to show Orwell's caring parenting skills and contrast with Koestler's point blank refusal to have children. I came to understand how Mamaine and Celia were two resilient women, one managing Koestler's dark moods and the other offering friendship, not love, to a lonely and needy Orwell.

The challenge for any writer when they start on a first novel is whether they can successfully complete it. Will they get stuck halfway? Will it peter out? How to avoid padding dialogue and keep suspense and drama alive to turn the pages? *Darkness in 1984* was a joy to write because of discovering such vivid characters and the conflicting emotions within friendships. Orwell's patriotism, practicality and socialism was a pleasure to explore, and Koestler's endless ideas and energy for progressive causes meant the storytelling felt as if I were inserted into Bwlch Ocyn's front living room for a week, listening to them bicker and laugh. Koestler would have been talking as a theoretical socialist while Orwell would have been reminding him of the need for practical improvements to people's lives.

On the way back from a family holiday in Abersoch in September, my wife and I did a slight detour to drive past the Bwlch Ocyn cottage (Well, I got lost and we happened to find ourselves close by …). On the spur of the moment I decided to visit and see if I could at least take some photographs from the outside that would help me picture scenes in my writing. When we drove along the main road to the turn off, I found that it was a narrow dirt track up a hill and I thought: 'Oh blow it, why not knock on the front door?'

From the driveway, I passed through a gate and walked up a winding gravel path past ferns, a pond and apple trees. There was the whitewashed stone cottage with a slate roof. I noted the slight name change on the plaque to Bwlch Iocyn. I stood for a moment, wondering what I was going to say, when I realised the timber front door was wide open and that I was probably being watched.

As I got closer, an older woman appeared, with that typical British polite smile and knitted brow reserved for complete strangers.

'Hello,' I said.

'Hello?' She pursed her lips.

'I'm awfully sorry to just turn up like this. Is this Arthur Koestler's home? I am a writer and …'

Mrs Brown turned and bellowed into the cottage: 'Dear, it's another Koestler fan.'

My first thought was to say: 'And a George Orwell fan,' but I didn't get a chance. My cheeks were now feeling very hot as a tall, older gentleman appeared and I started to babble my rather lame request when he said: 'Oh, come in.' Mr Brown explained that writers turning up was a not infrequent occurrence.

I stood in the wide living room with oak beamed ceiling and inglenook fireplace. I felt incredulous. It was just as Mamaine had described in her letters from eighty years ago.

'Do you want to have a look round?'

'Well, that's very kind,' I mumbled. 'Er, yes please, if it's no trouble.'

Mr Brown guided me around to the back dining room with the magnificent window looking out on to Welsh mountains and pointed to where Mamaine had sat as she read a book whilst leaning into where the old kitchen used to be, to stir ox heart's stew. I entered the floor-to-roof library with its minstrel's gallery. I could see the room where Orwell and Richard would have slept and I looked out on to the back garden where Mamaine grew vegetables they ate that Christmas. I followed in a daze through the new kitchen with a narrow doorway set in the side of the fireplace and, lo and behold, I was in Koestler's small study. I looked out of the window across fields to Blaenau Ffestiniog and imagined him scrawling his fountain pen as he wrote *Thieves in the Night*. I can't thank Mr and

ARTICLE

Mrs Brown enough for their hospitality that day and the willingness to embrace a random, unknown writer who turned up uninvited on the doorstep.

I identified the typical footpaths around the hills and fields full of sheep that Koestler would have taken Orwell. They would have climbed Big Manod and the locals in the Oakley Arms pub may have told them of the strange convoys that arrived at night during wartime with the rumours of things being taken down into the old mine workings for storage. After the war, it was revealed that paintings from London's National Gallery were brought up and taken by hand-hauled, narrow-gauge railway down into the old mines for safekeeping from nazi bombs and the likely invasion.

On those walks, I could well imagine that Orwell would have stood and breathed in the clean, breezy air and ached to find such a place of solitude and wilderness for himself, away from the polluted air and sooty grime of bombed-out London. Perhaps he could see Koestler and Mamaine had found happiness and imagined finding himself a new wife and living in the countryside? He certainly was attracted to Celia and quickly proposed to her when they were back in London (she said, 'no' – twice, but remained firm friends with him for the rest of his life).

I have tried to be faithful to the characters, (including their flaws), the actual timeline of known events and used real quotes to give an authenticity to the book. It is still historical fiction and minor details have been changed, such as adding a scene of Russell meeting Orwell that took place a few weeks later. However, I hope aficionado readers of Orwell will find *Darkness in 1984* believable and will encourage general readers to rediscover Orwell and Koestler's works, as they both have left powerful legacies that resonate in today's disturbing politics.

SOURCES USED AS BACKGROUND FOR THE NOVEL

Bankes, A. (2024) *The Quality of Love: Twin Sisters at the Heart of the Century*, Richmond: Duckworth Books

Bowker, G. (2003) *George Orwell*, London: Little, Brown

Cesarani, D. (1998) *Arthur Koestler: The Homeless Mind*, London: William Heinemann

Crick, B. (1980) *George Orwell: A Life*, London: Secker & Warburg

Fyvel, T.R. (1983 [1982]) *George Orwell: A Personal Memoir*. London: Hutchinson

Goodman, C. (ed.) (1985) *Living with Koestler: Mamaine Koestler's Letters (1945-51)*, London: Weidenfeld & Nicolson

Koestler, A. (1937) *Spanish Testament*, Left Book Club Edition, London: Victor Gollancz

Koestler, A. (1947 [1940]) *Darkness at Noon*, London: Penguin

Koestler, A. (1991 [1941]) *Scum of the Earth*, London: Eland

Koestler, A. (1946) *Thieves in the Night*, London: Macmillan

Koestler, A. and C. (1984) *Stranger on the Square,* London: Hutchinson

Orwell, G. (2013 [1938]) *Homage to Catalonia,* London: Penguin Books

Orwell, G. (1987 [1945]) *Animal Farm,* London: Penguin Books

Orwell, G. (1989 [1949]) *Nineteen Eighty-Four,* London: Penguin Books

Orwell, G. (2010) *Diaries,* Davison, Peter (ed.) London: Penguin Books

Orwell, S. and Angus, I. (eds) (1970) *George Orwell Essays, Journalism and Letters, Vol. IV, In Front of your Nose 1945*-1950, Harmondsworth, Middlesex: Penguin Books

Packer, G. (ed.) (2008) *George Orwell: Narrative Essays,* London: Harvill Secker

Rees, R. (1962) *George Orwell: Fugitive from the Camp of Victory*, Carbondale, Southern Illinois University Press

Scammell, M. (2009) *Koestler, The Indispensable Intellectual,* London: Faber & Faber

Shelden, M. (1991) *Orwell: The Authorised Biography,* London: William Heinemann

The *Observer* (2003) *Orwell, The* Observer *Years,* London: Atlantic Books

Also accessed were copies of the 'League for the Freedom and Dignity of Man' typed by Orwell and correspondence between Orwell and Koestler on the league. These are held in UCL Library Services and Heritage Collections, Edinburgh University Library.

## NOTE ON THE CONTRIBUTOR

Paul W.B. Marsden has sketched out further novels based upon George Orwell's life in World War Two and on the island of Jura. He has already written *Making A Moveable Feast*, dramatising the daily conversations of Ernest Hemingway and his first wife, Hadley Richardson, in Paris, in 1922. Paul is a former member of parliament and now works in construction. He is married to Elena and has three grown-up children. Further details of Paul's biography and his other writings can be found at https://www.paulwbmarsden.com.

# ARTICLE

# 'Our command is *"Thou art:"'* Winston Smith's Fabricated Life in George Orwell's *Nineteen Eighty-Four*

## JAN-BOJE FRAUEN

*This article reconstructs 'thought-criminal' Winston Smith's biography from the hazy memories and vague fragments which he presents to the reader in George Orwell's* Nineteen Eighty-Four *(1949). The investigation discovers a hidden, carefully constructed pattern in the armature of the novel revolving around the mystical number eleven.*

Eric Arthur Blair's, or George Orwell's, choice of date for his dystopian *Nineteen Eighty-Four* (1949) is a frequent topic of debate. Critics have theorised that the year may have deep religious significance as the completion of a Biblical seventy-year cycle starting at the beginning of the First World War or that it may be referring to other works of literature such as Jack London's *The Iron Heel* (in which, according to Dorian Lynskey, 'the year is a significant date') or G.K. Chesterton's *The Napoleon of Notting Hill* (which is set in the same year) or to a poem that Orwell's first wife Eileen O'Shaughnessy Blair wrote in 1934 (which is entitled 'End of the Century, 1984' and was preserved by Orwell 'until his death,' according to William Hunt) (Frothingham 1971; Richards 1976; Lynskey 2019: 81; Hunt 2013: 561). The latter claim has been powerfully reinforced recently by Anna Funder's controversial *Wifedom: Mrs. Orwell's Invisible Life* (2023), which makes a strong case for Eileen as the creative force behind much of Orwell's writings (Funder 2023).[1] According to Orwell's fellow novelist and drinking buddy[2] Anthony Burgess: 'Orwell had wanted to call it *Nineteen Forty-Eight*. But they [most likely referring to Orwell's publisher Fred Warburg] wouldn't let him' (Burgess 1987: 334; Burgess and Biswell 2013: 10; Frauen 2022b). However, Dorian Lynskey refutes all of these speculations: for the early drafts of the novel Orwell was still calling it *The Last Man* in Europe.³ Then, he wrote *1980*, then *1982* and only later *1984*. 'The most fateful date in literature was a late amendment' (Lynskey 2019: 167). And yet, that Orwell changed the year of (most of) the novel's narrated time several times also suggests that he was thinking about it very carefully as the novel took shape. After all, why would he change the year at all if it were totally arbitrary? Perhaps, then, the year 1984 had to fit into a hidden structure to be discovered in-between the lines of the hazy memories and vague recollections that the reader is presented with by the novel's unreliable narrator Winston Smith (via Orwell's third-person internal-focalisation technique)?

Besides general interest in the novel's overall structure, an inquiry into Winston's biography may be useful for the interpretation of Orwell's dystopia. O'Brien tells Winston in the Ministry of Love that 'the command of the totalitarians was "Thou shalt." Our command is "*Thou art*"' (Orwell 2000 [1949]: 231, italics in the original). Later, at a pivotal point during Winston's 'conversion' in the ministry, O'Brien announces that 'the heretic, the enemy of society, will always be there, so that he can be defeated and humiliated over again' (ibid: 242). Read in a certain light, O'Brien admits here that Winston's rebellion was never real, that it was a 'simulation of opposition' scripted by the Party to serve its totalitarian needs, as Vita Fortunati suggested (Fortunati 1987). Assuming that Winston the 'crime-thinker' is thus a fabrication by the Party 'so that he can be defeated and humiliated over again',⁴ a possible test to verify or falsify this hypothesis could be to reconstruct Winston's life and descent into 'thoughtcrime'. If his biography displays an unnatural, clearly artificially constructed pattern, this may be an indication that he is, indeed, unknowingly fabricated for 'crimethink'.

However, this is a difficult enterprise. In fact, it is precisely what Winston is struggling to do. In Lillian Feder's words: 'Relying on the only resources he has – dreams, memories of beauty, love, and sorrow, and fragments of history – Winston Smith tries to apprehend the intrinsic connection between selfhood, language, and objective reality' (Feder 1983: 394). Winston, in other words, attempts to step out of the Platonic cave of Big Brother's 'collective solipsism' and into empirical reality (Orwell 2000: 241; Yoon 2019; Dwan 2010, 2018; Howe 1956). The reader, in turn, sees Winston's world filtered through his eyes and is, thus, ultimately limited to what he can figure out about his past. As John Bowen states in his Introduction to the new Oxford World Classics edition: 'Orwell's book begins, ends, and is lived through an individual body and consciousness' (Bowen 2021: vii). The information from Winston, however, is fragmentary and riddled with doubt. For instance, Lavinia Marin and Jason Matthew Buchanan observe Winston's

ARTICLE

'trouble with the timeline' and his inability to reconstruct a 'coherent timeline' (Marin 2018: 192; Buchanan 2018: 102). In Winston's own words, 'everything faded into mist' whenever he attempts to put events into order (Orwell 2000: 69).

1984

Given the uncertainties in the timeline and Winston's doubts about his own memories, one has to identify some sort of focal point from which to reconstruct Winston's biography. This is not easy, as even the year 1984 is not entirely certain: 'To begin with [Winston] did not know with any certainty that it was 1984' (Orwell 2000: 10). However, we know from the slips of paper containing instructions on how to rewrite events which Winston receives from the 'pneumatic tube' in his office cubicle that 1984 is at least the official year (ibid: 37). Why a regime that intends to 'freeze history at a particular moment of time' still counts years is not clear; perhaps it is needed as a frame of reference for the rewriting of events (ibid: 195). However, the narrated time starts on 4 April 1984 according to Winston's diary (ibid: 10). This being somewhat early in the year, Winston receives three instructions on how to rewrite events in 1983 (17.3, 3.12, 19.12) followed by one 1984 event (14.2), which makes it implausible to assume that it is always 1984 in Oceania (ibid: 37). The implementation of Newspeak being an ongoing enterprise still, the arrow of time, apparently, has not yet come to a halt and history, while becoming increasingly relative, has not ended yet. The 'singularity',[5] the point at which our spatiotemporal laws no longer apply and time stands still, will only be reached in 2050, as has been argued elsewhere (Frauen 2022a). *Nineteen Eighty-Four*, most likely, starts in 1984 then.

1944

Assuming that the official year 1984 is also the actual year, we can infer Winston's year of birth. On 2 May 1984, Winston tells Julia: 'I am thirty-nine years old' (ibid: 110, 107). On 4 April, when the narrated time begins, he states that he 'was fairly sure that his age was thirty-nine, and he had been born in 1944 or 1945' (ibid: 10). Since he is thus 39 relatively early in the year already, it may be assumed that his birth year is 1944, rather than 1945. Possibly, his birthday is on 14 May since Orwell's adopted son Richard H. Blair was born on that day in 1944 (Taylor 2019: 60). Both the primary text and biographical parallels thus indicate that Winston Smith was born in 1944.

1955

Winston's childhood ends abruptly around eleven years later: 'He was not certain of the date, but he could not have been less than ten years old, probably twelve, when it had happened' (op cit: 146). Elsewhere, Winston states that 'he must, he thought, have been ten or eleven years old when his mother had disappeared' (ibid: 29). Besides his mother, his baby sister disappears on this day, his father having already disappeared at some unidentified point earlier. Winston steals his family's meagre chocolate ration due to 'the clamorous hunger in his belly' and runs away, 'starving the other two' (ibid: 147). When he returns, his mother has disappeared. Likely, his baby sister is killed by rats; a repressed memory that haunts Winston in his dreams (aided probably by the 'telescreen' in his room). Most likely, this plot feature is inspired by an actual event (of a child's face being attacked by rats) on the Scottish island of Jura while the novel's plot took shape, which is recorded in the 12 June 1947 entry of the 'domestic diary' Orwell kept on Jura (Taylor 2019: 83-84). The traumatic event, which Winston will be forced to retrieve and relive in Room 101, including the selfish 'murder' of his sister by his attempt to trade places with his beloved Julia, is the chronologically last childhood memory that Winston tells us about and likely the last that he can recall. After this, there is a gap in his biography of eleven adolescence years that are almost entirely unaccounted for besides a brief remark that he was sent to 'one of the colonies for homeless children' (op cit: 148). How the penniless orphan Winston became a somewhat privileged 'Outer Party Member' instead of a 'prole' later is unknown. In fact, it seems awkward given Oceania's strictly hierarchical society unless the Party had plans for him. If our earlier assumption that Winston's birthday was at some point later than 2 May 1944 is correct, however, the year of his mother and sister's 'murder' is very likely 1955 and Winston's age at that time eleven.

## 1966

The missing adolescence years end with a memory that prophetically foreshadows the final scene of the novel (ibid: 70). This memory is the beginning of Winston's story, according to Winston: 'But the really relevant date was seven or eight years earlier [before 1973]. The story really began in the middle 'sixties, the period of the great purges in which the leaders of the revolution were wiped out once and for all' (ibid: 69). At some point in 1965 or 1966, then, at the 'lonely hour of fifteen' when the 'yellow note' and the 'chestnut tree' rhyme were playing from the telescreen in the Chestnut Tree Café, Winston witnesses the three Ingsoc founding members Jones, Aaronson and Rutherford reach the final 'third stage' of their 'reintegration' (ibid: 236). Elsewhere, Winston states that 'it must have been in 1965 that these three had been arrested' and then 'had vanished for a year or two' in the Ministry of Love (ibid: 69). This suggests that Winston must have seen them in either 1966 or 1967. Given that 1966 is mentioned indirectly in both instances, the most likely year for Winston's Chestnut Tree Café awakening is 1966.

1973

1973, in turn, seems as certain as anything in the novel: 'Just once in his life [Winston] had possessed ... concrete, unmistakable evidence of an act of falsification. ... In 1973, it must have been' (ibid). The year is later confirmed by O'Brien in the Ministry of Love. Right at the beginning of Winston's ordeal, he states that 'eleven years ago you created a legend about three men who had been condemned for treachery. You pretended that you had seen a piece of paper that proved them innocent' (ibid: 233). Thus, we have established 1966 for the Chestnut Tree Café incident and 1973 for the photograph event. While the year 1973 seems somewhat out of place at first glance, one nevertheless cannot help but notice how peculiar it is that there are precisely eleven years between 1973 and the year of Winston's rebellion, 1984, also.

Besides receiving the photograph from the 'pneumatic tube' in his office, 1973 is important as it is during this year that Winston both marries and separates from his wife Katharine. Having married her 'three or four months' earlier, Winston recalls a 'sweltering summer afternoon, eleven years ago' during which he could have killed her by 'shoving her off a cliff' in Kent (ibid: 122). Living with the highly orthodox Katharine had become unbearable to Winston after the photograph event triggered his awakening earlier in the same year and 'Katharine would unquestionably have denounced him to the Thought Police if she had not happened to be too stupid to detect the unorthodoxy of his opinions' (ibid). One has to note here that Winston's memory that Katharine, like his mother and sister, merely disappeared after he did *not* kill her is not necessarily to be trusted. In this context, one also has to note that O'Brien clearly assesses Winston's state of mind from a medical standpoint at the secret meeting at his place. In response, Winston declares a shocking willingness to commit unspeakable crimes such as throwing 'sulphuric acid in a child's face' (ibid: 156). In the Ministry of Love, O'Brien repeatedly insists that the aim of Winston's 'reintegration' is to 'cure you, to make you sane' (ibid: 229). The difficulty to tell madness from fact in the novel has been dealt with by a number of critics and a final verdict, as David Dwan suggests, may just be impossible (Friis 2018; Mullen 2019; van Inwagen 2008; Yoon 2019; Dwan 2018).

However, assuming that the totalitarian dictatorship that Winston describes actually exists, Winston takes O'Brien's bait – marked by his 'failure in instinct' to dispose of the compromising material before it enters his conscious mind [6] – in 1973. Obviously, the only reason why this happens is that he had witnessed Jones, Aaronson and Rutherford's conversion experience in 1966 (the three being the three 'traitors' proven innocent by the photograph, of course).

## 1977

There is yet one more date that is of crucial importance for Winston's life between 1966 and 1984. It can be traced down with a high degree of certainty also. And, like the Chestnut Tree Café event, it is a prophecy of things to come: 'Years ago – how long ago was it? Seven years it must be – he had dreamed that he was walking through a pitch-dark room. And someone sitting to one side of him had said as he passed: "We shall meet in the place where there is no darkness." … It was O'Brien who had spoken to him out of the dark [meaning, of course, out of the telescreen in Winston's room]' (op cit: 25). 1977 as the year of the 'place-where-there-is-no-darkness' dream seems certain since O'Brien verifies the timeframe twice in the 'place where there is no darkness', meaning, of course, the Ministry of Love: 'For seven years I have watched over you. Now the turning-point has come. I shall save you, I shall make you perfect' and 'this drama I have played out with you during seven years will be played out over and over again' (ibid: 221, 242). The first passage is definitely shortly after Winston's arrest in August 1984 (ibid: 202).[7] The second quote, also, seems close enough to it to assume that it is still 1984 or, at most, early 1985, which makes the year of the prophetic dream very likely 1977.

## 1987

In the final chapter of the novel (excluding the Newspeak Appendix), we meet Winston again in the Chestnut Tree Café after his release from the Ministry of Love at the 'lonely hour of fifteen' (ibid: 259). Apparently, he has been released for some time already, as he tells of monotonous days spent between his flat and the café in a state of mind that is constantly hazed by gin (and probably worse mixed into it): 'In these days, he could never fix his mind on any subject for more than a few moments a time' (ibid: 260). He also tells of his lucrative but meaningless job in a 'sub-committee of a sub-committee,' which he goes to 'perhaps twice a week' for a couple of hours (ibid: 265). The narration ends here with Winston reaching 'acceptance' by 'winning the victory over himself' when the 'yellow note' plays from the telescreen, in the same way in which he had witnessed Jones, Aaronson and Rutherford reach 'acceptance' in 1966, the 'really relevant date' when 'the story really began' (ibid: 269, 69).

JAN-BOJE FRAUEN

While we cannot be sure for how long Winston has been released and pardoned at this point already, we know with certainty that the year is 1987. In the background of the café, the 'telescreen bulletin' announces the merry news that the 'Tenth Three-Year Plan's quota' has been 'overfulfilled' in the 'preceding quarter' (ibid: 261). We know from the very beginning of the novel that the 'overfulfilment of the Ninth Three-Year Plan' had been announced on 4 April 1984 in the same way (ibid: 6). Accordingly, it is 1987 and likely April, possibly the 4th.

### 1988

The last missing date, then, is Winston's death. O'Brien, after all, promised him in the ministry: 'Don't give up hope. Everyone is cured sooner or later. In the end we shall shoot you' (ibid: 248). Thus, his execution will be at some point after the narrated time ends. Since we witnessed the completion of his 'cure' on the final page of the novel (but before the Appendix), one may think that he will be shot or vaporised shortly afterwards. To arrive at the best possible estimate of just how shortly, then, one may analyse Winston's future in relation to Jones, Aaronson and Rutherford's fate.

We know that 'it must have been in 1965 that these three had been arrested' and that 'as often happened, they had vanished for a year or more' after that (ibid: 69). Then, they 'had suddenly been brought forth to incriminate themselves in the usual way' (ibid). After that, they had been 'pardoned, re-instated in the Party and given posts which were in fact sinecures' (ibid: 70). It is during this time, in 1966, that Winston witnesses their conversion in the Chestnut Tree Café. However, they were 'doomed with absolute certainty to extinction within a year or two' after their release, as Winston remarks while wondering what brought him to the doomed café in 1966 (ibid).

Indeed, 'a little later' the three traitors were 're-arrested and confessed to all their old crimes over again, with a whole string of new ones' at a 'second trial' (ibid: 71). However, 'a little later' does not mean within a couple of weeks nor even months: their 'execution' very likely took place in 1968 because 'about five years after this, in [presumably early] 1973', Winston receives the photograph that proves them innocent (ibid: 71).

Consequently, it seems most likely that Winston will die after a second arrest and a second trial in 1988. If he is actually executed in 1988, it is noteworthy that he would thus die at the age of forty-four, which is not only identical with his birthyear 1944 but also with Orwell's age when he wrote *Nineteen Eighty-Four* in 1948.

## 11

It seems that the cycles of Winston's life and rebellion revolve around the mystical number eleven from 1944 to 1988. At first glance, the out-of-place photograph event of 1973 that triggers Winston's descent into thoughtcrime and the year of his actual rebellion, 1984, itself do not seem to fit in. However, the importance of the eleven-year cycles is suggested here as well by the peculiar fact that there are eleven years between these two dates as well. Furthermore, it seems peculiar that Winston's active rebellion would start at precisely eleven o'clock on April 4, when O'Brien passes the 'unmistakable message' to Winston that makes him hurry home to write 'DOWN WITH BIG BROTHER' into his secret diary compulsively (ibid: 12, 19).

Taking a step away from Winston's life, it may or may not be a coincidence that the digit sum of 1984 is 22. However, it certainly does seem odd that time is supposed to end in 2050 with Newspeak 'finally superseding' Oldspeak with the adoption of its 'final, perfected version, as embodied in the Eleventh Edition of the Dictionary' (ibid: 270). It is not only peculiar that it is the Eleventh Edition of the Dictionary that is to sever 'the last link with the past' (ibid: 280). Furthermore, the year 2050 is precisely 66 years after 1984, which points to the eleven-year cycles again.

In any case, every one of the events in Winston's personal cycles seems to manufacture his future thoughtcrime and punishment. 1955 establishes the traumatic, repressed memory that Winston must relive in Room 101 (let us note that the room number includes an eleven also). In 1966, the 'yellow note' from the telescreen in the Chestnut Tree Café gives the starting signal for the crimethink game that will unfold over the next 22 years: it anchors the faces of the three traitors Jones, Aaronson and Rutherford deeply in Winston's psyche, thus making sure that he will take the bait from the pneumatic tube that proves them innocent in 1973, eleven years before he takes their place as he must, following the 'unavoidable order of things' (ibid: 29). 1977 is an explicit prophecy, when O'Brien tells Winston in his sleep through the 'telescreen' that they will meet 'in the place where there is no darkness' (ibid: 25). 1944 and 1988 are the beginning and the end. Winston dies aged 44, mirroring his birth year 1944. In Winston's words: 'The end was contained in the beginning' (ibid: 144). This timeline is so obviously unnatural that it strongly supports the thesis that Winston's rebellion is artificially constructed on a deep-structural level from beginning to end. Winston is more than merely manipulated. He is programmed for thoughtcrime: he actively participates in the structure of doublethink that he is usually said to resist and sabotages his own rebellion in cooperation with Julia and O'Brien (Frauen 2023). There are always three traitors in Big Brother's power game.

NOTES

[1] In the case of *Nineteen Eighty-Four* it must be taken into consideration, however, that Eileen died in 1945, before most of the book was written

[2] Burgess's biographer Andrew Biswell notes that Burgess may exaggerate his relation with Orwell (while their wives were befriended indeed). Possibly, the Mandrake Club (the real-world Chestnut Tree Café, according to Burgess) meeting that Burgess describes in the first book of his autobiography never happened (Biswell 2013: xv)

[3] This working title was a nod to Mary Shelley's final novel (Antal 2020; Cziganyik 2021; Bowen 2021; Gheran 2013)

[4] This author has proposed that Winston, like Julia and O'Brien, goes through several phases of rebellion and reintegration during his life. See Frauen 2023 (preprint)

[5] It has furthermore been pointed out that Room 101 represents a 'singularity' (Sandefur 2018)

[6] It is written in Goldstein's book that 'a Party member is required to not only have the right opinions, but the right instincts' (op cit: 190)

[7] We know that Winston and Julia are arrested soon after 'Hate Week' on an 'August evening' in 1984 (ibid: 202). Actually, it is morning, not evening, Winston and Julia having 'slept the clock around' from exhaustion after 'Hate Week' (ibid). However, this still means that they are arrested in August 1984, likely late August as the evenings and mornings are chilly and the light is 'fading at twenty-one hours' (ibid: 197, 202)

REFERENCES

Antal, Eva (2020) The Last Man and 'the First Woman': Unmanly images of unhuman nature in Mary Shelley's ecocritism, *Perichoresis*, Vol. 18, No. 2 pp 3-17

Biswell, Andrew (2013) Introduction, *1985*, London: Serpent's Tail

Bloom, Harold (ed.) (1987) *George Orwell's 1984*, New York: Chelsea Press

Bowen, John (2021) Introduction, *Nineteen Eighty-Four*, Oxford World's Classics, Oxford: Oxford University Press

Buchanan, Jason M. (2018) 24/7 newsleep, Di Nucci, Ezio and Storrie, Stefan (eds) *1984 and philosophy: Is resistance futile?*, *Popular Culture and Philosophy*, Vol. 116, Chicago: Open Court pp 95-104

Burgess, Anthony (1987) *Little Wilson and Big God: Being the First Part of the Confessions of Anthony Burgess*, London: Heinemann

Burgess, Anthony and Biswell, Andrew (2013 [1978]) *1985*, London: Serpent's Tail

Cziganyik, Zsolt (2021) The failure of progress and the example of fraternity in Mary Shelley's *The Last Man*, SFRA Review, Vol. 51, No 2 pp 227-233

Di Nucci, Ezio and Storrie, Stefan (eds) (2018) *1984 and philosophy: Is resistance futile?*, *Popular Culture and Philosophy*, Vol. 116, Chicago: Open Court

Dwan, David (2010) Truth and freedom in Orwell's *Nineteen Eighty-Four*, *Philosophy and Literature*, Vol. 34, No. 2 pp 381-393

Dwan, David (2018) *Liberty, Equality, and Humbug: Orwell's Political Ideals*, Oxford: Oxford University Press

Feder, Lillian (1983) Selfhood, language, and reality: George Orwell's *Nineteen Eighty-Four*, *The Georgia Review*, Vol. 37, No. 2 pp 392-409

Fortunati, Vita (1987) 'It makes no difference': A dystopia of simulation and transparency, Bloom, Harold (ed.) *George Orwell's 1984,* New York: Chelsea Press pp 109-120

Frauen, Jan-Boje (2022a) From Big Brother to the Big Bang: Self, science, and singularity in George Orwell's *1984, Utopian Studies,* Vol. 33, No. 3 pp 406-423

Frauen, Jan-Boje (2022b) Little Wilson and Big Brother: Anthony Burgess's answer to George Orwell's *Nineteen Eighty-Four* in *1985, Clio,* Vol. 50, No. 1 pp 19-40

Frauen, Jan-Boje (2022c) Winston's parallel universe: On history in George Orwell's *Nineteen Eighty-Four, The Explicator,* Vol. 80, Nos 1 and 2 pp 49-52

Frauen, Jan-Boje (2023) 'The unavoidable order of things': Fabricated resistance in George Orwell's *1984, Qeios,* 11 August. Available online at https://doi.org/10.32388/PG8V22

Friis, Jan Kyrre Berg (2018) The irrelevance of truth, Di Nucci, Ezio and Storrie, Stefan (eds) *1984 and philosophy: Is resistance futile?, Popular Culture and Philosophy,* Vol. 116, Chicago: Open Court pp 243-254

Frothingham, Richard (1971) 37. Orwell's *1984,* Part I, Chapter VIII, *The Explicator,* Vol. 29, No. 5 p. 72

Funder, Anna (2023) *Wifedom: Mrs. Orwell's Invisible Life,* New York: Random House

Gheran, Niculae (2013) The crisis literature of the last man: His individuality, memory and space: Mary Shelley's *The Last Man* and George Orwell's *Nineteen Eighty-Four, Transylvanian Review,* Vol. 22, No. 3 pp 159-169

Hietalahti, Jarno (2018) Hangings, shootings, and other funny stuff in *1984,* Di Nucci, Ezio and Storrie, Stefan (eds) (2018) *1984 and philosophy: Is resistance futile?, Popular Culture and Philosophy,* Vol. 116, Chicago: Open Court pp 145-152

Howe, Irving (1956) Orwell: History as nightmare, *The American Scholar,* Vol. 25, No. 2 pp 193-207

Hunt, William (2013) Orwell's commedia: The ironic theology of *Nineteen Eighty-Four, Modern Philology,* Vol. 110, No. 4 pp 536-563

Lynskey, Dorian (2019) *The Ministry of Truth: The Biography of George Orwell's 1984,* New York: Doubleday

Marin, Lavinia (2018) Through a telescreen darkly, Di Nucci, Ezio and Storrie, Stefan (eds) *1984 and philosophy: Is resistance futile?, Popular Culture and Philosophy,* Vol. 116, Chicago: Open Court pp 187-199

Mullen, Lisa (2019) 'The few cubic centimetres inside your skull': A neurological reading of George Orwell's *Nineteen Eighty-Four, Medical Humanities,* Vol. 45, No. 3 pp 258-266

Orwell, George (2000 [1949]) *Nineteen Eighty-Four,* London: Penguin Classics

Richards, David W. (1976) Orwell's *1984*: His choice of the date, *The Explicator,* Vol. 35, No. 1 p. 8

Sandefur, Timothy (2018) Love, truluv, Di Nucci, Ezio and Storrie, Stefan (eds) *1984 and philosophy: Is resistance futile?, Popular Culture and Philosophy,* Vol. 116, Chicago: Open Court pp 104-117

Taylor, D.J. (2019) *On* Nineteen Eighty-Four: *A Biography,* New York: Abrams Press

van Inwagen, Peter (2008) Was George Orwell a metaphysical realist?, *Philosophia Scientiæ. Travaux d'histoire et de philosophie des sciences,* Vol. 12, No. 1 pp 161-185

Yoon, Sarah (2019) History and truth-telling in George Orwell's *Nineteen Eighty-Four*, *British and American Fiction,* Vol. 26, No. 2 pp 117-139

ARTICLE

**JAN-BOJE FRAUEN**

NOTE ON THE CONTRIBUTOR

Jan-Boje Frauen is currently an Associate Professor in European Studies at Zhejiang International Studies University (ZISU). His academic background spans a wide variety of fields in philosophy, the humanities and the social sciences, which is reflected in his publications on a broad range of topics. However, the work of George Orwell more generally and *Nineteen Eighty-Four* in particular are never far from whatever it is he currently thinks about. A preprint of a much more elaborate and comprehensive interpretation of the novel building up on the thoughts presented in this article can be found (and reviewed!) at https://www.qeios.com/read/PG8V22.

# INTERVIEW

# Tracing the Ordinary Everyday (and the Importance of Chocolate) in Orwell

L.J. Hurst interviews Nathan Waddell, author of *A Bright Cold Day: The Wonder of George Orwell*.

LJH: George Orwell said of Charles Dickens that he was worth stealing, giving examples of Catholic writers who claimed he was almost Catholic and Marxists who claimed he was almost Marxist. Soon after Orwell died it seemed the same thing was happening to him – Christopher Hollis wrote a memoir claiming he was almost a Catholic, while George Woodcock claimed he was almost an anarchist. Do you think it is possible to write a neutral account of George Orwell?

NW: Orwell often came down quite hard on the idea of neutrality, and 'Inside the whale' (1940) insists that 'no book is ever truly neutral', so this isn't necessarily an ideal to aim for in Orwell's case anyway. But your question raises a related methodological query: what do we mean, on literary-historical grounds, by 'George Orwell'? Orwell's output is so large that the process of selection with which any account of it inevitably starts already makes neutrality impossible: our approaches to the man and to his work – our approaches to any writer and their work – are by definition biased, though they may not always be fully subjective. There's a lot of Orwell's fiction in *A Bright Cold Day*, for example, but comparatively less on books like *Down and Out in Paris and London*, *The Road to Wigan Pier* and *Homage to Catalonia* (even though they do appear). My book is concerned with the literary Orwell, because this is the Orwell in which I'm most interested. This closes certain avenues of interpretation even as it opens others. Where neutrality is concerned, we could think about related concepts like objectivity, impartiality and fairness. *A Bright Cold Day* is self-avowedly not an impartial account of Orwell: it's a book full of my own thoughts on what I call 'the unelaborate business of getting on with life'. Reading

**L.J. HURST**
**NATHAN WADDELL**

and writing about Orwell continually prompted me to think about how I live my own life and to reflect on what I find so fascinating about the ordinary habits of daily existence. *A Bright Cold Day* gave me the chance to incorporate these musings into a larger tapestry of writing about Orwell. So while I haven't pretended to detachment, I have tried to be fair, praising Orwell's work where it's due yet also taking him to task on his many xenophobias, for instance. This may or may not add up to an 'objective' rendering of the man and his work, but this wasn't my purpose. Neutrality, impartiality, detachment, objectivity: these things enable certain kinds of insight, but they can just as easily stop us from articulating a strong response that we genuinely feel and which may mean something to someone, somewhere, if conveyed in the right spirit.

**LJH**: Your book is organised by themed chapters – times of day and what they meant to Orwell, daily activities and what they meant to both Orwell and the characters of his novels. What was the advantage of this approach to – say – chapters on big themes such as politics, colonialism or crime?

**NW**: *A Bright Cold Day* could be thought of as a 'high concept' book in this sense. The Orwell I grew up with – and the Orwell I've tended to work with professionally – is the Orwell of big ideas: the writer who, as you say, addresses head-on the major political, social and moral questions of his time. There's still so much to learn and to enjoy about this Orwell. No doubt it's the Orwell most readers know and value. Yet while Orwell's fascination with the ordinary and the everyday is often mentioned by critics and biographers, it seemed to me that a book focusing on this topic – treating it as a 'big theme' equal in scope to things like colonialism, justice, criminality and surveillance – needed to be written. And written in a way that would complement some of the more settled modes of scholarly thinking about Orwell's life and work which have tended to be biographical and historicist in character. We wouldn't be anywhere without Orwell's many biographers, of course, nor without those critics, text-editing scholars centrally among them, who seek to place his life and thought in historical context of one kind or another. But I've always been intrigued by the possibilities of high-concept structures, not only because Orwell's most famous novels (*Animal Farm* and *Nineteen Eighty-Four*) are themselves high-concept works but also because I've been searching for years for a form in which to say something new about a man whose life and work we know so intimately. The form I've settled on in *A Bright Cold Day* freshens things up a bit, I hope. It's not a biography, but an attempt quasi-biographically to comment on how Orwell thought and wrote about living; not a book about how Orwell lived *per se*, but about how he tended to imagine what living is 'like'. The distinction is important because I wanted intentionally to collapse certain differences between Orwell's life and the life-worlds imagined in his fiction. Both are a product of how he thought about living as a thing that we do, rather than as something done to us: about the *performance* of living, which is such a crucial theme in his writing.

LJH: I doubt if we will have time to discuss this, but there were huge areas of his life that Orwell did not use in his writing. Despite his half a decade in the police there are few or no police officers, and there is nothing set in broadcasting. Certainly nothing told from the point of view of someone doing those jobs (while Winston Smith observes the telescreens, he does not write their output, for example).

NW: That's a really interesting point. Orwell does tend to surrender the perspective of authority, doesn't he? I suppose this may derive at some level from the fact that although in Burma he was empowered, that power nevertheless was subject to the larger weight of a certain tradition or framework of justice. Orwell's protagonists tend to look up at the world, rather than down at it. Indeed, the downward perspective enjoyed by 'the birds of the air' is depicted in *Keep the Aspidistra Flying* as a form of unbridgeable difference: an unencumbered position separated from humanity's necessarily ground-level being. John Flory, Dorothy Hare, Gordon Comstock, George Bowling, the animals on Manor Farm, Winston Smith: these are all figures looking up at and being pummelled by different kinds of crushing impress. So no police because Orwell's point of departure is those being policed. No broadcasters because he wants to think about being broadcasted *to*. No telescreen operators because the technology's mystique would be undone by peeking behind, or peeking too far behind, the veil.

LJH: *A Bright Cold Day* is divided into four parts: 'Morning', 'Daytime', 'Evening' and 'Night'. Would you say that any one of them is more significant than the others? 'Daytime' contains as many chapters as the other three altogether, yet it is Winston Smith's dreams (title of one of the chapters in 'Night') that cause so much of his aspiration and unhappiness, and are, in fact, the motor of the novel, that I wondered if perhaps the three divisions of the book should not have been the gerunds 'Living', 'Sleeping' and 'Dreaming'. What do you think?

NW: That's a fair point. From the start of thinking about *A Bright Cold Day*, I wanted to trace an arc moving across the ordinary flow of a twenty-four-hour period – not least because Orwell

**L.J. HURST**
**NATHAN WADDELL**

himself so often makes the day, as a unit of time, central to his storytelling. It's there right in the title of *Burmese Days*, but all his fiction communicates a strong sense of daily time: how mornings are different from afternoons, how evenings have their particular pleasures and how the night is so fruitfully ambivalent. This is why I wanted to emphasise the gerundive activity *within* the temporal categories of 'Morning', 'Daytime', 'Evening' and 'Night': I wanted to linger on how Orwell writes about the daily things we do (washing, eating, walking, having hobbies, etc.) and about the daily things we do *in time* (eating at specific moments, moving about in the morning and in the evening, a nap versus the overnight sleep). My literary agent challenged me to align all of this with the trajectory of Orwell's life and career, too, as a way to map this sense of the daily onto the flow of his preoccupations. There's more about *Burmese Days* in the earlier parts of *A Bright Cold Day*, for instance, and more about *Animal Farm* and *Nineteen Eighty-Four* in its latter stages. One of the problems I had here was ensuring that I wasn't just flipping randomly between the life and the work in service of this high-concept structure; that there was a logic to it, in other words. How successful I've been in this regard is for readers to decide.

**LJH:** Incidentally, did you start any chapters but decide not to continue on those lines, or perhaps include the material in another chapter?

**NW:** Looking back at the proposal for *A Bright Cold Day*, I'm reminded that originally there were going to be chapters on 'Gardening', 'Clubs', 'Alcohol' and 'Retiring'. These became the chapters on 'Greenery', 'Hobbies', 'Pubs' and 'Dinner'. There were remarkably few changes otherwise, and by 'remarkably' I mean 'remarkably for me'. I tend to change the structure of anything I write continually as I write it, a method which has the advantage of ensuring flexibility throughout the writing process while having the disadvantage of lacking a road map. Yet once the high-concept structure of *A Bright Cold Day* occurred to me, and here I should credit conversations with Chloe Currens (Penguin) and Emma Smith (University of Oxford), the writing of the book followed the sequence of chapters as I first envisaged it. I always knew there was going to be a chapter on ablutions, a chapter on lunch and one on sleep, for instance. The only substantive alteration came in writing the 'Walking' chapter, which grew so big that I decided to make it a two-parter. One of the most enjoyable aspects of writing the book was knowing ahead of time that there were certain set pieces I wanted to write about and then finding the right chapter in which to place them. Some of this was straightforward: I knew I wanted to write about the sticky heat in *Burmese Days* and the restaurant scene in *Keep the Aspidistra Flying*, and I also knew how I wanted to write about them. Some of it was complicated: I agonised for a very long time over how to write about and also where to place the material on Orwell and Jacintha Buddicom before deciding to channel most of it into the second chapter on walking, because walking, as an idea and activity, captures at least part of the doubleness in their relationship – the ordinariness of how they spent their time, meandering through the countryside, and the trauma of what happened between them, during one such jaunt, before Orwell went to Burma.

**LJH:** If we throw ourselves so early in this discussion into one of your later themed chapters (in fact, it is called 'Walking (Again)' as you have two chapters on walking) is it possible that your treatment underplays Orwell's seriousness? I am thinking of sentences such as 'Orwell spent a lot of time walking through London during the Blitz, which is one reason why *Nineteen Eighty-Four*, a Blitz book by any measure, contains so many scenes of urban sauntering.'

**NW:** Seriousness isn't all it's cracked up to be. I mean that quite seriously, if you'll forgive the glib joke (such as it is). I've been trained as a literary scholar and I earn my living from inhabiting, pursuing and defending certain standards of literary scholarship. Yet I also feel very strongly that the tone of intellectual seriousness academics and other kinds of scholar are obliged to adopt can be a hindrance. The literary philosopher Steven Connor has written recently about the work *performed* by seriousness, about how seriousness is something we do or wear, rather like a costume. Who's to say that one kind of treatment opens up a literary text more effectively or legitimately than another? Why is seriousness in analysis better than playful techniques of interpretation? *Nineteen Eighty-Four* is largely a grim book about grim things, but I also think it's a text that's been allowed to acquire a certain mysteriousness. Puncturing some of that charisma may help to keep the novel fresh and fascinating, and even to keep it political. *Nineteen Eighty-Four* is a work of satire in the mould of Jonathan Swift's *Gulliver's Travels*, a work of serious play hailing from the tradition of *serio ludere*: a mode of seeing serious things, or seeing things seriously (or even seeing serious things seriously), through playful, mischievous means, such as those characterising Thomas More's *Utopia* and perhaps even the entire tradition of utopian speculation itself, to which *Nineteen Eighty-Four* is a response. I intend *A Bright Cold Day* to give its readers licence to think about Orwell's seriousness in ways that sidestep the burden of his reputation as the 'wintry conscience of a generation', however treasured it is, and to enjoy some of the humour, and sometimes the gallows humour, in Orwell's mind. I suppose what

**L.J. HURST**
**NATHAN WADDELL**

I'm saying is that the charge of underplaying Orwell's seriousness hooks on to a truth. Part of my objective in writing *A Bright Cold Day* has been to show that the seriousness we find in Orwell may reflect a desire to *find* seriousness in his work, even when it's us putting the seriousness there to begin with. I find certain aspects of and episodes in *Nineteen Eighty-Four* hilarious, and I say so in *A Bright Cold Day*, but this won't stop the novel from being taken seriously. Our cultures of critical esteem are too invested in Orwell's seriousness for that to change.

**LJH:** In several places Orwell insisted on finding the criticisms hidden within humour, as you say, exemplified by his line: 'When the Red Queen remarks, "*I've* seen hills compared with which you'd call that one a valley," she is in her way attacking the bases of society as violently as Swift or Voltaire.'

**NW:** I like Orwell's claim, a few lines before this passage in 'Funny, but not vulgar' (1945), that 'there are subtler methods of debunking than throwing custard pies', to which he adds: 'There is also the humour of pure fantasy, which assaults man's notion of himself as not only a dignified but a rational being.' Then again, in the Dickens essay he says that there's 'always room for one more custard pie' when it's a matter of 'revolt against authority'. Orwell also states in 'The art of Donald McGill' (1941) that whatever is funny is subversive, and that 'every joke is ultimately a custard pie'. (Who knew Orwell had such a specific interest in clownish weaponry?) There aren't any custard pies in *Animal Farm*, not openly, at any rate, but there's a lot of subversion, and much of that comes from a sense that the humour – think of Napoleon's hangover – has a serious purpose: to identify and to puncture authoritarianism's many hypocrisies. One more example: the moment in *Nineteen Eighty-Four* when Winston wakes up with the word 'Shakespeare' on his lips. In *A Bright Cold Day*, I poke fun at this episode because it's so often seized on as an indication of everything Winston, and the national memory he represents, has to lose. It may be this, for sure, but it's also inherently ridiculous, as an image, and I think its ridiculousness is its point. Winston may utter Shakespeare's name because it means something important in the face of Ingsoc's encroachments on everything England once held dear. But it may also just be a bit of froth. Having Shakespeare on your lips, after all, is little more than symbolic resistance to a totalitarianism caring nothing for, and unintimidated by, culture.

**LJH:** Obviously Orwell was not a *flaneur* in the style of Walter Benjamin, but could he have been a predecessor of analysts such as Stephen Graham, author of *Cities Under Siege: The New Military*

*Urbanism* and editor of *Disrupted Cities When Infrastructure Fails?* Your Introduction begins with the blocked drains of Mrs Parsons, while Graham's contributors deal with not just super-floods but sewers choked by cooking fat devastating city blocks. The relationship seems very similar to a phrase you use in variations, 'the big in the small'. Is that why you began with the Introduction you have?

**NW:** I always wanted to start with that example, with Winston repairing the blocked sink in his neighbour's flat, because it so economically captures everything about Orwell's writing that makes it last – i.e. his ability to make resonant, small-scale encounters evoke large political or philosophical processes. It also struck me as a way to attend to Orwell's writing at the level of literary form. Why is it that so many of his essays and stories include these resonant or epiphanic moments of big meaning contained in the small occurrence? Part of an answer to this question involves some consideration of what Orwell calls, in 'Politics and the English language', 'loss of vividness'. His efforts to avoid such loss take many forms, including a reliance on the symbolic moment or evocative incident: the big in the small. To my mind, this is a *literary* characteristic of his writing, a noticeable part of its texture.

**LJH:** Orwell several times uses examples of micro-behaviour to exemplify far worse evils (a ship's steward with an illicit custard tart, or a lord of the manor refusing to allow one of his cricketers to be bowled out, are Orwell's examples). Do you think these fit 'the big in the small'? What other examples did you find? Are there more of even greater significance?

**NW:** There are too many to mention, really. I love the micro-behavioural details in Orwell's poetry, some of which I include in *A Bright Cold Day*, and I remain fascinated by Orwell's attention to how malign purpose can be divulged by apparently innocuous action – a good instance being that moment in *Nineteen Eighty-Four* when O'Brien forgets (or appears to forget) Syme's name and, in that forgetfulness, discloses the intolerant apparatus of the power he serves. Another example would be the surreal image of Orwell trying to chase a soldier, bayonet drawn, in *Homage to Catalonia*, a book full of small-scale encounters in weird conditions that point to larger realities. As a technique, it feels like a signature: Orwell's representational autograph, as it were. I often try in my teaching to get students to pay attention to these little moments of condensed meaning, not only because they're inherently fascinating but also because they tell us something important about Orwell's style. He preferred the direct statement over the loquacious detour, or at least

INTERVIEW

**L.J. HURST**

**NATHAN WADDELL**

claimed to, but he was also inclined towards a quasi-modernist symbolism. He imbued small acts with big meanings because, as I say in the 'Coda' to *A Bright Cold Day* (and here I should credit Andrzej Gąsiorek for helping me to clarify this aspect of the book's argument), the local and the personal are the little worlds in which most people live and the *only* spaces in which so many can act.

LJH: Orwell as a nature writer has come into public consciousness, especially through Rebecca Solnit's *Orwell's Roses*, which you mention. In the 'Greenery' chapter you write: 'There's a gardener's mind at work in *Animal Farm*, which treads a fine line between taking a view of planting and weeding as good things in themselves and questioning them as tools of power.' Is that not limiting, or failing to criticise Orwell, for thinking as a 'gardener' when if he were to think on a large scale he should have thought as a farmer? A farmer's responsibilities are far greater than a domestic gardener's. Orwell draws attention to this distinction in his long essay on Rudyard Kipling where he compares the Anglo-Indians who built the railways with lesser spirits who would have achieved nothing 'if the normal Anglo-Indian outlook had been that of, say, E.M. Forster'. Or did Orwell unknowingly condemn himself?

NW: There's a critique to be made of Orwell for being, as he remarks of Kipling in the same essay, 'too much of a highbrow'. As I've already said, I've always thought that Orwell's various analyses of power begin in the local and particular – that they move from the ground, or the soil, up. But what Orwell understood as 'the local and particular' was conditioned by the fact that he was an outsider by temperament, and an outsider of privileged origins, to boot. He so often hits his targets, but occasionally I get the sense that the targets have been quite conveniently chosen from within a frame of barely palpable 'advantage'. *Keep the Aspidistra Flying* is a good example: its basic point, that capitalism shapes life, is hard to argue against, but the novel's lack of a persuasive answer to that situation is, I think, tied to its critique's lack of financial specificity. *Keep the Aspidistra Flying* is, in many respects, a novel about capitalism understood in general terms abstracted from the political and policy-based strategies needed to 'correct' it. Orwell's goal was not to provide such specificity, of course. It's a novel about Gordon Comstock's limited, abject understanding of the world, which proceeds from a basis of feeling rather than from knowledge. And I wonder in any case whether we should look to Orwell's novels for solutions to socio-political problems. Orwell's gardening- or ground-level perspective enabled him to write persuasively about person-to-person quandaries, but arguably equipped him less well, in his fiction at any rate, to be a major critic of *systems*. I can already anticipate the cries of objection to this statement, which I don't mean as a dismissal. I go to Orwell's essays for insights into systems and to his fiction for insights into life, assuming those things are neatly differentiable (which they probably aren't).

**LJH:** One of the future pleasures of *A Bright Cold Day* will be opening it at a random page and re-reading your observations, thoughts going out into the world. Meanwhile, re-reading your chapter on 'Pubs' – it is interesting that you draw attention to pubs as vehicles of democracy, where talk is free, mentioned repeatedly by Orwell – I have also noticed that Orwell says very little about the product sold in pubs – beer. Many years after Orwell's death one of the leading figures in the Real Ale movement was Roger Protz, editor of the *Good Beer Guide*, who had also been active in the International Socialists (later the Socialist Workers Party): when Orwell wrote about individual items of English cooking, should he not have also been able to write about individual beers, if someone like Protz was able to cross the line?

**NW:** I do miss in Orwell's work that attention to the individual natures of this or that beverage. Throughout the writing process I scoured the essays for insights about beer and wine only to come up relatively empty-handed. Again, the novels contain a lot of phenomenological detail – the wateriness of terrible beer and the sharp tang of bad gin in *Nineteen Eighty-Four*; the fuzzy stink of whisky in *Burmese Days*; the social implications of wine in *Coming Up For Air*. But there isn't an essay on beer or wine, strangely, even though there are many passing references to both throughout his journalism. When Orwell writes in 'A nice cup of tea' (1946) that tea 'is meant to be bitter, just as beer is meant to be bitter', I want to know more: about the judgement itself and about the standards of comparison enabling it. My interest here lies in a sense of personal connection. I was introduced to alcohol relatively early in much the same way that French children are (with a water-diluted glass of wine on a Sunday afternoon). I enjoy beer and I've tried over the years to cultivate an amateurish appreciation of wine, and I'm intrigued to know more about the Orwell who could write so confidently, as he did in 1946, about the 'rather inferior wine' made by the French in colonial Morocco. Was its inferiority commonly acknowledged? Or was Orwell making a more personal judgement (and why)? These asides are what give Orwell's prose so much of its character, even though they also pose so many unanswerable questions.

**LJH:** You deal with students now in your role as Professor of English at the University of Birmingham. How far do you find you have to explain terms that have been forgotten, or idioms that

**L.J. HURST**
**NATHAN WADDELL**

younger people have never learned? I notice that you use modern barbarisms such as 'train station' rather than 'railway station'. On the other hand, going back to pubs, you give no explanation of a 'beer house' (a public house with a licence to sell beer but not wines or spirits; usually an indicator of a very poor business). What are the difficulties of terminology in teaching Orwell?

**NW:** I remember once being advised by the late David Bradshaw (the esteemed Oxford scholar) that we should think about anything older than roughly twenty years ago as ancient history. David said this to encourage in literary scholarship a fine-grained attentiveness to historical difference: never to assume that the past can be understood properly just because in some superficial ways it resembles the present. How successfully I've lived up to this standard in my work is not for me to say, but it's certainly a goal or an attitude I try to convey to my students, especially given that the twenty-first-century society of spectacle – with its cultures of informational instantaneity – so remorselessly threatens to erode our historical knowledge. *A Bright Cold Day* isn't meant to educate people in historical difference, nor is it meant to grapple with the problem of terminology. Nevertheless, both questions are central to my pedagogical approach, particularly when it comes to thinking about Orwell's so-called timelessness. To my mind, this is one of the least helpful ways of thinking about him, despite the lure of the idea. Orwell seems time-bound: a figure writing in and about specific historical situations. *Nineteen Eighty-Four* can be, and so often is, taken as a general warning about totalitarian power, but it's much more fascinatingly read as a 1940s-specific response to where politics appeared to be heading immediately after the Second World War. Part of the challenge – and the fun – in teaching Orwell is getting students to acknowledge this sense of historical particularity and, more importantly, to use it as a springboard for thinking creatively about how and why his work matters to us now, almost a century after the main phase of his writing career got underway.

**LJH:** When you mention the 'society of spectacle' are you using that phrase generally, or alluding to a connection between Orwell and Guy Debord, the author of *The Society of the Spectacle* (1967)? Are students today aware of the Situationists?

**NW:** I'm using it generally, but there are lots of connections to be made between Orwell and Debord (and through Debord, between Orwell and a figure like J.G. Ballard). *Nineteen Eighty-Four* is a novel about the spectacle's primacy over genuine, verifiable experience (or what Debord calls the receding of direct life into representations), but then again *Keep the Aspidistra Flying* and *Coming Up For Air* are also stories about social unreality. Here I'm thinking about the culture of advertisement against which Gordon Comstock rails, and George Bowling's anxious reflections on streamlined emptiness. Students today wouldn't necessarily encounter Debord's work, or the wider context of the Situationist International, on a straightforward English Literature degree unless they happened to access it through a module on critical theory, say, or in the wider context of secondary reading for post-war fiction and culture. Yet they live their lives in warrens of representations. They're also often keen, with varying degrees of concern, to connect Orwell to depthless social-media existence. And for some students, the society of spectacle isn't a condition to lament but a fact to accept, and maybe even to enjoy: I'm the dinosaur, they're the *virtuosi* surfing the wave of unbreathable, intangible illusion.

**LJH:** Given Orwell was born in 1903, what differences are there between Orwell's mind and that of someone born in 1953? And what about someone born in 2003?

**NW:** All the differences in the world, I should imagine – and I suppose that's the point: it's very difficult to *know* these differences with any certainty. This is one reason why I remain sceptical about wanting to 'claim' Orwell for our own time (e.g. in order to make him an ally in a fight against this or that twenty-first-century cause) when his circumstances differ so radically from ours. This sits in tension slightly with what I've just said about Orwell and the society of spectacle – we clearly can learn a lot about the world today by reading and thinking about Orwell's work, but only so much, in my view.

**LJH:** I am a little worried that you might contribute to a false impression of Orwell's time in Paris – it was not all penury and misery, which came later when his money was stolen. His first year when he had his savings from his police job and was introduced to the world of Esperantists must have been more comfortable, but that did not become part of *Down and Out in Paris and London*. Anna Funder's recent book, *Wifedom*, about Orwell's first wife, Eileen O'Shaughnessy, of course, has done something far worse. Should we blame Orwell or should we blame his critics?

**NW:** Another fair point. Some of the explanatory short-cuts I've taken in the book will possibly make some Orwell enthusiasts wince, the biographers especially, although I've tried not to take any short-cuts that lead simply to incorrect commentary. The word 'impression' is apposite, though, because as I was writing *A Bright Cold Day* I had the work of the novelist Ford Madox Ford at the back of my mind (a consequence, perhaps, of the fact that I'm a scholar

INTERVIEW

**L.J. HURST**
**NATHAN WADDELL**

of twentieth-century literary modernism by training). Ford writes in his memoir, *Ancient Lights and Certain New Reflections* (1911), that his text is 'full of inaccuracies as to facts, but its accuracy as to impressions is absolute.' It's a beautifully judged bit of have-your-cake-and-eat-it bombast, openly admitting to the charge of factual inaccuracy in order to enshrine the unassailable claims of feeling. We don't tend to read Orwell for sentiment, or for impressions for that matter, but a lot of his writing is recuperable within something like the impressionist mode Ford and many other modernist writers favoured – what Orwell calls, in 'Charles Dickens' (1940), the 'impressionistic touch'. Factual imprecision is something I tried very hard to avoid in writing *A Bright Cold Day*, throughout which I relied on the scholarship of superb biographers like Bernard Crick, D.J. Taylor, Robert Colls, Sylvia Topp and Darcy Moore. But I also wanted to prioritise Ford's sense of an 'accuracy as to impressions', to try to respond faithfully to the impressions of life and living that Orwell had and conveyed through his books, many of which blur the lines between fact and fiction. I advise at the outset of *A Bright Cold Day* that the book blends the factual and the fictional, not to minimise or to dismiss the charge of inaccuracy but to caution people that my avowed purpose has been to relate fact and fiction in a subjective, non-linear, associational way.

**LJH:** Chocolate provides a good subject for examination. Chocolate is one of the themes of *Nineteen Eighty-Four* (and again if it is not the big in the small, then it is two images running in parallel: public announcements of the chocolate ration in Winston's present, versus Winston's childhood memory of stealing his sister's share of their chocolate). As I have mentioned terminology, I should note that contrary to 'chocolate', Orwell also talks about 'chocolates' (for instance, throughout 'Such, Such were the joys') by which he means individual sweets sold by weight (the precursors of *Black Magic* and *Milk Tray* sold in boxes). Orwell condemned Shakespeare's *King Lear* for its parallel plots yet here he is doing the same thing in *Nineteen Eighty-Four* – what does this tell us about him, or his methods of construction?

**NW:** It may be that he's trying to have his cake (or his chocolate) and eat it, though at the same time Orwell may have been locating the operations of power at multiple levels. The snatched chocolate in *Nineteen Eighty-Four* is, in its way, an echo of the 'snatching' of chocolate from the wider citizenry evident in the alterations made by the Ministry of Truth to the 'categorical pledge' not to reduce 'the chocolate ration during 1984'. I note, too, that Winston can't help 'snatching' a 'sidelong glance' at Martin's 'Mongolian face' in

O'Brien's apartment, which suggests a trace of Winston's childhood misdemeanours in his adult behaviours. There's a patterning of imagery, in other words, in *Nineteen Eighty-Four*, and it's precisely Orwell's tendency to 'pattern' his books that gives the focus to so much of what I've written about them.

**LJH:** Going back to my gardener/farmer division, I wonder if this can be applied to 'Orwell's list', which you mention in the 'Hobbies' chapter. That is, was Orwell determined that government needed figures on whom it could rely? There was a similar period during the World War when he was contacted by RAF security to provide references for figures such as Georges Kopp, who had escaped from Vichy France. Was he not used to being in that environment?

**NW:** It's a very odd list. And a very odd moment in Orwell's life, too. The exact details of what transpired in this situation may never fully be known, but I don't get the sense that he was at home in such circumstances. It's an uncomfortable alignment. Did some of this make its way into how he wrote about Winston's incorporation into state power? Or, indeed, about the broader scenario of *Nineteen Eighty-Four*, in which the providing of information about 'figures' leads inexorably to vaporisation? Your question has made me think that part of what *Nineteen Eighty-Four* may be enacting, or trying to enact, is self-satire, and possibly even self-exculpation. Although Orwell's list comes after the novel, the notebook on which the list is based precedes it. Is the novel's depiction of snitching on your comrades, and even on your parents, related in some way to Orwell's feelings about how he kept watch on others?

**LJH:** When I first read Orwell's war-time diaries in the *Collected Essays, Journalism and Letters* his list had not been published. I was surprised, though, to find that he was accessing figures in the Civil Service such as Sir James Grigg as an everyday activity. Was he never totally out of that social class to which Eton had given him access, even when he was living in a cottage with an outside toilet?

**NW:** I don't think so. Eton followed Orwell to Paris and to Spain, and it's there in *Nineteen Eighty-Four*, too, in the novel's depiction of the 'aristocratic' O'Brien; it may also be there in the 'top hats' recalled by the old prole in the pub. Many commentators find a contradiction in Orwell's Etonian background – a tension between his socialism and the school's elitism. It would be just as plausible to construct Orwell's Etonian roots as the source of the experiences that gave rise not only to the socialism but also to his networked placement in English life (and, in that sense, to his work as a sociopolitical commentator).

**L.J. HURST**

**NATHAN WADDELL**

LJH: Half-way through your book you quote a letter to his friend Eleanor Jaques written in 1936: 'I have been skating a number of times at the Streatham ice rink. It is great fun but very shame-making, because in spite of the most desperate efforts I still can't learn to skate backwards.' Orwell would have been 32 at the time – do you think he was slow in growing up, or does this indicate something else about him, his ability to take pleasure in youthful things? Pleasure in ice skating does not seem like the 'gloomy George' that we often encounter.

NW: One of the joys in reading about Orwell in the 1930s has been accessing this lighter side of his character. I've never quite understood this idea of the 'gloomy George', not least because *Animal Farm*, routinely constructed as a tragic work, is (for me) so hilariously funny. There's a schoolboy naughtiness in many of his novels, *Keep the Aspidistra Flying* being the text where he satirises schoolboyishness (or maybe 'immaturity' would be the better word) at greatest length. I've tried repeatedly to convey this sense of the *humour* in Orwell to my students, with varying degrees of success – though one of my most recent undergraduate students has written about humour in Orwell to good effect, and Luke Seaber has a brilliant chapter on 'Orwell the Humorist' in *The Oxford Handbook of George Orwell* (2025). But I think your sense that Orwell takes *pleasure* in youthful things is precisely the right way of putting it, and here I think of the youthful exuberance discernible in his love of small creatures. The attention Orwell devotes in his diary to that moment in October 1939 when he encountered a 'phosphorescent worm', for instance, which I write about in my chapter on 'Animals' in *A Bright Cold Day*, evokes a specifically childlike fascination with nature. The same exuberance motivates 'Some thoughts on the common toad' (1946).

LJH: You have had access to the two recently discovered sets of letters to Eleanor Jaques and Brenda Salkeld, now in the Orwell Archive. I wonder if there are documents in the National Archives of the UK or Burma revealing more of Orwell's life in the 1920s and wonder if someone will ever have access to the time and finance needed to make that search given the pressures on all academic research. What new discovery would you like to be made? What is preventing the investigation?

NW: I would dearly like to know more about Orwell's time in Burma. This is such an absence in the record, despite the tireless efforts of so many scholars to reconstruct it: we know a lot, but we don't know as much about his life in the mid-1920s as we should. Given the importance of the Burma 'episode' for everything that comes after it, in his writing and in his life and career, this is a tantalising problem for Orwell scholarship, and particularly for Orwell biographers. There's a book to be written about the 'Burmese Blair'. Not by me, though.

LJH: Nathan Waddell, thank you.

- *A Bright Cold Day: The Wonder of George Orwell*, by Nathan Waddell, is published by Oneworld

INTERVIEW

## POETRY INSPIRED BY ORWELL

THE SPECIAL PATIENT
Was he well enough, I wonder, for fresh air
or for a trip to the Knoll, and along the common
Was there a nurse, or orderly, interested and strong enough
to wheel him up Cranham hill
He weighed very little
Was he well enough to be outside in the evening
as the sun, setting, flamed Painswick's spire
flooded Laurie Lee's valley, with the glow of childhood
as he pointed out, between the wooded hills
the Black Mountains, just a distant smear
Perhaps another time, after breakfast
he was returned to the ridge
when the sun was enough to tempt the adders
into its warmth
and to lift the mist off the forest trees
In the clearings
where the sun arrives later
it still slowly rose
to escape like smoke
he imagined
from campfires, of hunters, of poachers, of anglers
from charcoal burners, smoked black and telling tales
from coal-fired funnels – starboard out port home
from Dacoit bands, sharing spoils and schemes,
from the unnoticed, dans les ruelles, and alleyways, warmed by
    poor ragged flames
from the convivial fug of a black-gowned common room
from coal-black chimneys of terraced colliers
from a gardener's steaming compost
from the smoked remains of the bombed and the burnt
from a cold cold crofter's smouldering peat

Returned to the sanatorium
through pools of summer orchids
past the school in silent study
all downhill

## POETRY

HE ROSE ABOVE
a dark dark sea
of Maafa pain
spade-black
blood that flowed
thick as molasses
wide-eyed souls
of broken coolies
made Morpheus playthings
through thoughtless cruelty
entitled indifference
thorough administration

He floated

on this ancestral
sea of cess
adrift
An unformed baulk of Indian mahogany
blown westward
to thin veneers of pale English oak
thrown back east
through rough cut Burmese teak
washed up
with charred remains of twisted olive
carried back to seek
coarse-cut timber
darker oak
knotted pine
brash and bramble
weeping
willow

Left the flotsam
drifted north
to fresh water
clear air

Finally

fine-grained
polished
carried
across

CLASS
nobility smells

of coal dust and sweat
of steel blasts and sweat
of canals and barges and the sweat
of horses
of dogs and uncleaned bairns
of the senile
and the incontinent
of bleach and donkey stones
of cabbage boiling
on smoky fires
of beer and vomit
of a leather belt flying
and the blood of violent retribution
and curses
and childbirth
of hunger
of death

a noble acceptance


ROOM 101
the walls appeared slowly
and silently crept to enfold him
uninvited and unexpected
and he began to face his fears

what if wicked leaders
are replaced by the more wicked
what if they aren't in charge
what if they lie
what if all truth is lies
what if peace means war
plenty means none
what if news is fantasy
what if programmes are programmed
what if everyone is watching you
betraying you
to someone who wants you to be betrayed
what if it is your big brother
what if the poor are noble

what if the rich aren't
what if meeting a party girl
is a worrying thing
what if thoughts
are policed
and memories are given
what if light
is permanent and painful
if every week is hate week
if good and evil
friends and enemies
are the same
what if my language is old-speak
because I'm old
what if I am less equal
or the least equal

he saw the future
in a ball of crystal clarity
what fear could be a greater

## POETRY

RAILROAD TO WIGAN

Steam and smuts drifted through the station. Striding down the platform
looking for a seat, he stepped into the last carriage,
as the guard slammed the doors with a flourish,
blew his whistle and waved his flag.
Sadly not red.
They staggered away from Kings Cross.

Carriages filled,
with smoke of Chesterfields and Balkan Sobranies,
smells of brilliantine, wet tweeds, and Dubbin.
He stood in the corridor, alone,
compartments all filled with Oxbridge reunions.
Readers, through tortoiseshell frames, of 'Kampf' and 'Kapital'
and Plato, in the Greek of course.
Some clutched the soft black leather of bibles,
seeking to convert the heathens.
While others sought the titillation of tough 'lads',
or rough 'lasses'.

Chaps checked their Leicas.
Gals checked their chalks and charcoal
expecting mostly black and white.
Fat Sheaffer pens, Giannini Firenze notebooks, Castell pencils.
Hidden luxuries: a spirit burner and green tea, silk and cologne,
hock and a syphon of seltzer (they'll have refills up there, surely).

With every sway, anticipation swilled through the train.
A descent into the caldera of northern ferment,
expectation of the heat and fissures of anger and injustice.
Hoping to capture the eruption, the start of the revolution,
a republic, a Reich, socialism, communism, or anarchy
It must be there; it must be now.

He braced himself against the carriage wall,
not his first train journey spent standing.
Tired tweeds, knitted tie, soft collared shirt, and smoking roll-ups
He had lived with the poor and dispossessed.
Not giddy, nor expectant,
he went to search, to find, and to understand.

He strode from the station.
In his canvas satchel, a handful of pencils, reporter's pads,
and all his belongings.
It was only half full.
From the top deck of a trolleybus, he saw the others
waiting for taxis,
and brushing smuts from their hair.

'Railroad to Wigan' was inspired by a quotation from Professor Robert Colls on a 'Rest is History' podcast: 'You could hardly get on the train north, in the nineteen thirties, for middle class boys going north to write about how awful it was, but also how authentic it was.'

Rob Joyson wrote poetry for 50 years with no intention of publication. For the last few years as a member of writing groups in Louth, Lincolnshire, he has decided to expose his work to the critical gaze of the wider world. He published his first poetry collection *Of Life and Love and Interludes* in 2020 and has since been published by the *Ekphrastic Review*. He is an enthusiastic reader of his work at many events throughout greater Lincolnshire.

SHORT STORIES

# Holding Up His Sky: Stories of Women in the Life of George Orwell

**ANN KRONBERGS**

FOREWORD

This collection of Orwellian short stories has grown from the germ of an idea planted over thirty years ago when I was living in Church Stretton, Shropshire. In a local newsletter I read a cricketing memoir written by a retired gentleman recalling his boyhood days in the village of Ticklerton between the wars. He wrote: 'I still have memories of a tall, saturnine character who turned out regularly each summer for Birtley whilst staying with his friend …at Ticklerton. To us he was chiefly notable for his habit of always fielding on the boundary to facilitate his non-stop production and consumption of hand-rolled "fags"; we knew him simply as Eric Blair.'

Without tracking down so much as an old score card, I tried in vain to trace Eric Blair's cricketing form in the 1920s. Finally, I came to the conclusion that this intriguing eye-witness account must have been a false memory, a fusion of fact and fiction. Nevertheless, it had set me on a peculiar trail, leading me to peer through a keyhole into the past, at the lost world of Ticklerton Court, owned by the Buddicom family. Here Eric had stayed during his school holidays from Eton at the invitation of his friends, the young Buddicoms, honing his skills of shooting and fishing with Prosper and Guinever, sharing his love of books in the library of the old house with their sister Jacintha. And somehow that image, of a detached observer watching a game of cricket from the boundary line, stayed with me over time; almost like a ghost, turning up unexpectedly, causing a stir and then disappearing. Sprinkling the seeds for these stories.

Spool forward to A.L. Kennedy's Orwell Memorial Lecture of 2017, 'Orwell with Women'. Here Kennedy adopted a snapshot approach to her discussion of Orwell's relationships with women, exploring a selection of moments in time, whether caught on camera or in letter form. With a formidable eye for detail, she analysed the photograph of Orwell on the beach in Southwold with Eleanor Jaques. With forensic attention to body language and clothing she discussed more photographs – of Orwell with his first wife Eileen, for example. With sensitivity to language and tone, she scrutinised the letters he wrote to his girlfriend Brenda Salkeld in the early thirties. It seemed to me that Kennedy's snapshots were like oral tales, representing the female perspective for moments in Orwell's packed life. These tales were pithy, rooted in the detail of a particular time and place, and they showed how the short-story form might be used to de-centre Orwell from his own story and allow a few of the women in his life to be foregrounded.

So, I attempted to turn detective once again, with the intention of writing individual stories focusing on significant women in the life of George Orwell. I scoured biographies and photographs, listened repeatedly to taped interviews, visited relevant archives in an effort to pin down evidence about each one at specific times and in particular places. I stumbled on surprising facts such as Ida Blair's presence at Ticklerton Court in the summer when her son returned from Burma, as recorded in the diary entries of Lilian Hayward for August 1927, and Avril Blair's unsung catering career in the Copper Kettle in Southwold, making her the ideal contender for the role of chief housekeeper and cook when her brother finally settled in the remote farmhouse on Jura and completed *Nineteen Eighty-Four*. Furthermore, I learned virtually all of these women close to Orwell were skilful writers in their own ways: we have Jacintha Buddicom's *Eric & Us*, a memoir covering her meeting and early friendship with Eric Blair; Lilian Hayward's notebooks, diaries and photograph albums; the few surviving letters and Esperanto articles of his aunt Ellen Limouzin and Eileen Blair's letters to her husband and also to her friend Norah Myles; Inez Holden's published writings of the war years as well as her unpublished diary with the account of Orwell's visit to her flat in late March 1945; and Sonia Brownell's diaries, letters and *Horizon* articles also.

Whilst I have used the historical record to guide how I represent each of the women, my main aim has been to dramatise moments in their experience, to show their reality within the overarching story of George Orwell's own life, without allowing them to be overshadowed by this literary giant. The title, *Holding Up His Sky: Stories of Women in the Life of George Orwell*, argues an untold truth about these women's lives: that just as influential men in high places, like Sir Richard Rees or David Astor, helped smooth Orwell's entry into the world of letters, so too, collectively, these women were also significant at crucial times in his journey as a writer, providing a degree of psychological and moral support, secretarial and editorial input, sexual pleasure and cultural companionship, domestic and even nursing care up to the last days of his life.

I hope these stories offer an insight into their significant input into the phenomenon that is George Orwell and the development of the man who was Eric Blair.

## TICKLERTON, SHROPSHIRE, AUGUST 1927

Aunt Lilian thought the motorcar was a much over-rated vehicle, not that she would dare express such a view nowadays. For her there was no better mode of transport on a fine summer's day than the horse and trap the gardener, Lewis, had brought round to the front of Ticklerton Court. She stroked Polly's muzzle and patted her neck, deftly lifting her skirt before nimbly stepping up, gathering the reins in her right hand as she sat down. Meanwhile Mrs Blair, helped by Lewis, climbed with an effort into the trap, making the springs compress on the passenger side. With a gentle shake of the reins they were off, the horse's hooves scrunching on the gravel, mane rippling in the breeze. Aunt Lilian nodded a goodbye to her house guest, Mr Dolby, who was polishing the bodywork of his new Ford. The shining black carapace reminded her of an over-sized beetle. Something about it made her shudder. So funereal.

**SHORT STORY**

Perfect timing for the drive, warm late afternoon sunshine with a light breeze. Mrs Blair sitting back enjoying the ride beside her. She was a pleasant enough companion, very good at bridge it would appear. Sometimes given to unsettling outbursts if people grated on her. Like Mr Dolby. She was so obliging and helpful in the garden. Doesn't seem to mind spending hours with the shears and secateurs, cutting back the shrubs and dead-heading the perennials. Lewis happy for her to do his work for him, no doubt. She misses having a big garden in Southwold, she says, after their Shiplake days. Oh well. We can't have everything. That's how life is.

Polly broke into a brisk trot as they pulled out onto the lane. Clip-Clop. Clip-Clop. Aunt Lilian loved this point of acceleration, the fresh air blowing her hair and the rhythmic jolting of the trap tilting her gently this way and that. Why did people want cars when they could have this motion instead? She glimpsed the hedgerows speeding past, noticed the greenish pink blackberries plumping up. Not ready for picking yet. A few more weeks to go. She'd asked Cook to bake a pie for supper, using a few ripe cookers from the orchard. She seemed to remember Eric liked that: a crusty apple pie with lashings of custard.

He was due to arrive at the station at 6.40 p.m. on Tuesday 23rd August, so the latest telegram had stated. His journey back from

## ANN KRONBERGS

Burma through France had taken inordinately long, especially since he'd made a detour to Paris to visit his Aunt Nellie, Mrs Blair's older sister. Odd of him to want to see the aunt before his own mother. Odder still, in the circumstances, that he should wish to travel the distance to Ticklerton before making his way home to Southwold, especially when she wasn't there this summer. Jacintha that is. Still, he would find her brother and sister, Prosper and Guiny Buddicom and Laura their mother. They would make him welcome. Make him feel at home.

Out on the main road with the slow incline towards Church Stretton, Aunt Lilian marveled, as she always did, at the magnificent scenery on all sides. The sun was quite dazzling at this point in the day, casting its long rays of light across the fields, cottages and gardens which slipped by on either side of them. Up ahead the hills of the Long Mynd were in shadow as the sun slipped lower in the sky, the whale-like bulk of Caer Caradoc looming closer as the pony and trap trundled on, the wooden wheels rumbling beneath them and the pace of Polly's strides quickening as the reins urged her on to a canter.

Soon enough they reached the bend in the road when suddenly the picture postcard view of the small market town appeared ahead: the railway line cutting a clear boundary to the town in the foreground, the bridge crossing it towards Sandford Avenue lined with the handsome Victorian town buildings, the fine church spire of St Lawrence in the near distance and the wooded hillside beyond. Here Aunt Lilian halted the trap and helped poor Mrs Blair disembark. This proved to be quite a task. She was a little red in the face and ruffled by the exertion. Aunt Lilian advised her to take a soothing stroll in the little park near the station, watch some tennis on the courts or bowls on the green. Or she could sit quietly on a bench. Get her thoughts together before his train arrived.

Five minutes later Aunt Lilian was back with the reins in hand, urging Polly on to a trotting pace, passing the Post Office and shops en route for the crossroads at the end of the street. She had one purpose in mind: to get a view of the Long Mynd from the Burway before the sun dipped below the crest of the hills. There was a special area of scrubby grass where she could allow Polly to stand and wait in her harness, whilst she allowed herself a short stroll up the narrow track to reach her favourite viewpoint. Here the steep hillside covered in gorse bushes and rough grass pitched down on her right, forming one side of the fault line of Carding Mill Valley whilst the other side mirrored this one, dotted with a few straggling sheep and one or two stray Mynd ponies. She cast her eye towards the old Carding Mill building, now Pearson's café, where tired walkers could enjoy a pot of tea and scone on most days of the week. Beyond it were the scattering of ramshackle cottages and remote houses before the track curled towards the reservoir and the range of hills rolled away into the far distance, a steady stream curling and swirling its way down from the Lightspout Waterfall.

Here in this place she could stand, reading the landscape as if it were an open picture book, the images changing hour by hour as the sun moves in the sky, clouds subduing the light. Nowhere like the Burway to calm a troubled mind. It would be awkward seeing Eric after all this time. Difficult to know quite what to say, or what not to say, more to the point. There were some stories one could not tell.

NO GOING BACK
*Southwold, September 1927*

Moments before waking she was a child again, on a woodland walk. From high above her head came a loud tapping.

**SHORT STORY**

'It's a woodpecker, Av. Look up there.'

And her eyes followed where he was pointing. Nearly camouflaged by green leaves, there was the bird's head, hammering at the tree trunk.

'It's a mating call. That's what it is.'

What was a mating call? The knocking continued, occasionally interrupted by a sliding sound. But this was no beak on wood. This was the sound of the metal keys of her brother's typewriter hitting the page, waking her up at 6.30 a.m.

What on earth did he have to say, so early in the day? He had plenty of words, to put down on paper, but scarcely any for her, or her parents, these days. Not since the disastrous holiday together in Cornwall and his shattering revelations. Shattering where her father and mother were concerned because they had sunk all their hopes in him. Not particularly shattering for her, his younger sister. She didn't really care if the truth were told: Eric must do as he liked. She had better things to think about.

As Avril's feet touched the bare floorboards of her bedroom, she ran through the checklist in her mind: cakes (two Victorias and one Lemon); scones (plain, fruit and cheese – a dozen of each); jam tarts (half a dozen, using up a jar of blackcurrant jam). Her confections were lined up on the kitchen table on trays, covered in linen cloths, ready to be carried next door before opening time. Surely Eric could help her with this task? No good sitting pounding away at the typewriter all day long. He should get on and do something practical for a change. She also needed help with the washing-up.

Pulling open the curtains she saw Queen Street slowly coming to life. The milk cart was doing the rounds, a delivery boy was shifting

**ANN KRONBERGS**

boxes of fruit and vegetables into the greengrocers across the street. Better get a move on.

The keys of the typewriter sounded louder as she passed by Eric's closed door on her way to the bathroom. Occasionally he allowed their mother Ida to read what he was writing, by special request. Afterwards she always made encouraging remarks:

'Beautifully written, Eric. Quite amusing. But I'm not sure I understand the ending: what really happened there?'

The answer would depend on his mood: a clear and rational explanation, or a sullen shrug of the shoulders before he left the table, his mood swings casting a dreary shadow over them all. Avril had too much to occupy her in the real world and did not have time for his fictions. Nor did their ageing father who, whenever Eric entered the sitting-room, quickly reached for *The Daily Telegraph*. His son's writing ambitions were a great disappointment to him.

By 7.00 a.m. Avril had returned to her bedroom. The catches and hinges of the mahogany wardrobe were rusted with age and, as she pulled open the door, it squeaked and rattled noisily, exhaling the combined scent of damp and mothballs. She reached up for the hanger of well-pressed clothes for the working day: black skirt, white blouse, a linen half-apron. Neat and smart, that was the look she cultivated.

As she zipped up the skirt and tucked in the blouse, Avril glanced in the full-length wardrobe mirror and liked what she saw. The tailor round the corner had done a good job: the skirt was a snug fit; the pleats flattered her shape. Turning sideways she studied her profile view. Slim. Few curves. Her mother often commented that Avril reminded her of Aunt Nellie when she was a younger woman. How, she wondered, could she have anything in common with this batty old aunt who had recently stunned them all by joining her lover in Paris? She knew love could make people behave oddly, but Aunt Nellie was in her late fifties, she was much too old to be in thrall to a younger man. It was so undignified! Eric had visited the couple in July on his journey back through France. Not that he had said much about it.

Moving to the dressing table Avril stared at her reflection in the small mirror: a rosy-cheeked china doll with wavy, light-brown hair, pretty in a quiet way. She must try to look a bit older if she was going to win the respect of the customers. Picking up her powder compact and flicking open the lid with a few deft taps, she powdered her nose and cheeks. Then she applied a dash of eyeshadow and a few strokes of mascara. Better. Less like a schoolgirl. She was still thinking about her aunt and her habit of caking her face in thick layers of face powder and rouge and spraying herself liberally with cheap perfume. She had an infectious laugh, loved entertaining people with her scandalous anecdotes from her life as an actress. Then there was her special bond with Eric, their trips together to the theatre and the literary soirées where she introduced him to famous writers of the day. How come Nellie had never invited her to the theatre, to these parties? She always missed out on the fun.

The previous week a letter had arrived from Nellie addressed to Eric. Avril had recognised the neat cursive handwriting and the French stamp on the envelope as she picked it up from the hall mat. So she chose to write to her nephew, instead of her own sister? There was some kind of a conspiracy afoot. Typically, Eric had not shared the contents of the letter when he sat reading it over breakfast. The family had watched him in silence, expecting a summary of the contents at the very least. He had said nothing, merely folding the letter and tucking it away in the breast pocket of his jacket.

The sound of a chair scraping on bare floorboards and the clicking of the keys of the typewriter ceased abruptly. Avril heard her brother's firm footsteps crossing the passageway to the bathroom, a door closing, a pause and then the clank of the toilet chain being pulled. Perhaps she had disturbed his train of thought. Time to head down to the kitchen and put the kettle on.

**SHORT STORY**

* * *

Avril's new place of work, The Wistaria (sic) Tea Rooms, was immediately next door to the Blair family home. Privately she told herself she could do better, at least by spelling the name correctly on the sign over the door. A blue colour theme prevailed throughout, which she thought was moderately tasteful, if a bit heavy-handed. She was not averse to the willow-patterned china either. What did seem incongruous was the glass cabinet beneath the main counter where crocheted and knitted toys shared space with her homemade cakes. Rattles, miniature dolls and teddy bears were piled on top of each other in a wicker basket and whenever a customer asked to see one, the whole lot would have to be lifted out and churned over. But Miss Smythe liked making these items and she thought her customers appreciated them. Did they? Avril wondered about that.

So far, morning business was going well. One or two customers for an early coffee or tea, no cakes served as yet. Strange to be on her own inside this confined space, one large room divided in two by dark wooden panelling, crammed to bursting with sets of tables and chairs.

Seconds leaked away invisibly, marked by the loud tick of a carriage clock, which stood among the bric-a-brac in the middle of the mantelpiece. Occasionally Avril broke the silence with the chink

ANN KRONBERGS

of china as she stacked a tray, the sound of her heels echoing on the wooden parquet floor when she crossed to the kitchenette to the rear of the Tea Rooms.

At the age of twenty Avril had not really seen herself having a career in catering. Both her years in a girls' school and her elder sister Marjorie's example, had led her to expect marriage as her ultimate career option, but before the right young man of handsome looks and status came along, she supposed this was as good a way as any to spend her time. The job opportunity had come about by chance. For a while, as something to keep her busy, and admittedly to earn some pocket money, she had started to bake cakes to order for a number of local families. Birthday and Christmas cakes were her speciality, and in addition she had also mastered a range of recipes from Mrs Beeton's, which had become very popular with her growing customer base in Walberswick. In the spring the news had spread about her cakes to the proprietor of the Wistaria Tea Rooms, and overnight Avril had become Miss Smythe's chief cake and biscuit supplier.

In June, before Eric's return to the family nest, Miss Smythe had recruited Avril to work in the Tea Rooms, for a reasonable wage, on Mondays, Wednesdays and Fridays. After a short, and rather tense, training period Avril was judged to be capable of coping by herself. In general, she liked the work and the attention from the customers. She hoped, with her mother Ida's financial help, to take on the lease herself in due course, to be her own boss.

On the dot of 10.45 a.m. two of her regular customers arrived after their Monday morning circular walk down to the harbour and back along the Promenade. Retired schoolteachers, they were pillars of the church community and the Southwold W.I. They made a big entrance, noisily opening the door, making the bell ring repeatedly.

'Good morning, Avril. It's very breezy out there today. We were nearly blown off our feet, weren't we, Joan?' Nancy handed her coat to Avril whilst Joan contemplated the blackboard listing of the cakes and scones on offer. Avril resented assuming the servile role they made her play, as if she were their paid servant. But she had to grin and bear it, she had no option. They were regular customers and must be humoured.

Once seated at the window table, Nancy tidied her hair with her hands and continued her account of the weather.

'Yes. It was a real North wind: sign of things to come I'm afraid. What will you order, Joan?'

'Well, I would like a pot of Earl Grey and a slice of your delicious lemon cake, please dear. And you, Nancy?'

'A piece of Victoria sponge and I'll share a pot of Earl Grey with Joan, please, Avril.' Both women shook the starched linen serviettes and spread them over their laps in a synchronised action. Nancy posed the question she had been dying to ask since her arrival.

'And how is your brother settling into life in our little town? Quite a shock to his system, I imagine, after life in Burma?'

The question stalled Avril for a second.

'Yes. He likes it very much, thank you. I'll fetch your tea.'

No point whatsoever telling them the truth when they would prefer an unvarnished lie. As Avril busied herself behind the counter, scooping tea from the Earl Grey caddy into the teapot, she bristled internally at the way Eric's presence at home had caused such a stir in the town. Was he really that important? Why did people appear to care so much about his sudden change of direction? As if her thoughts had conjured him out of thin air, Avril looked up from her work and caught sight of her brother strolling past the bow-fronted shop carrying a fishing rod.

'Quick, Nancy. Look!' Joan was pointing towards the window in a very indiscreet manner, Avril thought.

'It's him. Eric Blair.' With mounting irritation, she heard the words spoken in a hushed undertone and saw Nancy raising her index finger to her lips as she slyly shifted her gaze sideways in time to see Eric's tall figure striding by outside. Avril approached the table with her loaded tray, pretending not to have seen him.

'Perfect, dear. This will warm us up.'

Nancy set the teapot, cups and plates on the table whilst Avril returned to the counter to cut segments of the required cakes. The drop in tone of the ladies' voices was all too obvious, she knew they were exchanging words about her brother. It was deeply humiliating, especially as Eric was making a spectacle of himself at this very moment. In plain sight, visible for everyone to see, he had stopped on the corner opposite the Wistaria Tea Rooms to roll a cigarette. He had taken out the tattered tobacco pouch from one pocket of his tweed jacket and was now ferreting in the other for the Rizla cigarette papers. It was excruciating to watch him. What a clown he was. What a total embarrassment!

**SHORT STORY**

\* \* \*

Eric headed in the direction of North Parade, the smell of singeing tobacco winning over the stench of hops from Adnams Brewery. He tried to feel pity for his sister, empress of the homemade scones and slices of sponge cake. But maybe, after all, it was Avril who had the right idea and he who had made the biggest mistake of his life so far, giving up a well-paid job with benefits to sit in a room in his parents' house for hours on end, bashing away at the typewriter, filling pages and pages with complete drivel. Where was the fun in this, or the money?

# ANN KRONBERGS

The piercing shriek of gulls overhead interrupted his thoughts, they were circling about, squawking loudly, one of them had landed on a chimney pot and was sitting aloof, beak clamped shut. Eric accelerated his pace, reaching the junction with the Promenade to stand by the railings and look out to sea. Puffing on the remaining stub, he felt a gratifying burst of adrenalin from the shot of nicotine. Thick clouds were covering the sun and far ahead the sea and sky merged into one another as if someone had drawn a horizontal line in charcoal pencil across it.

Eric made his way down the shallow steps onto the beach, tossing away the butt end. The tide was coming in, waves churning up the brown sand before breaking on the shore, where they unfurled in thick sheets of foaming bubbles. He glanced towards the pier in the distance, spotting a couple of fishermen installed, waiting for a catch. He was a relative newcomer to sea fishing, would have to ask one of them a few questions at the start, only now his enthusiasm was waning.

A few yards away was an old chap standing behind an easel, squinting as he stared out to sea. Something of a Monet, perhaps, with his white hair and long beard. Next moment he was busily squeezing blobs of colour from metal tubes onto his palette, dabbing his brush into the little pools of black and white, a dash of blue. Eric walked over so he could watch the artist's hand move from paint to paper, making light, deft strokes. Very soon the noisy scene in front of them took form as slate grey lines with shots of turquoise. About right. Much easier to smudge paint on paper than fill a page with words which mean what you want them to.

Burma. Bright oranges and fierce pinks. Red. Of silk. Of blood. Grey. Of elephant's skin. Yellow of bright sun. The stink of the marketplace, the sandalwood scent on the skin of the little Burmese girls. Hard to paint the smells, the noises, the oppressive heat. The oppression. In a moment of madness, in Cornwall on holiday, he had tried to tell his father why he had had to leave, but it was no good.

'You're a self-deluded wordsmith.'

The old man did not understand. It was a waste of words, trying to explain to him why he wanted to be a writer.

'A dilettante, more likely. No money in writing, that's for sure. I have given you an education fit for a prince, Eton and the rest, and now you're giving up a fine career as a colonial Police Officer to become a penniless scribbler.'

Eric sat down on the beach and abandoned any intention of using the fishing rod. He knew he was a complete misfit, wherever he went. Stuck in some kind of no-man's land where anyone could take a pot shot at him: he was twenty-something without a job.

An object of contempt and ridicule here in Southwold, especially given his privileged education and posh gentleman's accent. No-one wanted him, least of all women. Or rather, least of all one woman, his 'childhood sweetheart', Jacintha. Three letters he'd written to her from Burma and only received one in return, which had so infuriated him with its note of cheery stoicism that he'd torn it up in a fury; she did not have a clue what he had gone through out there. The fact that she had never replied to his other letters, leaving him to suffer in silence, had made his blood boil. Surely, she, of all people, ought to have understood how much he loathed the Service and what it did to people? What it had done to him.

Through the sweltering heat and dog days in Burma he had clung on to the belief that one meeting with her after all these years would be enough to make her say yes; all he had to do was establish contact with her Aunt Lilian in Ticklerton. She'd be delighted to hear from him. Of course, he had known it would be awkward meeting Jacintha after all these years. His clumsy assault on her that last summer seven years earlier was not a good memory. Christ, what a fool he'd been. He'd lost control, tried to clamber on top of her, trapping her tiny body beneath his. She'd cried out, struggled, pushed him off. Run away. But he'd been only a boy. They were both such innocents in those days. She would see it that way, surely? He had learned all a man needed to know in Burma.

Now his stomach lurched at the thought of his visit to Ticklerton on his return. One of the most excruciating experiences of his entire life. He supposed, in retrospect, he had naively expected something of a hero's welcome from the Buddicoms. Here, with the tumult of the waves in front of him, he replayed one ghastly scene in his mind after another. Wasting no time, he had travelled direct to Shropshire on his arrival back in England in late July, taking the train from Paddington. He had secretly hoped for a hero's welcome as he stepped down from the train at Church Stretton: a line-up of the three Buddicom siblings perhaps, with Jacintha in her prettiest summer frock. Nothing had prepared him for the reality: his mother, Ida Blair, hot and flustered in the heat, calling out his name from the doorway of the ticket office in a loud, imperious voice and following this greeting, as he approached, with an uncustomary maternal embrace reminding him how he loathed shows of familial affection. Then there had been the physical discomfort of the ride to Ticklerton, perched between his mother and Aunt Lilian, quietly in charge, on the narrow bench seat of the pony and trap. He sat in silence, scarcely hearing his mother's lengthy explanations, overwhelmed by feelings of disappointment.

As soon as the pony steered up the driveway of Ticklerton Court, the ivy-clad house and well-planted shrubbery loomed into view,

**SHORT STORY**

as the cawing of crows in the tall trees and the rustle of the leaves stirred memories of his visits long ago.

Quickly Aunt Lilian had stepped down from the trap to assume her role as hostess, opening the front door and standing with back and neck stiff and straight like a poker.

'Eric! Welcome. Dinner will soon be served. Please come on through.'

She had led him across the large hallway towards the deserted drawing room where the door stood open. The heavy mahogany furniture, the portraits and photograph frames, the ceramic table lamps and mantelpiece candlesticks were all exactly as he remembered them. Only there was more dust on the surfaces. It felt colder. The shutters had cut out the light.

'Eric. Mrs Blair. Make yourselves at home. The others will join you any moment. Excuse me for a few moments. Do take a seat meanwhile.'

Soon they would be reunited. He would look at Jacintha's face as she entered the room and stare into her eyes, feel that spark of recognition. How might she have changed, he wondered? In the old days she had been so tender-hearted towards animals, but her feelings had not extended to humans, or so it had seemed to him from the flint-hearted absence of replies to his letters from Burma.

His pulse had quickened at the sound of loud steps echoing the hall, but the sight of her brother Prosper a moment later, caused Eric to modify his expectations.

'Eric, how are you? How was the journey? Good to see you, old chap.' They had shaken hands with Eric bending forward slightly. Prosper was plumper in the face, he'd already developed a paunch.

'I see you're as thin and wiry as ever, Eric, but as you can see, too much fine wine and good food at Oxford has done for my waistline! How was Burma, old fellow? I understand you've only just got back?'

Eric nodded, quickly turning his attention to Aunt Lilian, who had re-entered the room with a tray of delicate glasses etched with the family crest. At this prompt, Prosper fetched the sherry decanter from the sideboard, removing the stopper and pouring generous quantities into each of the five glasses. Surely one was missing, there should be six people altogether counting Prosper, Guiny and Jacintha, Aunt Lilian, himself and his mother? Meanwhile Aunt Lilian was gently issuing orders for Prosper to open the shutters, explaining:

'We have to keep them closed, Eric, to save the fabric.'

As the light streamed into the room, he had noted the sun-bleached curtains and streaked upholstery. The rich colours of the linens and silks had faded with time.

'Guiny will be back any moment. She decided to take the dogs for a walk at teatime. Sherry? Nuts? Eric, Mrs Blair?' Jacintha was not mentioned.

Prosper had enjoyed his varsity years a little too much, it seemed. He'd only decided to settle down to work in the last term, by which time it was already too late to make up lost ground. Some City connections had come out of it, though, and his sisters had enjoyed themselves while he was there: May balls, concerts, undergraduate productions, punting parties. Perhaps Jacintha had met a Prince Charming in his absence? Eric had tried to press him for more information but Prosper was in mid-flow and appeared not to hear him.

With the entrance of Guiny, followed by two dogs, their conversation ended:

'Eric! Lewis said you were in the house! Good to see you! When did you arrive? I would have been back sooner, but the dogs nearly got lost chasing rabbits in the woods.'

Eric stood up to greet her. She was taller, and with windswept hair and cheeks flushed from the walk, she looked prettier, more womanly, less of a tomboy than in the old days, when she'd roamed the countryside with him and Prosper, shooting rabbits and pheasants.

'Didn't Cini join you on the walk?'

His innocent question went unanswered as she looked over at her brother, then gestured to the decanter on the sideboard.

'More sherry, Eric? Supper won't be long. You look as though you need feeding up.'

She indicated to Prosper to top-up Eric's glass.

'No. Cini couldn't get away from London. She'll probably be coming at Christmas. We'll see.'

A sidelong glance across at Aunt Lilian prompted agreement from her.

'Yes. She's a bit bogged down with things at the moment. I hope she'll be visiting before too long. Nowadays it's unusually quiet here, Eric, as you can imagine. Did you know I'm putting together a book of local walks?'

Here, on the hard pebbles of Southwold beach, his dream of marriage and a life with Jacintha broke into a thousand pieces all over again. If she had had any fragment of feeling left for him, she would not have stayed away leaving him to face them all alone. He cringed when he recalled the way he had lit a cigarette under their piercing gaze, how he had sat there smoking it in sullen silence, allowing the burning ash to crumble onto the rug at his feet. Then had followed the ultimate humiliation: a telling-off from his mother.

**SHORT STORY**

## ANN KRONBERGS

All he had wanted, at that moment in time, was to leave Ticklerton Court and never go back.

Now, putting his hand in the pocket of his jacket he took hold of the small box he had intended for her. Embossed in gold lettering on the lid was the name of the jewellers in Katha where he had bought the ring in a moment of impetuosity months before he left. A Burmese ruby flanked by diamonds. In his mind he had pictured her surprise as he presented it to her, watching her slipping the ring on her finger, speechless with emotion.

But Jacintha had moved on. He was an irrelevance now.

Eric stood up, his hand still clutching the box like a bowler holding a cricket ball. Ahead of him were two gannets riding the waves a short way out. With one sharp overarm movement he could hurl the missile and watch it plummet into the sea, startling the birds into flight.

Instead, he picked up his rod and headed towards the pier. The ring box remained in his pocket.

* * *

Jacintha pushed the pram along the Bayswater Road in the direction of Lancaster Gate. As usual she was not wearing a watch, but she guessed from the traffic and the people up ahead entering the Tube station that this was mid-morning. She thought with envy of the office workers, people with proper jobs to do, struggling to understand how she fitted into any of this anymore. Under foot, the pavement was strewn with sodden sycamore leaves, which reminded her of the disgusting wet nappies draping the sides of metal buckets in the sluice. Dank and messy.

Last night had been stormy with rain battering the windowpanes and wind rattling the tall sash windows of the Home. She had sat on the edge of her bed, breast-feeding the baby in the dark, listening. She was not very good at any of this. As usual she had not been able to fall asleep easily after she had settled her in the cot, too many thoughts whirling round her head. She was exhausted, she craved sleep, but all too often she heard the office clock downstairs striking the hours until the baby woke at the crack of dawn for another feed. She tried to comfort herself with the reminder that it would soon be over, this nursing stage. Then when she looked down at the cot, at her sleeping baby, how could she not hate herself?

Chilly October. Nearly time for the clocks to go back. Turning into Kensington Gardens she made her way along the path as far as the Peter Pan Statue, following the same route she took every day. It was a ritual almost turning into an obsession. The baby was stirring. Soon she would open her eyes, but before she did, Jacintha saw the bronze figure of the boy suddenly appear in the distance, playing his pipe. Perched high on the tree stump, above the fairies, mice and squirrels, the boy was free, absorbed in the pleasure of his tunes, unaware that out of earshot and invisible, the crocodile with the ticking clock was skulking about, ready to pounce.

At a bench nearby she parked the pram and saw the baby moving her head from side to side, kicking her feet under the covers. Looking into her little daughter's cornflower-blue eyes, Jacintha fought with herself to avoid the steady gaze. Quickly she bent over and lifted her out of the pram, wrapping her tightly in a blanket and placing her on her shoulder, rubbing her back as one of the nurses in the Home had shown her how to do. She crossed the grass to the statue to stare upwards at the boy from NeverNeverland, her single moment of escape.

The baby was sucking her little fist and beginning to murmur. Soon she would be howling at her mother for a morning feed. Tucking her under the covers again, Jacintha turned the pram to continue the walk as far as the entrance gates on the far side of the Gardens. Grey storm clouds were gathering, she was cold and exhausted, but resistant to returning too early, she carried on. As usual other mothers and uniformed nannies were pushing their charges in the finest models of Silver Cross carriage prams and pushchairs, making the one she was using, standard issue to residents, look even more battered and old. She avoided meeting anyone's eye, she did not want to answer questions.

The black cast-iron gates near the Albert Monument were an odd source of comfort to her, and her secret pleasure was to read the footplate sign with its reference to the Coalbrookdale Company, Shropshire. At least they stayed the same, these gates, they did not exclude her or her baby. Unlike her own family: her parents, Aunt Lilian, Guiny and Prosper. They had found her this private maternity hospital and hatched the plan: she must have the baby there and, after six months, hand her over for adoption. That was the understanding. The deal. She had no option but to stick with it.

Already three months had gone. The family had kept away.

**SHORT STORY**

\* \* \*

At lunchtime, when the baby was asleep, Jacintha checked her pigeonhole and found a letter from her sister and a message to say someone (no name) had called whilst she was out. Perhaps they would ring back, this mystery caller. She had almost forgotten how to have a phone conversation, what was there to say?

Back in her room she sat down at the small table she used as a writing desk. She had done her chores for the baby, fed her and settled her for an afternoon sleep, and she had the time now to read Guiny's letter and write a reply. Her news was always about her little

# ANN KRONBERGS

daughter: her cooing and murmuring, the flicker of her smile, the tiny fist clutching a rattle and the weather in London, the winter coming on. She had also kept a diary, starting at the end of July with an account of the baby's birth, the full day and night of excruciating pain and agony, leading to the horrific moment of delivery with the midwife wielding forceps when she was too weak to push anymore.

She heard the shrill, repetitive phone ringing in the distance, and moments after, a rap at the door:

'Miss Buddicom, there's a call for you. The caller, a gentleman, rang earlier. You may take it in the office.'

She opened the door and quickly followed the nurse along the corridor. The caller must be her father or brother, she thought. Perhaps they were in London and would actually come to see her. Unlikely, on second thoughts. The office was empty. Jacintha picked up the receiver on the secretary's desk and heard a deep breath at the other end of the line, someone talking in a whisper, speaking her name, sounding every syllable, tagging on her nickname.

'Jacintha – Cini?' Only the family called her this, or childhood friends she never heard from these days. Four, maybe five people at most.

'Sorry. Please can you speak up? This is a bad line. I can hardly hear you.'

He was repeating himself, sounding her names once more.

'Jacintha? Cini? It's me, Eric.'

Unmistakably this was his voice speaking that unlikely name which had never suited him. But what could she possibly say to him?

'Eric? I thought you were in Burma …'

Her voice tailed off. How arrogant she must have been, so insensitive to his suffering, so blind to what it was like to be caught in a trap with no way out. She had mocked his anguished letters to her, had found no words of comfort for him. Eventually she gave up replying to him. Forgot.

He was talking very quickly, explaining himself.

'When I got back, I went to Shropshire, hoping I'd see you at Aunt Lilian's – only you weren't there. It was obvious they were all hiding something: what on earth's going on? Where are you? Have you had some kind of accident?'

There was a pause, he expected her to reply, but how could she begin to tell him? He continued.

'I managed to persuade Prosper to give me this number, but I don't have your address, you see. I'm in London, Notting Hill, in fact. My aunt has let me use her flat for a short while. She's in Paris you see.'

She was trying to make sense of what he was saying. Eric was only a five- or ten-minute walk away. No time at all. Her soulmate from that other time and place when amber shafts of sunlight cut through the branches of woodland trees on a summer's evening. But this was London. Autumn. How could she begin to share with him the facts? Tell him what had happened that night in Oxford, what an idiot she'd been?

Wait – what was he saying now? Something about wanting to see her. There was real urgency in his voice, he was pleading with her to allow him this one visit.

'Please, before I leave for Paris.'

Jacintha ached to say yes. To give in. She'd show him the baby, even let him hold her. He'd understand without judgement, not like all the others. But in her mind, she was closing the gate, shutting him out. She could never let him see the mess she was in. The milk was seeping through her blouse, tears streaming down her cheeks. No. Eric must never see her here, in this place.

She had no idea what to say to him, only managing to stammer out a few words of absolute finality.

'Listen, Eric. I'm sorry. There's no going back. It's impossible.'

Hastily she replaced the receiver and ran back to her baby.

**SHORT STORY**

**Ann Kronbergs was Education Trustee for The Orwell Society from 2017-2023.**

# REVIEW ESSAY

**'Perfidious Albion': Britain and the Spanish Civil War**
Paul Preston
London: The Clapton Press, 2024 pp 282
ISBN: 9781913693350

Paul Preston is arguably the most important historian of the Spanish Revolution and Civil War writing in Britain today and so anything he has to say about George Orwell and his Spanish experiences and writings is inevitably of great interest. His new collection of essays, *'Perfidious Albion': Britain and the Spanish Civil War*, contains two essays that deal with Orwell: 'Light and shadows in George Orwell's *Homage to Catalonia*' and 'The Cold War, Anglo-Saxon historians and the Spanish conflict'. They are both unremittingly hostile, so much so that the book has predictably received a very favourable review by John Green in the *Morning Star* titled 'Orwell got it wrong' (22 February 2024). The *Morning Star*, it is worth remembering, still routinely refers to the great working class revolt against communist tyranny in Hungary in 1956 as a 'counter-revolution'!

Regardless of this, we still have to take Preston's discussion seriously, but exactly how useful is his attempted demolition of Orwell's reputation? A good case can actually be made that in his eagerness to discredit Orwell, he on occasions completely throws overboard the academic standards that inform the rest of his work.

The book is mainly concerned to explore the British government's role in helping bring about the triumph of the nationalists. Preston certainly exposes 'Perfidious Albion' to good effect, but what about his assault on 'Perfidious Orwell' (my phrase, not his)? Preston's main grievance against Orwell is that, instead of celebrating the Popular Front as republican Spain's only hope, he condemned it as a Stalinist front that rolled back the revolution, crushed the revolutionary left and weakened the fight against Franco. What makes it even more galling is that *Homage to Catalonia* is 'almost certainly the most sold and most read book about the Spanish Civil War'. He acknowledges how 'vivid and well-written' it is but, nevertheless, the book is 'deeply flawed by his acceptance of the partisan views of anarchist and POUM comrades as well as ignorance of the wider context'. *Homage to Catalonia* is, in fact, written 'from a political angle by a cocksure partisan telling the reader what to think'. Preston's obvious sympathy for the Popular Front is clearly not partisan presumably because it is supported by academic research, but Orwell's hostility apparently is partisan because it is the result of firsthand experience! He actually favourably quotes historian Robert Stradling's hilarious criticism of Orwell's failure to conduct any research while he was in Spain (pp 160, 161, 163, ibid). He was, of course, too busy getting shot in the throat by a fascist sniper and escaping from the communist secret police!

Leaving this aside, Preston goes on to try to strengthen his case by discrediting Orwell. He discusses the question of whether or not Orwell understood Spanish and Catalan well enough to be a reliable witness to what was actually going on, concluding that John McNair's assertion that he did was 'implausible'. McNair, it is worth remembering, was with Orwell in Spain and fled the country alongside Orwell and his wife, Eileen, in June 1937 who all faced possible murder during a communist clampdown. So what did he know about it? Indeed, Orwell's claim to understand Spanish actually 'throws doubt on his honesty'. He also quotes Frank Frankford's assessment of Orwell, to the effect that he was a 'supercilious bastard' who 'really didn't like the workers'. Moreover, Frankford thought 'he was on the wrong side' (pp 163, 170).

While McNair is implausible, Frankford, who had accused his POUM comrades of being allied with the fascists in the *Daily Worker* on 14 September 1937, is presumably credible. Frankford actually claimed to have seen Georges Kopp, Orwell's POUM commander, returning from a meeting with the fascists behind their lines where they had been planning the May events in Barcelona. Orwell responded ferociously, writing a detailed repudiation of Frankford's allegations that was signed by another fourteen militia veterans and published in the *New Leader* on 24 September. At the time, Kopp was still being held in prison in Spain, starved and brutally mistreated. For some reason, Preston does not mention this and it obviously does not throw any doubt on Frankford's honesty.

He is also guilty of selective quotation when it serves to discredit Orwell. He quotes Bob Edwards dismissing Orwell as 'a bloody scribbler with no actual experience of the working class struggle other than as a journalist observer' (p. 168). This was during a heated argument regarding Orwell's determination to transfer from the POUM militia to the communist-run International Brigades in Madrid. Now Edwards's quote comes from his Introduction to the Folio edition of *Homage to Catalonia* (1970) and, it has to be said, it gives a rather misleading impression of Edwards's view of Orwell. Let us consider Edwards's assessment of the man. He first met Orwell when he transferred from the mainstream POUM militia, where he had been serving as a corporal, into the Independent Labour Party (ILP) contingent. Orwell had been training Catalan volunteers who, according to Edwards, 'idolized him' (ibid). One

**REVIEW ESSAY**

can only wonder what this contributes to the debate regarding Orwell's grasp of Spanish and Catalan! Edwards notes their political differences with Orwell arguing that 'the Spanish social revolution had gone too far and had to be halted if the war was to be won' (ibid). In fact, at this time Orwell was sympathetic to what he understood to be the Popular Front position and was, as we have seen, determined to join the International Brigades on the Madrid front. This disagreement precipitated Edwards's diatribe.

Edwards goes on to write of how Orwell suffered terribly from the cold and had 'a great phobia against rats'. On one occasion, his shooting of 'a particularly adventurous rat' precipitated a major exchange of fire with the fascists that left two POUM buses and 'our treasured cook-house … destroyed'! And then there were his excursions, crawling on all fours, under machine gun fire, to collect potatoes from an abandoned plot a couple of hundred yards into no-man's land. Edwards refused to join him in this particular enterprise, although presumably he helped eat the potatoes! More seriously, he tells of how on another occasion, he and Orwell had strapped a badly wounded comrade to a donkey, but when they were taking him back to a first-aid post, they got lost and found themselves in a village occupied by the fascists. They quickly made their escape. Their comrades found the whole episode extremely amusing, but it left him with 'an insight into the absolute dependability of George Orwell and his supreme fearlessness in crisis'. Edwards also describes how what Orwell saw in Barcelona in May 1937 impacted on him. He saw firsthand how 'the hard-won gains of the workers and peasants in Catalonia, and particularly in Barcelona itself, had been whittled away' and this convinced him to 'set himself firmly against the view that he had previously held' and to become 'an open opponent of Stalinism'. The May events, as Edwards puts it, ended Orwell's 'temporary flirtation with the Stalinists. From practical experience he soon realized that they were a party of counter-revolution and were fearful of the power that had been placed in the hands of the workers'. He sums Orwell up as 'a brave, indomitable fighter for human freedom' (ibid: 5-11). Preston, of course, ignores all of this in favour of relishing the description of him as 'a bloody scribbler'!

While the May events may have had a massive impact on Orwell's political trajectory, Preston dismisses them as 'a confused, unimportant and obscure incident in a war he did not understand'. They were, in fact, 'provoked by the need to remove obstacles to the efficient conduct of the war'. Orwell's understanding of the episode, indeed of the whole conflict, was flawed, wrong-headed, mistaken. And Preston cannot resist abusing both the POUM and the anarchists for committing terrible atrocities that Orwell ignored. He accuses the POUM of 'imposing a wave of criminality' on the city of Lerida, effectively abandoning the war effort because they 'seemed most concerned with leading the good life in the requisitioned homes of the wealthy'. As for the anarchists, in Barcelona by early August 1936, 'they had committed many crimes and over five hundred civilians had been murdered'. At the same time as he abuses the anarchists and the POUM, Preston at every stage gives the communists the benefit of the doubt, certainly playing down whenever possible the terror they unleashed against the revolutionary left, a terror that he puts down to 'Russian paranoia' whereas it was, in fact, one of the very cornerstones of Stalinism. And, of course, when Orwell and his wife, Eileen, 'left Barcelona in a hurry, believing that they were being pursued by the Republican security police', there is no evidence that they were actually in any danger at all (pp 172, 175-176, 179, 182, 187)! While Preston certainly acknowledges that the Stalin regime was only helping the republic in pursuit of its own strategic objectives – that had seen it earlier ally with fascist Italy and would soon see it ally itself with nazi Germany – nowhere does he really grasp the enormity of Stalinism, either in the Soviet Union itself nor on the international stage. Orwell, of course, did not have this problem after Spain and, instead, dedicated himself to fighting communist influence on the left, fighting it by polemical argument and discussion and in his later fiction, rather than intimidation and slander.

REVIEW ESSAY

Preston goes on to argue that Orwell later recognised that he had misunderstood what was going on in Spain. He acknowledged that the crushing of the revolutionary left and the rolling back of the revolution was not responsible for the republic's downfall, but never amended *Homage to Catalonia* to reflect this understanding. The reason he gives for this failure is that Orwell was very likely content to leave the book as it was so it could serve as a weapon in the Cold War. Before we examine this proposition, however, it is worth considering whether or not Preston has got Orwell's later understanding of the Spanish Revolution right. He focuses on Orwell's essay, 'Looking back on the Spanish War', written in the autumn of 1942, where he acknowledges that the outcome of the war was in reality decided by the Great Powers. Even if the revolution had triumphed in republican Spain, Franco would still in all likelihood have won because of the military strength of the nationalist forces, following the assistance they received from fascist Italy and nazi Germany.

Preston draws the wrong conclusion from this assessment, however. Orwell had actually concluded that the republican cause was doomed to defeat whether or not the revolution triumphed. Presumably, Preston would agree with this, but as far as Orwell was

**JOHN NEWSINGER**

concerned this was certainly no reason to rally behind the Popular Front nor to seek reconciliation with the Stalinists. If the republic was doomed to defeat anyway, why should he compromise his politics by supporting the Popular Front? While Orwell no longer considered revolution as having been the recipe for victory in Spain, he remained a socialist and what he had seen during the May events and afterwards demonstrated that both the Popular Front and more particularly the Stalinists had nothing to do with socialism. Rather, the Stalin regime's supporters back in Britain, who were covering up events in Spain, had to be fought if a genuine socialist movement was to be built.

Instead of recognising that Orwell's anti-Stalinism was motivated by his socialist politics, Preston seems to endorse the proposition that it was all to do with his embrace of the politics of the Cold War. He supports the contention that *Homage to Catalonia* 'took an essentially Cold War line'. Now to argue that a book published in 1938 took a Cold War line does seem somewhat ahistorical even without bothering to read the actual book. And any serious reading of the book makes the contention positively ridiculous. But Preston is so determined to discredit Orwell on the Spanish Revolution that he ploughs on regardless. Apparently, Orwell's indictment of Stalinism in Spain was useful to his new friends in the US and British secret states, so the book was left as it was, a condemnation of the Popular Front and Stalinism. As Preston puts it, a picture 'has emerged in recent years of an Orwell who compromised his personal integrity by allowing himself to become part of the Cold War offensive of both the CIA and the British Security Service's Information Research Department' (pp 207-208).

Certainly, Orwell's involvement with the IRD, forwarding to them his infamous 'little list' of crypto-communists, was appalling. But not only does this have nothing whatsoever to do with *Homage to Catalonia*, Orwell's politics at this time cannot be reduced to just this. He remained a strong defender of civil liberties, including those of communists, and an opponent of any anti-communist purges in the civil service, insisting that communist influence within the British left had to be fought by polemical argument and discussion.

To be fair, Preston does make clear that Orwell never became pro-Franco, unlike the US and British governments, but this is faint praise. In fact, Orwell remained determinedly anti-Franco, something that Preston manages to ignore. Let us look at some of the evidence of his continuing hostility to the Franco regime and support for the resistance. In 1941, he had published Arturo Barea's *Struggle for the Spanish Soul* in the Searchlight series of short radical books that he and Tosco Fyvel edited. Here, Barea urges that it was essential for Britain to make clear its war was against fascism and that included the Franco regime. He pointed out that it was only fear of the 'defeated Republican masses' rising up again that prevented Franco from declaring war alongside the nazis, the Spanish people serving as 'a sheet anchor to prevent any bellicose adventure of their betters at Germany's side'. The Spanish people were Britain's 'silent ally'. Barea insisted, somewhat over-optimistically, that the defeat of the nazis would inevitably lead to the overthrow of Franco's regime (Barea 1941: 115, 122). Later, after the war, Orwell reviewed the third and last volume of Barea's autobiography, *The Clash*, in the *Observer* (24 March 1946). Here, he wrote, Barea recounted his experiences in Madrid during the revolution and civil war: '… the wild enthusiasm and chaos of the early period, the expropriations, the massacres, the bombing, and shelling of the almost helpless city, the gradual restoration of order, the three-sided struggle for power between the common people, the bureaucracy, and the foreign Communists'. He worked in the Radio Service, but found his own position increasingly difficult as communist influence increased. As Orwell points out: 'Mr Barea's wife was a Trotskyist. That is to say, she was not a Trotskyist, but she was an Austrian Socialist who had quarrelled with the Communists, which, from the point of view of the political police, came to much the same thing. There were the usual episodes: sudden incursions by the police in the middle of the night, arrest, reinstatement, further arrest…' Barea and his wife fled the country in the summer of 1938. Orwell praised Barea's 'exceptional book, and the middle section of it must be of considerable historical value' (*CWGO* XIX: 166-168).

**REVIEW ESSAY**

A few days after the review appeared, on 26 March 1946, Orwell was one of the speakers at a meeting called by the Freedom Defence Committee, a civil liberties organisation that he had helped set up, demanding the release of 226 Spanish republicans, including communists, being held prisoner in a camp at Adlington, Lancashire. These men had fought fascism in Spain, had been used as slave labour by the nazis in occupied France and had been imprisoned in Britain for eighteen months awaiting deportation back to France. The meeting was chaired by Fenner Brockway and among the other speakers was Victor Gollancz.

This was not the end of his interest in Spain. Later, on 3 March 1949, the *News Chronicle* published a letter from Orwell protesting against the death sentence that the Franco regime had just imposed on the Spanish anarchist trade union leader, Enrique Marco Nadal, arrested and tortured after clandestinely entering the country from France where he had fought in the resistance. As Orwell observed, he 'was sentenced to death without trial' and 'has probably not done anything that would constitute a legal offence in any democratic country' (*CWGO* XX: 51). It was commuted to an indefinite term

**JOHN NEWSINGER**

of imprisonment and he was eventually released towards the end of 1964. Two days later, Orwell wrote to his friend David Astor, editor of the *Observer*, turning down his request for an article on the Spanish Civil War. He had already written on the subject for the newspaper on a number of occasions and, anyway, was currently not well enough to do any writing. Instead, he recommended Astor try Franz Borkenau, Arturo Barea or Gerald Brenan. Most interesting, he wrote that if Astor wanted an article on the International Brigades then he recommended Tom Wintringham, Humphrey Slater or Malcolm Dunbar, all of whom had served in the brigades in senior positions.

All this is certainly not what one would expect of the Orwell whom Preston constructs. And let us end with noticing the setting up in Paris of a committee for the help and protection of Spanish democrats that was reported in *Tribune* on 2 September 1949. Among the signatories were Albert Camus, Jean-Paul Sartre, André Gide, Jef Last, Ignazio Silone, Stephen Spender, Pablo Casals, André Breton, François Mauriac, Carlo Levi ... and George Orwell (*CWGO* XX: 164). Orwell died soon after on 21 January the following year.

REFERENCES

Barea, Arturo (1941) *Struggle for the Spanish Soul*, London: Searchlight

Edwards, Bob (1970) Introduction to Orwell, George, *Homage to Catalonia*, London: The Folio Society

Orwell, George (1998) *The Complete Works of George Orwell: Smothered Under Journalism, 1946, Vol. XVIII*, Davison, Peter (ed.) London: Secker & Warburg

Orwell, George (1998) *The Complete Works of George Orwell: Our Job is to Make Life Worth Living 1949-1950, Vol. XX*, London: Secker & Warburg

**John Newsinger, a retired academic and the author of *Orwell's Politics, Hope Lies in the Proles: George Orwell and the Left* and *Chosen by God: Donald Trump, the Christian Right and American Capitalism***

# REVIEW ESSAY

**George Orwell and Russia**

Masha Karp

London: Bloomsbury Academic, 2023 pp 294

ISBN: 9781788317122

The Soviet Union was central to George Orwell's thinking and writing, and it is quite remarkable that it is only now, more than 70 years since his death and after a veritable torrent of books and articles about him, that a book has appeared devoted to his thinking, writings and actions on this topic.

Masha Karp first encountered Orwell and his *Nineteen Eighty-Four* in her home town, then known as Leningrad, in 1980, when she read a clandestine copy of this strictly forbidden work that her friends had managed to obtain. They were all impressed by the way that Orwell, who had never visited the Soviet Union, presented in the novel's fictional Oceania various aspects of their personal experiences, such as the wearisome official propaganda and the shortage of consumer goods. What impressed them most of all was his ability 'to piece together their psychology' and thereby present 'the inner monologue of a secret "thought-criminal"' (p. 234). They were not alone: this was a common response of other readers across the Soviet bloc. Karp has since written a substantial Russian-language biography of Orwell and has translated many works, including Orwell's *Animal Farm*, into Russian. She is also the editor of the biannual Orwell Society *Journal*.

This book covers a great deal in its 294 pages. It starts by investigating the possible influence upon Orwell in the early 1930s of French dissident communists, via their personal connections with Orwell's aunt Nellie Limouzin, the partner of the French left-wing Esperanto buff Eugène Adam, who worked under the name Lanti.[1] Orwell's Hampstead landlady and employer in the 1930s, Myfanwy Westrope, was a member of the Independent Labour Party and an early critic of Stalinism. Another possible influence was Reg Groves, one of the pioneer Trotskyists in Britain, who had met Orwell when working in Westrope's bookshop. A common belief amongst them was that the Soviet regime had become a dictatorship *over* the proletariat, an idea that was central to Orwell's subsequent thinking on the topic.

We then come to Orwell's public emergence as a socialist in the mid-1930s, with *The Road to Wigan Pier*. Karp shows that this book not only contained the well-known excoriations of the left and in particular the official communist movement, with his recoiling from 'Bolshevik commissars (half gangster, half gramophone)', 'shock-headed Marxists chewing polysyllables' and 'the stupid cult of Russia', but also took aim at Sidney and Beatrice Webb and George Bernard Shaw, strong admirers of Stalin's Soviet Union, with their idea of socialism as 'a set of reforms which "we", the clever ones, are going to impose upon "them", the Lower Orders'. Orwell's adventures in Spain come next, which not only confirmed in a most vivid manner his existing fears about the conduct of the Soviet regime, but also brought home to him the degree to which Stalinist behaviour had infected the official communist movement as a whole, not least the Communist Party of Great Britain.

Orwell's near-fatal experience of Stalinism in Spain led to his developing a long-lasting interest in the mechanics of totalitarianism in the Soviet Union and nazi Germany and the motives of the intellectuals in Britain who fell for the lure of Stalinism during the 1930s and 1940s. Karp covers this in considerable detail, and introduces the Austrian thinker Franz Borkenau, a former member of the Communist Party of Germany now resident in Britain, 'whose influence upon Orwell's development as a social thinker is impossible to overestimate' (p. 186). Borkenau's works, three of which Orwell reviewed,[2] contended that pre-1917 Bolshevism had little to do with Western socialist movements, but stood in the tradition of authoritarian, violent Russian nihilist intellectuals such as Nechayev and Tkachev,[3] and that the Soviet Union and nazi Germany were essentially identical societies with a collectivised economy and totalitarian political system. Another influence upon Orwell whom Karp covers at some length is Eugene Lyons, a disillusioned US fellow-travelling journalist, whose hefty account of his times in the Soviet Union, *Assignment in Utopia*,[4] brought to a Western readership the infamous '2+2=5', which Orwell turned from a witty propaganda slogan – having the First Five-Year Plan completed in four years – into the symbol of Winston Smith's abject defeat at the hands of the Ingsoc regime in *Nineteen Eighty-Four*. Other influences, such as André Gide, another disillusioned supporter of the Soviet Union, and Bertrand Russell, are also covered, if in less detail.

We then come to World War Two, during which Orwell dealt with at length and with increasing disquiet the upsurge of pro-Soviet propaganda, both in left-wing publications and in the mainstream media and official war propaganda, and the way that its uncritical nature required writers consciously to deceive their readership, to tell lies and to suppress facts that were politically inexpedient to broadcast. Orwell's refusal to go along with the lionisation of

Stalin and the Soviet Union culminated in his allegory of the Soviet experience, *Animal Farm*, which faced many obstructions before it was finally published, not least those placed by Peter Smollett, a Soviet agent who had managed to obtain an official government job and used it to promote a rosy view of the Soviet Union.

Orwell's final years in the immediate post-war period are covered next, with an emphasis upon his continued ruminations around the questions of economic collectivism and democracy, the writing and reception of *Nineteen Eighty-Four*, and his continued polemics against Stalinism and its supporters in Britain. Also investigated in some detail is his cooperation with Arthur Koestler in the abortive League for the Rights of Man.

A chapter that will bring previously little-known information to many readers looks at the background to translations of *Animal Farm* that were aimed at a Soviet bloc readership. A Polish edition, translated by Teresa Jeleńska, was published in London in late 1946, and Ukrainian and Russian language editions were to follow, the former published by Prometheus (Prometey) in Munich, the latter by Possev, also in Germany.[5] Both the Ukrainian and Russian editions were subject to cuts; the Introduction to the former was abridged,[6] whilst the latter was outrightly censored by Possev's editors on the grounds that they objected to Moses the raven, the symbol of religious obscurantism. Karp also looks at the Russian-language editions of *Nineteen Eighty-Four*, which first appeared in 1955 in four issues of *Grani*, an émigré journal and then, helped by a grant from Orwell's widow Sonia, published by Possev as a book, and at the official Soviet translation of the novel, a very limited edition published exclusively for the higher echelons of the élite in order that they be acquainted with foreign publications. Karp informs us that it was not until 1988 that *Animal Farm* and *Nineteen Eighty-Four* were officially published in the Soviet Union, and even then not in Russia but in Latvia and Moldavia respectively, serialised in small-circulation journals.

## CLAIMING ORWELL

This book, however, is not just a detailed account of Orwell's writings on the Soviet Union and the related topics of the official communist movement and totalitarianism. It is a polemical work, one which stands within the longstanding tradition of liberal and conservative writers of championing Orwell for their own political purposes.[7]

It is a pertinent question as to why Orwell, alone amongst radical socialists, has become a hero for so many writers who do not endorse his political outlook. Let us now investigate Orwell's engagement with the topics discussed in this book and, in so doing, assess the validity of this long-running liberal and conservative claim upon him.

## DEMOCRACY, TOTALITARIANISM AND THE SOVIET UNION

Karp shows that Orwell clearly recognised a central feature of Stalinist society, indeed of totalitarian societies in general: the contrast between the absolute infallibility of the regime and the infinite malleability of its ideology within the scope of an intensely politicised social framework. Various observers had noted during the Moscow Trials the regularity with which yesterday's heroes became today's villains; Orwell understood that such dramatic shifts were a *necessary* feature of totalitarianism, that they could not be avoided as the leadership was forced to deal with the complex needs of the day.[8] This was perhaps the most perceptive of Orwell's political observations. Following from this, he made much of the manner in which apologists for totalitarian regimes were obliged faithfully to follow these twists and turns in their paeans to them, often with risible and far-reaching *volte faces*, especially when major policy shifts took place. Moreover, when writing about the Soviet Union, Orwell insisted, any writer or journalist who was 'fully sympathetic' to it needed 'to acquiesce in deliberate falsification on important issues', not merely in respect of present-day events but also when discussing its past: history itself needed to be infinitely malleable.[9] Here, I feel that Orwell showed a sharper understanding of the question, especially in respect of the need to revise the historical record, than many other commentators of that period.

Karp also notes that Orwell took a great interest in ascertaining why British intellectuals came to subscribe to the 'cult of Russia' during the 1930s, and again I would add that his writings were more perceptive than those of many of his contemporaries. He concluded that, disillusioned with crisis-ridden Britain, they found in the Soviet Union 'a Church, an army, an orthodoxy, a discipline ..., a fatherland, a Fuehrer..., patriotism, religion, empire, military glory..., father, king, leader, hero, saviour', that is, '*something to believe in*'. This was the 'patriotism of the deracinated', the substitution of the seemingly dynamic, vibrant Soviet Union, thrusting ahead, brushing aside all obstacles, for the capitalist world which was struggling to pull itself out of economic slump, with country after country descending into fascist obscurantism. It was easy for middle-class youngsters to see in the Soviet Union all the certainties that Britain provided their fathers and grandfathers but which it could no longer supply. At this juncture, Orwell tended to view pro-Soviet attitudes amongst British intellectuals as the result of their naïveté, that they could 'swallow totalitarianism' because they had 'no experience of anything except liberalism'.[10] All the same, his understanding that they recognised that, compared to the ineffectual floundering of Britain's rulers, in Moscow there was an élite which could really rule, prefigured his subsequent conviction that they possessed a predilection for authoritarianism. Before long he was detecting amongst pro-Stalin intellectuals a decided tendency towards power-worship that was no different to that expressed by supporters of Hitler or Mussolini, with a 'cult of power' which was 'mixed up with a love of cruelty and wickedness *for their own sakes*'.[11]

However, when it came to his understanding of Soviet society, what it was and how and why its rulers had betrayed the Soviet republic's founding principles and came eventually to head a totalitarian state, Orwell's writings were far weaker, with certain important matters only lightly touched upon.

Orwell barely discussed the key question of the Soviet economy, although the idea of economic planning and the Soviet Five-Year Plans were topics of wide discussion at the time. He staunchly rejected the validity of the Moscow Trials but, beyond passing remarks, he wrote little on the topic other than the superb parody to which Karp refers (p. 100) and in two pieces on Koestler, in which he presented some rather tentative explanations as to why the defendants made such abject confessions.[12] However, one needs to be fair to Orwell, as quite a few other commentators who attempted to ascertain the rationale of the trials were equally nonplussed by the horrific spectacle.[13]

As for the socio-economic nature of the Soviet Union, in the late 1930s Orwell wondered if it was 'a peculiarly vicious form of state capitalism' which 'does not seem to be very different from fascism'.[14] Here, Orwell was swimming with the tide, as the idea that the Soviet Union had evolved into a state capitalist society and comparisons between Stalinism and nazism were by no means uncommon at various points of the political spectrum by then.[15] By 1940, he had concluded that the Soviet Union and nazi Germany were 'rapidly evolving towards the same system', a collectivised society, neither capitalist nor socialist, ruled by a totalitarian dictatorship.[16] Although this idea was already in circulation in Britain during the late 1930s and had been given a major boost by the Molotov-Ribbentrop Pact in August 1939, and Orwell was thus following a trend of thought that was increasingly common,[17] there can be little doubt, as Karp states, that Borkenau exerted a considerable influence upon him. Whether he was actually responsible for Orwell's shift in outlook is unclear, but some of the key ideas expressed in his *The Totalitarian Enemy* emerge in Orwell's subsequent writing.[18]

Orwell insisted that democracy was a fundamental requirement of a genuine socialist society, as it was the only means by which a

REVIEW ESSAY

collectivised economy could escape a totalitarian outcome, although he remained vague about the actual nature of popular control of the economy and the state.[19] He rooted the rise of totalitarianism in the Soviet Union. Hence he wrote in early 1939: 'The essential act is the rejection of democracy – that is, of the underlying values of democracy; once you have decided upon that, Stalin – or at any rate someone *like* Stalin – is already on the way' (italics in the original). He rejected Trotsky's criticisms of Stalinism, stating that the exiled Bolshevik could not avoid taking responsibility for the evolution of the Soviet regime, and there was no certainty that 'as a dictator' he would have been preferable to Stalin,[19] for 'all the seeds of evil were there from the start and … things would not have been substantially different if Lenin or Trotsky had remained in control'.[20]

But why did the Bolsheviks abjure democracy? Except for one brief moment, in 1946, when he considered that the rise of Stalinism was the result of the almost impossible objective conditions facing the Bolsheviks,[21] he generally endorsed the view of Borkenau and John Plamenatz, that in 'a backward country like Russia', with a tiny working class, Marx's concept of 'an overwhelmingly powerful proletariat sweeping aside a small group of opponents, and then governing democratically through elected representatives' was impossible, whereas we had 'the seizure of power by a small body of classless professional revolutionaries, who claimed to represent the common people but were not chosen by them nor genuinely answerable to them', and the Soviet republic thus could not avoid being 'the dictatorship of a handful of intellectuals ruling through terrorism'.[22]

Karp investigates the possible influence upon Orwell of French dissident communists, some of whom developed a libertarian outlook, often close to anarchism, and notes his contact with anarchists during the Spanish Civil War and afterwards in Britain. Worth noting in this respect is a wartime anarchist tract in Orwell's possession, which declared that 'the present state of Russia' was 'the inevitable result … of the Marxist-Leninist practice of centralisation and dictatorship' of the Central Committee of the Communist Party:

> Bolshevist tactics wherever they are applied will always lead not to the emancipation of the workers from the chains which now enslave them. … They lead inevitably to the absolute of the totalitarian state. *By allowing power over the instruments of production to pass out of their own hands into those of a so-called revolutionary government,* the workers will achieve not liberty but a slavery as bad or worse than that they sought to escape from.[23]

The emphasised passage shows the essential difference between the anarchist analysis and that of Borkenau and Plamenatz. Despite the concurrence in placing the blame upon the Leninist style of party, the former considers the central problem to be that *the workers let power slip from their hands*. It also provides a strong clue to Orwell's thinking behind *Animal Farm*, for this is what he recognised had occurred in the Soviet Union, what he saw occurring in Spain, and what he subsequently portrayed in the novel. It is a question of control within a revolution – the masses or the leadership? – not the legitimacy of the revolution itself.[24]

This brings us to a fundamental problem for liberal and conservative champions of Orwell: that, for all his rejection of Bolshevism, he never disavowed the October Revolution itself. Although liberals will sympathise with the downtrodden poor and oppressed, a revolution that aims at replacing capitalism with a socialist society will always be as unacceptable to them as it is to conservatives. However critical Orwell was of the Bolsheviks, however pessimistic he was about the fate of the Russian revolution, he never disavowed the revolution that put the Bolsheviks in power, nor did he reject the idea of radical social change. In *Animal Farm*, the animals' revolt against Farmer Jones is celebrated in no uncertain terms: there is no criticism of the animals' expropriation of the farm nor of revolutionary violence. A key factor in Orwell's condemnation of official communism was that it was *counter-revolutionary*. Karp cites Orwell's 'Spilling the Spanish beans' (p. 87) to this effect – 'communism is now a counter-revolutionary force…'[25] – but does not develop the question, nor notes how this sits uncomfortably with the liberal and conservative championing of Orwell. In *Animal Farm*, the tragedy is not that the animals seized power, but that their revolution was purloined by the leadership, which then became a self-conscious ruling élite. It is the *betrayal* of the revolution that is central to Orwell's writings.

## ORWELL THE NEO-CONSERVATIVE?

Karp investigates in some detail Orwell's pondering over the question of economic collectivism and the need for popular control, but she keeps her ideas within the paradigm adhered to by quite a few other liberal and conservative champions of Orwell, of questioning his continued allegiance to socialism by, on the one hand, referring to his worries about the dangers of undemocratic collectivism and, on the other, projecting him into the future, with the implication that eventually he would have in effect rejected the very idea of socialism, even if he retained some vestigial formal attachment to it. Here she draws heavily upon an essay by the neo-conservative Norman Podhoretz, which claims that the post-war development of capitalism would have undermined the basis for Orwell's opposition to the capitalist system,[26] adding that Orwell's insistence that capitalism leads to dole queues and wars did not take into consideration the welfare state capitalism that emerged after the Second World War (p. 191). But the Keynesian phase of capitalism was transient, a product of the post-war recovery and boom, lasting but a few decades as not merely liberal and conservative currents but also right-wing social-democrats came to turn their back on it and to subject the welfare state to sustained attack, starting in Britain in the late 1970s under a Labour government. Podhoretz made his assertion in the early 1980s, precisely the period when, for the first time since the 1930s, we had the spectacle of homeless youngsters living on British city streets. The idea that the author of *Down and Out in Paris and London* would have endorsed the kind of capitalism favoured by Podhoretz & Co. – the blatantly inegalitarian, socially disintegrating, privatised, deregulated, anti-welfare, anti-union, neo-liberal capitalism of the last four decades – really does beggar belief.

Karp does not demur from Podhoretz's conviction that Orwell would have adopted the neo-conservative stance in respect of the Soviet Union on the international scene, that he 'would have felt a greater kinship with the neo-conservatives' on this topic than with those favouring *détente* or nuclear disarmament.[27] However, the idea that Orwell's opposition to Stalinism would have led him to adopt the Cold War orthodoxy of the perpetual 'Soviet threat' is a big assumption.

Orwell's siding with the USA if it and the Soviet Union came to blows – in March 1947, Orwell felt that the Soviet Union was 'preparing for war against the Western democracies'[28] – had a definite reluctance about it, harking back to his choosing of the lesser of two evils in 1939: liberal-democratic Britain versus nazi Germany. What we had with right-wing social-democracy was, after a brief flirtation with a 'third way' between the USA and Soviet Union, the adoption of Atlanticism, a strong identification with the USA and especially with its foreign policy. It was one thing to side – and reluctantly at that – with the USA as a lesser evil in a direct confrontation between it and the Soviet Union, and quite another to adopt an Atlanticist policy of ideological, diplomatic and political subordination to Washington. It was perfectly possible, on the one hand, strongly to oppose the repressive internal procedures of the Soviet bloc and be critical of the activities of the Western Communist Parties and, on the other, also to view the Soviet Union, once it had marked out its domain and East-West tensions had settled, as effectively a status quo power and to reject the idea that Moscow represented a constant deadly threat to the world. This is, more or less, the standpoint of much of the Labour Party left: a democratic socialist road, between Stalinism and Cold War orthodoxy.

Twice – in his withheld preface to *Animal Farm*[29] and replying to Randall Swingler in 1946 – Orwell strongly insisted (to cite the latter) that whilst the 'dominant brand' of orthodoxy was 'not criticising Stalin', he felt that this could – indeed, probably would change and it would then be *de rigueur* 'to attack him': 'But,' he added, 'I should not regard this as an advance. Nothing is gained by teaching a parrot a new word. What is needed is the right to print what one believes to be true, without having to fear bullying or blackmail from *any* side' (italics in the original).[30] Karp seems surprised by this (p. 131), but it is not at all out of character.

Just as the pro-Soviet lobby indignantly rejected even the slightest criticism of the object of their adoration, the more fervid Cold Warriors branded as 'soft on communism' anything that did not present the Soviet Union as an inexorable totalitarian threat to the West. Even *détente*, an attempt to reduce tensions within the Cold War global division, was seen by Podhoretz & Co. as a dangerous concession to Moscow. Orwell lashed out at what he called the 'smelly little orthodoxies' of his time:[31] why should the subsequent Cold War orthodoxy, a mindset that was immeasurably more pervasive than the transitory pro-Soviet sentiments of the Popular Front days and World War Two – and, let us remember, one whose credibility was undermined by the events of 1989-1991, with the collapse of the entire Soviet bloc and the élites' jettisoning with indecent haste their long-proclaimed Marxist-Leninist ideology – be exempt?

It is true that Orwell demonstrated a pessimistic and even fatalistic streak when looking at the prospects for socialism, not least when he wrote in 1938 that 'it would seem that what you get over and over again is a movement of the proletariat which is promptly canalised and betrayed by astute people at the top, and then the growth of a new governing class'.[32] It is equally true that Orwell's vagueness on the question of democratic control of a collectivised economy, combined with his insistence that workers were by and large unable theoretically to grasp the ideas of socialism and that workers who became union officials or labour politicians or who made their way into the radical intelligentsia were merely joining the middle-class socialists thus forming an élite-in-waiting,[33] led him into a political blind alley and must have reinforced his pessimism. Yet to go from there to consider that the development of capitalism in the post-war era would have encouraged Orwell to make his peace with the system he so disliked is to make too great a leap of faith.

## PAUL FLEWERS    TOTALITARIANISM AND BRITISH INTELLECTUALS

Karp follows Robert Conquest in disagreeing with appraisals of *Nineteen Eighty-Four* which see the book as not merely a description of Stalinism but also a comment upon trends within Western society. She writes that, in theory, it should be possible to see the book as a critique of both, but, 'in real life, turning Orwell's satiric lens on different worlds inevitably meant turning it *away* from the one he tried to attract attention to' (p. 246, italics in the original). Although Conquest correctly argued that the society portrayed in the novel was based upon the Soviet Union, and that it came into being through the overthrow of capitalism rather than through its development,[34] it is clear that Orwell was also concerned about the trends towards totalitarianism within society *as a whole*. He hit out hardest at Stalinism because it represented to him the furthest development of the trend. But state censorship and self-censorship in wartime Britain worried him greatly, as he wrote in 1944:

> The MoI [Ministry of Information] does not, of course, dictate a party line or issue an *index expurgatorius*. It merely 'advises'. Publishers take manuscripts to the MoI, and the MoI 'suggests' that this or that is undesirable, or premature, or 'would serve no good purpose'. And though there is no definite prohibition, no clear statement that this or that must not be printed, official policy is never flouted. Circus dogs jump when the trainer cracks his whip, but the really well-trained dog is the one that turns his somersault when there is no whip.[35]

Karp cites this passage to claim that Orwell's disgust with the servility of intellectuals towards the Soviet Union was aimed 'of course' at 'left-wing intellectuals' (p. 128). But surely Orwell was directing his fire well beyond the left. Orwell was not talking here about Stalinists nor, more broadly, left-wingers; rather he was addressing what he felt was a potentially dangerous frame of mind at large within Britain, and especially its official structures, one which was not enforced by fear or fiat, nor commanded by a party line dictated from Moscow, but was voluntarily adhered to by those concerned. Despite the infiltration of Soviet agents such as Smollett into the British state and the fondness of adherents of the pro-Soviet lobby for a country under totalitarian rule, it would surely be the case that the offices of state in Britain were overwhelmingly supervised and staffed by people who, whatever their political outlook, would not under normal circumstances be sympathetic to Stalinism. Orwell here was concerned about British official thinking and the ensuing practice adhered to, something that went a lot further than the influence of Stalinism in Britain. We have seen that he was worried that the lionisation of Stalin might merely be replaced by some other orthodoxy: it was not just the uncritical support for one particular totalitarian state that perturbed him; more important was the mindset of ideological conformity and closed dogmatic thinking that underpinned both this example of state-worship and the surreptitious censorship and guidance exercised by the British state during the war.

All the same, it does seem that there were occasions when Orwell was losing his sense of proportion, such as when he wrote in May 1944 that the bulk of the intelligentsia in Britain was 'perfectly ready for dictatorial methods, secret police, systematic falsifications of history, etc'.[36] Some of Orwell's critics have considered that he exaggerated the influence of Stalinism upon Britain's intellectuals. The anarchist George Woodcock claimed that those under the spell of official communism 'had always been a minority'.[37] Robert Hewison stated that notwithstanding the relegitimisation of the Soviet Union after June 1941, there had been a steady drift away from the official communist movement on the part of British intellectuals since 1939 because of the Molotov-Ribbentrop Pact and the 'slow seep' of information about the grim realities of Stalinism.[38]

Certainly by the late 1940s Orwell was kicking at an open door. It is true that during the 1930s praise for the Soviet Union – or at least for aspects of it – went beyond the CPGB and fellow-travellers, and that after June 1941 the Soviet Union was highly respected as a wartime ally. But outwith the pro-Soviet lobby much of the pre-war praise was, as Karp notes (p. 43), predicated upon the introduction there of welfare schemes and economic administration that did away with unemployment, and the wartime respect was a refracted form of British patriotism. All this went after the war; indeed, it is significant just how rapidly pro-Soviet sentiments faded away once hostilities ceased. Official Britain, with Labour in government, quickly adopted a hostile stance towards Moscow. Stalinism had discredited itself through acts great and small, from clamping down upon democratic rights within its newly obtained domain in Eastern Europe – the Stalinist takeover in Czechoslovakia stripped any remaining respect for Moscow from most of the Labour left – to petty acts of bureaucratic cruelty, not least the 'Soviet wives' episode. The group of actual pro-Soviet Labour MPs who so worried Orwell and were expelled from the party numbered a mere four. Soviet welfare schemes and economic administration lost their allure once the Labour government's programme of reforms and the revival of British capitalism led to a steady amelioration of the onerous condition of the 1930s. By the time *Ninety Eighty-Four* appeared, few beyond the declining CPGB and the shrivelled fellow-travelling scene adhered to an unblemished vision of Stalinism. Karp's

REVIEW ESSAY

contention that in 1943 'the majority of the British intelligentsia still believed in the need to support "the Soviet experiment"', is not unreasonable if one takes into account the wartime atmosphere; her assertion that this was still the case at the time of Stalin's death in 1953 (p. 152) is certainly wrong. Had he lived longer, Orwell, with his keen eye, would surely have noticed, even from his remote island home in Jura, the steady disenchantment with the Soviet Union within left-wing circles.

As for the impact of Soviet infiltration into the British state upon public opinion, Karp makes much of the activities of the Soviet spy Smollett in building up the pro-Moscow atmosphere during the war, not least in the almost certain role he played in obstructing the publication of *Animal Farm*. But Smollett was riding the tide. Although, as Karp notes, there was official disquiet about the pro-Moscow fervour, hailing 'our brave Soviet ally' was nonetheless part of the wartime ethos – one account states that 'criticism of the USSR became tantamount to treason'[39] – and as Orwell wrote in his unpublished preface to *Animal Farm*, it just was not done to point to the embarrassing aspects of Soviet society.[40] It certainly seems that Jonathan Cape, initially enthusiastic about publishing it, had been 'got at' by Smollett. On the other hand, Faber & Faber's rejection seems not to have been the result of any intervention on his part, but rather because Orwell's novel ran very much against the prevailing wartime atmosphere, not merely on the left but within British society as a whole. Smollett's role was insidious, but he would not have been able to use his official position to promote the Soviet Union and in so doing to 'advise' Cape unless British government policy itself allowed someone of his views to do that. And, as we have seen, this situation came to a sudden end with the onset of the Cold War after 1945.

HOW TO SEE ORWELL

As we have seen, Karp's book stands within the genre of conservative and liberal claiming of Orwell. To do this his non-socialist champions home in on various facets of his writings, especially his defence of aspects of bourgeois society, his incessant criticisms of other left-wingers, his deradicalisation, his wartime patriotism and his last two novels. Let us consider them in turn.

Orwell certainly defended many aspects of bourgeois society, and he excoriated left-wingers who disparaged them: 'Any Marxist can demonstrate with the greatest of ease that "bourgeois" liberty of thought is an illusion. But when he has finished his demonstration there remains the psychological *fact* that without this "bourgeois" liberty the creative powers wither away' (italics in the original).[41] This was in line with his insistence that a socialist society needed to maintain the better aspects of a liberal democracy. He was presenting his defence of 'this "bourgeois" liberty' not out of any desire to maintain a bourgeois society but in order to emphasise that socialism had to be built upon the gains of the capitalist era, and socialists could not reject them without courting disaster.

That Orwell was very critical of aspects of fellow socialists is undeniable. But this did not mean that he was forsaking the left. Alex Zwerdling put it well, writing that 'his aim was to reform and strengthen, not to discredit the world to which he pledged his loyalty: he was the left's loyal opposition ... his criticism was always designed as internal'.[42] Orwell did, indeed, take pleasure in 'rubbing his own cat's fur backwards', as Bernard Crick put it,[43] but there was a purpose in this. Orwell was so critical of the left *precisely because* he was a left-winger: he considered it necessary to point to the various self-damaging and self-defeating foibles of which the left was guilty in his day (and – one must admit – remains guilty, *mutatis mutandis*, to this day). It was not evidence of any renunciation of socialism on his part.

The radicalism that marked Orwell's socialism into World War Two, peaking with *The Lion and the Unicorn*, had subsided somewhat by the end of hostilities. All the same, Crick argues convincingly that despite this, 'Orwell never changed his values after 1936'. What we had was the replacement of 'the wild hope that he had from 1936 onwards that "the revolution" ... was around the corner' by a 'more realistic' view 'in considering time-scales' of radical social change.[44]

When we come to Orwell's patriotism, as most openly expressed in *The Lion and the Unicorn*, we find that far from being 'king and country' flag-waving, it was based upon two factors that were central to his concept of the struggle for socialism. Firstly, he considered that an internationalist appeal was ineffective, especially to the middle-class people whom he wanted to win to socialism; and secondly, he wanted to defend those aspects of British life that he felt were worth preserving, such as the 'liberty of the individual' and 'the respect for constitutionalism and legality'. He recognised that they were a product of Britain's specific historical development, rather than springing from innate national characteristics and would be threatened by the British ruling class were its power and privileges threatened. As he considered that the aim of socialism was 'a world-state of free and equal human beings' and not any kind of nationally-oriented affair not peculiarly British venture, it is clear that he saw these aspects as necessary features of a socialist society on a global scale, that is, in all countries.[45]

The use in *Animal Farm* of different sorts of animals to represent various social strata coincides neatly with political theories that view

REVIEW ESSAY

the Bolsheviks not as a militant trend within the socialist movement but as a discrete body led by a clique of intellectuals, an élite-in-waiting even, parasitic upon the working class, who consider the rise of Stalinism as the inevitable result of this leadership's coming to power, rather than primarily as the unintentional consequences of the harsh objective pressures upon the Bolsheviks once they were in power. Although Orwell was worried about *Animal Farm* being exploited by the right, as the novel was intended to show the need for a libertarian brand of socialism, the novel became popular with liberals and conservatives *precisely because* it sees the pigs' ascendancy into a ruling élite as an ineluctable process. If it did not, it could not be used as a pro-capitalist work.

The problem with *Nineteen Eighty-Four* is of a different nature. Here, the memory of the revolution that put Ingsoc into power a mere four or so decades in the past, exists in a few fragmentary childhood memories on Winston Smith's part that barely go beyond the hardships caused by social dislocation. The revolution itself – surely an epochal event – hardly exists in the narrative or in Goldstein's 'Book', or for that matter in Ingsoc's own propaganda; the British equivalents of the Russian soviets, factory committees, strikes, demonstrations, passionate debates at mass meetings and street-corner speeches of 1917 are conspicuous by their absence. Smith's journey from a homeless waif to Outer Party member and Minitrue clerk is not traced; it is as if great chunks of his own memory have been eradicated. How we get from the revolution to the situation in 1984 remains a mystery.[46] The theoretical exposition in Goldstein's 'Book' – a series of timeless clichés of ineluctable processes, the struggles amongst 'the High, the Middle, and the Low', with the Middle disingenuously eliciting the help of the Low against the High in order to become the new élite, with 'the same pattern' always reasserting itself – is banal even when compared with those of Cold War or anarchist thinkers.[47]

Moreover, the course of history in the Soviet Union was quite different to that of Oceania. Unlike Borkenau, who insisted that it faced a future 'of terror without end, of hostility towards everything human, of horrors that carry no remedy and which can be cured only *ferro et igni*',[48] Orwell did not feel that the totalitarian stranglehold of high Stalinism was immutable; the world of *Nineteen Eighty-Four* was one which Orwell insisted '*could arrive*' but which was not inevitable.[49] Indeed, within three years of Orwell's death, Stalin was dead and his successors embarked upon a programme of liberalisation. There could be no 'Thaw', no 'Secret Speech', in Oceania. The post-Stalin leadership did not introduce a liberal democracy, let alone a socialist democracy, repression and censorship remained prominent features of the regime but Stalin's successors, nonetheless, steered Soviet reality to some degree away from the dystopia presented in *Nineteen Eighty-Four*, not ever closer to it.

In his essay on the Russian writer Fyodor Sologub, Yevgeni Zamyatin declared:

> The whip has not yet been given its full due as an instrument of human progress. I know of no more potent means than the whip for raising man from all fours, from making him stop kneeling down before anything or anyone. I am not speaking, of course, of whips woven of leather thongs; I am speaking of whips woven of words, the whips of the Gogols, Swifts, Molières, Frances, the whips of irony, sarcasm, satire.[50]

*Animal Farm* and *Nineteen Eighty-Four* were satires. Yet they failed in their purpose because they could only *describe* the phenomenon they were satirising, were unable convincingly to *explain* it – that is, to explain it in a way that differed from the explanations offered by anti-socialists – and therefore they could be – and, indeed, have been – misused.

Orwell's 'whips woven of words' fell readily into the hands of his political opponents, those who were and remain opposed to his vision of a democratic, libertarian socialism. Orwell did protest against the way in which his last novel was used as anti-socialist propaganda but, compared to the millions of people who have read *Animal Farm* and *Nineteen Eighty-Four* within the ideological framework of the Cold War, how many – or, better put, how few – have seen his protests or consulted his writings which provide a far broader and clearer idea of his overall political outlook?

Masha Karp's book contains much of value to all those interested in George Orwell and his thoughts and writings, but in this reviewer's opinion it is unduly coloured by the author's insistence upon championing Orwell for her own political viewpoint, one which is a considerable distance from his. She concludes by appealing to Orwell in her quest 'to keep the liberal tradition alive' (p. 273). Orwell, indeed, wished to preserve the positive aspects of capitalist society, but his aim, as we have seen, was not to preserve capitalism, even in its liberal form, but to help ensure that capitalism would be replaced by a socialist society that was more democratic, more human, than anything that preceded it. Orwell's writings on the Soviet Union, the official communist movement and, more generally, totalitarianism, with all their perceptive insights and for all their shortcomings, were part of that quest, and should be considered as such.

## PAUL FLEWERS

### NOTES

[1] Karp reminds us that Orwell had a lifelong aversion to Esperanto and that Newspeak, Oceania's debased new language in *Nineteen Eighty-Four*, was heavily based upon it

[2] Borkenau 1937, 1939, 1940

[3] Borkenau was not the originator of this theory, which was to become a central factor in Cold War orthodoxy; it had been expressed by, for example, the Czech democrat Tomáš Masaryk and the Russian populist Benedict Myakotin during the early years of Bolshevik rule: Masaryk 1922; Myakotin 1924. Borkenau presumably adopted the theory only after leaving the official communist movement in 1929

[4] Lyons 1938

[5] Karp notes that Possev was the publishing house of the National Labour Alliance of Russian Solidarists, a far-right organisation, but unfortunately does not mention that Prometey was the publishing house of the Ukrainian Revolutionary Democratic Party, a left-wing organisation formed in Germany in 1947 by longstanding Ukrainian leftists and people who moved leftwards from the Ukrainian nationalist milieu

[6] Karp explains that Orwell allowed the translator Ihor Szewczenko to trim, if he so wished, a few sentences from his preface which he, Szewczenko, thought unsuitable for West Ukrainian readers. As the original English typescript has gone astray and we are reliant upon a re-translation from the Ukrainian, we no longer have the full text of the Preface. Szewczenko subsequently regretted his wielding of the editorial scissors

[7] For a detailed account of the championing of Orwell by liberal and conservative commentators up to the late 1980s, see Rodden 1989; this phenomenon has continued unabated over the ensuing three and a half decades

[8] *The Listener*, 19 June 1941

[9] The prevention of literature, Orwell 1984a [1968]: 85; Karp views this as one of his best essays

[10] Orwell 1940: 166-169

[11] Raffles and Miss Blandish, Orwell 1946: 218

[12] *New Statesman*, 4 January 1941; Arthur Koestler, Orwell 1946: 185-201

[13] Flewers 2008: 145-154, 169-171

[14] *New English Weekly*, 9 June 1938

[15] Flewers 2008: 72, 107-108, 131-133, 143-144

[16] Review of Borkenau, *The Totalitarian Enemy*, Orwell 1984a [1968]: 40-41

[17] Flewers 2008: 131-133, 184-200

[18] Although James Burnham's popular work *The Bureaucratic Revolution* did not appear in Britain until 1942, and thus could not have influenced Orwell's change of view on the nature of the Soviet Union, it was nonetheless a major influence on him; much of Goldstein's 'Book' in *Nineteen Eighty-Four* reads like a paraphrase of it. Unfortunately, Karp does not write much on Burnham's book nor his ensuing treatise on the prevalence of power-seeking in political life, and their influence on Orwell's thinking and writing: Burnham 1942, 1943

[19] *New English Weekly*, 12 January 1939

[20] Catastrophic gradualism, Orwell 1984c: 35

[21] What is socialism?, Orwell 1998a: 61-62. It is not clear what caused this uncharacteristic assertion. Although Orwell knew Trotskyists, such as Reg Groves, and was long familiar with Trotskyist ideas, he never at any other time subscribed to anything resembling the Trotskyist analysis of the rise of Stalinism

[22] Marx and Russia, Orwell 2003: 72-73

[23] Anonymous 1942: 28, my emphasis; Orwell's pamphlet collection, Orwell 1998b: 282

[24] As Orwell informed the American libertarian Dwight Macdonald, stating that he was referring in *Animal Farm* to a revolution led by 'unconsciously power-hungry people', and presenting the moral of the book: 'You can't have a revolution unless you make it for yourself; there is no such thing as a benevolent dictatorship' — letter to Dwight Macdonald, Orwell 1998a: 507

[25] *New English Weekly*, 29 July 1937

[26] Podhoretz 1986: 66-67

[27] ibid: 63

[28] Burnham's view of the contemporary world struggle, Orwell 1984c [1968]: 365

[29] *New Statesman*, 18 August 1995

[30] Annotations to Randall Swingler, The right to free expression, Orwell 1998a: 443

[31] Charles Dickens, Orwell 1946: 75

[32] *New English Weekly*, 16 June 1938

[33] Orwell 1983: 44, 117, 154-155, 189-195

[34] Conquest 1989: 88

[35] As I Please, Orwell 1984b: 212

[36] Letter to Noel Willmett, Orwell 1984b [1968]: 178

[37] Woodcock 1970 [1966]: 198

[38] Hewison 1988: 25-26

[39] Northedge and Wells 1982: 151

[40] *New Statesman*, 18 August 1995

[41] Orwell 1940: 172-173

[42] Zwerdling 1978: 5

[43] Crick 1983: 4

[44] Crick 1989: 201; see also Newsinger 2018: 107-108

[45] *The Lion and the Unicorn*, Orwell 1984a [1968]: 78-81, 93, 102

[46] I thank Mike Belbin for pointing out to me the absence of the Ingsoc revolution in *Nineteen Eighty-Four*

[47] Orwell 1969 [1949]: 162-166

[48] Borkenau 1949: 120

[49] Letter to Francis Henson, Orwell 1984c [1968]: 564

[50] Zamyatin 1991: 221

## REFERENCES

Anonymous (1942) *The Russian Myth*, London: Freedom Press

Borkenau, Franz (1937) *The Spanish Cockpit*, London: Faber & Faber

Borkenau, Franz (1939) *World Communism: A History of the Communist International*, London: Faber & Faber

Borkenau, Franz (1940) *The Totalitarian Enemy*, London: Faber & Faber

Borkenau, Franz (1949) Stalin im Schafspelz, *Der Monat*, No. 14 pp 203-210 (I thank Mike Jones for the translation)

Burnham, James (1942) *The Managerial Revolution*, London: Putnam

Burnham, James (1943) *The Machiavellians: Defenders of Freedom*, London: Putnam

## PAUL FLEWERS

Conquest, Robert (1989) Orwell: *1984, Tyrants and Typewriters*, London: Hutchinson pp 86-96

Crick, Bernard (1983) Introduction, Orwell, George, *Nineteen Eighty-Four*, Oxford: Clarendon

Crick, Bernard (1989) Orwell and English socialism, *Essays on Politics and Literature*, Edinburgh: Edinburgh University Press

Flewers, Paul (2008) *The New Civilisation? Understanding Stalin's Soviet Union, 1929-1941*, London: Francis Boutle

Hewison, Robert (1988) *In Anger: Culture in the Cold War, 1945-60*, London: Methuen

Lyons, Eugene (1938) *Assignment in Utopia*, London: Harrap

Masaryk, Tomáš (1922) The Slavs after the war, *Slavonic Review*, June

Myakotin, Benedict (1924) Lenin (1870-1924), *Slavonic Review*, March

Newsinger, John (2018) *Hope Lies in the Proles: George Orwell and the Left*, London: Pluto

Northedge, F.S. and Wells, Audrey (1982) *Britain and Soviet Communism: The Impact of a Revolution*, Basingstoke: Macmillan

Orwell, George (1940) *Inside the Whale*, London: Gollancz

Orwell, George (1946) *Dickens, Dali and Others*, New York: Harcourt Brace

Orwell, George (1969 [1949]) *Nineteen Eighty-Four*, Harmondsworth: Penguin

Orwell, George (1983 [1937]) *The Road to Wigan Pier*, Harmondsworth: Penguin

Orwell, George (1984a [1968]) *Collected Essays, Journalism and Letters, Vol. 2*, Harmondsworth: Penguin

Orwell, George (1984b [1968]) *Collected Essays, Journalism and Letters, Vol. 3*, Harmondsworth: Penguin

Orwell, George (1984c [1968]) *Collected Essays, Journalism and Letters, Vol. 4*, Harmondsworth: Penguin

Orwell, George (1998a) *Complete Works, Vol. XVIII*, London: Secker & Warburg

Orwell, George (1998b) *Complete Works, Vol. XX*, London: Secker & Warburg

Orwell, George (2003) The Observer *Years*, London: Atlantic

Podhoretz, Norman (1986) If Orwell were alive today, *The Bloody Crossroads: Where Literature and Politics Meet*, New York: Simon & Schuster pp 50-68

Rodden, John (1989) *The Politics of Literary Reputation: The Making and Claiming of 'St George' Orwell*, New York: Oxford University Press

Woodcock, George (1970 [1966]) *The Crystal Spirit: A Study of George Orwell*, Harmondsworth: Penguin

Zamyatin, Yevgeny (1991) *A Soviet Heretic*, London: Quartet

Zwerdling, Alex (1978) *Orwell and the Left*, New Haven: Yale University Press

### NOTE ON THE CONTRIBUTOR

Paul Flewers is a freelance historian. He received a PhD in history from the School of East European and Slavonic Studies, University College London. He is the author of *The New Civilisation? Understanding Stalin's Soviet Union, 1929-1941* (2008), the editor of *George Orwell: Enigmatic Socialist* (2005), *1933: Warnings from History* (2021) and co-editor, with John McIlroy, of *1956: John Saville, E.P. Thompson and* The Reasoner (2016). Email: trusscott.foundation@blueyonder.co.uk.

BOOK REVIEWS

A Jura for Julia
Ken MacLeod
Illustrations by Fangorn
Newcon Press, 2024 pp 219
ISBN: 9781914953828

In April 1943, when he reviewed Tangye Lean's *Voices in the Darkness* for *Tribune*, George Orwell asked of broadcasting: 'Is it better from a propaganda point of view to tell the truth or to spread confusing rumours and promise everything to everybody?' (*CWGO* XV: 85). The reviewer of Orwellien (if I can distinguish in this way from 'Orwellian') writing, particularly fiction, has to ask: 'Is it better to avoid spoilers?' That is, if a story has a plot or a revelation, should it be shared before the potential reader has taken up the book in question? In the best spirit of British compromise, I must do both: avoid spoilers and reveal the truth where relevant.

Like much science fiction published in Britain today, Ken MacLeod's collection of short stories comes from a specialist small publisher who have produced a work of excellent quality. The title story has not appeared before, but it is a sequel to MacLeod's 'Nineteen Eighty-Nine', which was first published in *Parsec*, the online 'zine, in 2021; the two stories top and tail the new book. In 2023, the anthology, *Parsec in Print*, included the first story in a *best-of* anthology from the publisher. Forgetting I had read this left me wondering if I was experiencing *déjà vu* for a few pages. Since I can report that 'Nineteen Eighty-Nine' has a sequel, the story clearly is not a last word. This, in turn, puts us in confrontation with Orwell, who quoted from Yevgeny Zamyatin's *We*, when he reviewed that in 1946, but rejected the argument in his novel published three years later. Orwell countered Zamyatin's '... Numbers are infinite. There can't be a last one.' 'Then why do you talk about the last revolution?' with *Nineteen Eighty-Four*'s boot stamping on a face forever. Some critics such as Thomas Pynchon, in his Introduction to the 2000 reprint of *Nineteen Eighty-Four*, have referred to the 'Principles of Newspeak' Appendix being written in the past tense as evidence that all the events of the book are past, but that ignores Orwell's typical writing techniques – he never wrote in a future tense and almost never wrote in the present tense. Only two years later, after reading Orwell's novel closely, John Wyndham was able to include a chapter on economics (of the Triffid oil society) within the body of his novel, *The Day of the Triffids* (1951). Narrative tense is unlikely to be a clue to the future or no-future of Winston Smith's world.

So let us have a first, perhaps only, spoiler. In MacLeod's year 1989, Winston Smith has not been shot and is back in his miserable job. Things seem to have changed a little – or perhaps Orwell did not have space to mention them – and the telescreens are broadcasting images from Eastasia, where anti-authority rioting has broken out. Two characters from the past re-appear, one of whom – Syme – Winston thought had been vaporised, though without any proof, while the other is O'Brien who – it turns out – has access to a very different underground.

The grounds on which MacLeod's revolution takes place, (this is my spoiler), reveal an extremely close reading as his tipping point depends on sections of *Nineteen Eighty-Four* almost one hundred pages apart (pages 192 and 296 of the first edition). He also gives an interesting reason why the revolution should be driven by events overseas, as O'Brien reveals to Winston where his images of the 'Golden Country' originated, and why Winston has that association.

Twenty-two years have passed between the events of 'Nineteen Eighty-Nine' and the story 'A Jura for Julia'. Julia Hobbs is now (after her eventual release from joycamp she went back into education) a professor of Computational Literature at University College London, studying the books written by the kaleidoscopes of the Ministry of Truth during the INGSOC period. MacLeod then throws in another clever mind-meld: using modern terminology Julia reveals that the machines had to be trained by 'large language models', such as today's AI systems. Party members, though, would have watched their language, so the systems would have been limited: what was there instead? To take the language of the proles and feed that much richer diet into the maws of the machine learning systems. It was not true that the proles were not surveilled, but equally how could they be sold prolefeed if the machines did not use their language? Like the tipping point in 'Nineteen Eighty-Nine', MacLeod has been able to bounce off another little-thought-of few lines in Orwell's original novel.

There are no oligarchs mentioned in Julia's world, but just as quickly as the Soviet Union was broken up and exploited have the tools of the Ministries been re-purposed. The telescreens have been reduced in size, for instance, and now everyone carries a miniscreen for instant communication. Sounds familiar? Perhaps the revolution has not been betrayed, but Julia ends by feeling that.

The story is set on the remote Scottish island of Jura as Julia determines to go to Barnhill where Orwell lived on and off after the Second World War. Julia, though, does not know that – she is in a different time stream, remember, the one where the world was devastated by atomic wars and then divided by three superpowers, before further revolutions. Julia does know something affects her about the place, and in the final pages of the story we enter a different type of science fiction, one of parallel worlds, as she discovers (if only we could!) Orwell's carbon copy of the typescript he sent to his publishers, and finds herself there. Julia looked at a photograph of Winston Smith in the first paragraph of the story, and he is in her mind in the last sentence. According to MacLeod things will end very differently.

There are thirteen stories in *A Jura for Julia* and some of them feel light-weight, while others will have a greater reference for those interested in the politics of Scottish Nationalism (or for those who feel they have been excluded from Scottish Nationalism), but 'Nineteen Eighty-Nine' and *A Jura for Julia* are stories to read and re-read.

**L.J. Hurst maintains The Orwell Society website and Facebook page.**

## Orwell's Ghosts: Wisdom and Warnings for the Twenty-First Century

Laura Beers

W.W. Norton & Company, New York, 2024 pp 240

ISBN: 9781324075080 (hbk)

In an interview promoting her compact but rich and illuminating book, *Orwell's Ghosts*, Laura Beers identifies the 6 January 2021 violent insurgency at the United States Capitol as the event that 'crystallized the importance of understanding Orwell and reading Orwell in our current political moment'. Yet, she clarifies, her realisation came not so much from the attempted insurrection itself, but its aftermath – specifically claims of 'Orwellian censorship' from the likes of Donald Trump, Jr. when his father was expelled from Twitter (now X) and US Senator Josh Hawley, whose book contract with Simon & Schuster was cancelled due to his apparent solidarity with the rioters. These instances, Beers explains, called to mind a 'tension, effectively, between ideas about liberty and freedom of speech, but then also the importance of truth in speech, both of which are very much emphasized by Orwell throughout his career'. Confronting and understanding this tension prompts Beers's timely and highly readable book.

*Orwell's Ghosts* deftly traces the ways that this core question – how to negotiate the right to expression with a commitment to intellectual and ethical honesty – stands at the heart of so much of Orwell's thought, and Beers brings her readings of Orwell to bear on the dominant political, social and economic issues confronted by Western liberal democracies today. 'Why does Orwell matter now?' is an evergreen question, but Beers's insightful answers, crafted for Orwell specialists and general readers alike, make for a key intervention within Orwell scholarship and a lively addition to the wider public discourse. If Beers wrote her chapters to be accessible to audiences 'who have not read Orwell at all, but who are familiar with the term Orwellian and curious to learn more about its origin and meaning' (p. 18), her analysis provides insights and new contexts that will make the book fresh for Orwell experts and aficionados. Moreover, her attention to topics – notably Orwell's views on women and feminism – in which Orwell's relevance emerges from his ideological blind spots helps fill a gap in Orwell criticism.

# BOOK REVIEW

As her title suggests, in *Orwell's Ghosts*, Beers sets her eyes on the various ways in which Orwell's preoccupations, ideas and political engagements haunt the twenty-first century. The book's Introduction and initial chapter lay groundwork by establishing its exigence and providing some key historical and biographical background. In her Introduction, Beers cycles through several of the countless examples in which Orwell is invoked by politicians, pundits, activists and other public figures, as well as prevailing issues of today – concerns about disinformation, a wave of rising authoritarian regimes, neo-imperial global conflicts – that create 'uncanny parallels between the inter-war decades and our present political moment' (p. 14). The visibility of Orwell in public discourse and the resonances between his era and ours 'give Orwell's writing a renewed salience in the twenty-first century' (p. 14). In terms of her book's structure, after an initial chapter, 'From Eric Blair to George Orwell', which provides an account of Orwell's life and career – focusing on his ties to the British Empire, his education and vexed class identity, and the creation of his major works – Beers turns to how Orwell refracts today.

This project begins in earnest starting with Chapter 2, 'The thought police: Censorship, cancel culture, and "fake news"'. Like subsequent chapters, this one covers considerable historical, biographical and literary ground. Beers's references range from Orwell's writings about his experiences in Burma, northern England and Spain, to 'The list', Orwell's infamous catalogue of authors whom he believed were excessively sympathetic to the Soviet Union. Unifying Beers's accounts of these topics is the apparent conflict found between two iconic Orwell quotations: first, 'If liberty means anything at all, it means the right to tell people what they do not want to hear', and, second, liberty 'is the freedom to say that two plus two make four' (p. 43). These two ideals of freedom – the ability to say what one pleases and the commitment to upholding truth – were 'frequently in tension in Orwell's time, and nowhere is a similar tension between truth and liberty clearer than in recent debates over political censorship and cancel culture' (p. 44). At first, the chapter's attention to social media and online speech may seem to raise low stakes. However, Beers explains that not only are debates over free expression versus intellectual honesty the main sites for contemporary invocations of Orwell, but also that the moderation of online content and social media's dissemination of information sits on a spectrum with legislative book bans, control of school curriculum and repressive censorship in authoritarian regimes. The full implications of debates over truth and speech on social media, then, are varied and profound.

To be sure, Orwell abhorred censorship, a commitment forged in part by occasions upon which he directly saw or experienced some form of it, whether from a publisher fearful of legal action or from the Soviet-backed Spanish government's persecution of left-wing militias. Yet, surprisingly, Beers points us to Orwell's notorious list of potential fifth columnists – for many commentators, an unforgiveable instance of Orwell betraying his commitment to free expression – as the key to understanding where Orwell would stand on contemporary questions of censorship and so-called cancel culture. According to Beers, Orwell's willingness to draw up 'The list' 'reveals his privileging of truth over freedom of speech when the two came into direct conflict' so he was 'willing to do his part to ensure that authors whom he perceived to be knowingly mendacious were not offered a platform to voice their untruths' (p. 55). Drawing again on *Nineteen Eighty-Four*'s memorable maxim, Beers writes: 'In a free society, citizens should theoretically be able to proclaim 2 + 2 to be whatever they want it to be. But that is not Orwell's idea of freedom from censorship. Orwell believed in liberty above all else, but liberty, in his view, was predicated on an assumption of personal and social responsibility' (p. 57). When this critical facet to Orwell's understanding of free speech is taken into account, Beers continues, the 'weight of evidence suggests that Orwell would have been more disturbed by the mendacity of those claiming to have been canceled than he would have been by the decision of some media not to publish them' (ibid). Reassessing 'The list' helps Beers split the difference between Orwell's twin values of free expression and truth.

From this determination, Beers turns to Orwell's writing on political language. Starting with two of Orwell's most enduring essays, 'Politics and the English language' and 'Why I write', Beers then turns to the appendix to *Nineteen Eighty-Four*, 'The principles of Newspeak'. The logic behind Newspeak for the Party, famously, is that 'if certain language could be eliminated, the realities it had described would in effect cease to exist' (p. 66), a project with which Beers finds resonance in Russian state control of media. Newspeak logics are not exclusive to outright authoritarian regimes, though. Beers suggests that in the US, principles of Newspeak sit behind recent state laws that restrain how teachers address the history of slavery and LGBT issues. Beers cycles through additional examples from the UK and France, all mobilised to conclude that Orwell 'believed that any society held a potential for tyranny, and that it was important to be vigilant against abuses of power by regimes of all political persuasions, including purported democracies' (p. 74). Understandably, Beers never pronounces what Orwell would think on any given contemporary issue. Instead, she draws out how the underlying conflicts behind her examples chime with the political problems and questions to which Orwell's writing responded, sketching the parallels between Orwell's time and our own and, from there, how Orwell's perspectives offer guidance.

Beers brings similar depth and nuance to her next two chapters, respectively focused on a rising tide of populist authoritarian political movements and on class inequality. In Chapter 3, 'Isms', Beers begins once more with her book's central Orwellian tension: 'Because Orwell valued truth and liberty so highly, he was determined to expose the assault on those values from both the Stalinist totalitarianism of the left and the fascist totalitarianism of the right' (p. 76). Her survey of Orwell's writing on tyranny traverses the spectrum between these poles, noting how Orwell attended not only to despotisms abroad but also at home. In particular, despite his frequent casual racism, Beers places Orwell's hostility to the British Empire in which he served, and his wider anti-imperialism, alongside his denunciations of totalitarian regimes. Such a perspective on Orwell allows Beers to use his anti-authoritarianism as a lens to view twenty-first century authoritarian societies, such as Russia, as well as tyrannical histories and tendencies in the UK and US. After that chapter, Beers turns to questions of inequality. Here, Beers's main contemporary context is the prevailing neoliberal order in Western liberal democracies. She shows how economic, cultural and political inequalities soared over the past few decades, accelerating in the austerity conditions following the 2008 financial crisis. This portrait resembles similarly intense levels of inequality during Orwell's lifetime. While Beers never lets Orwell off the hook – she makes clear how Orwell's distance from working class experience often expressed itself as condescension towards the poor – this chapter by and large reads Orwell's analysis and prescriptions as directly applicable today.

Contrasting with Beers's general endorsement of Orwell's view on inequality is her subsequent chapter about Orwell on women, feminism and gender relations. In what might be the best chapter in *Orwell's Ghosts* – at least, the most lively and necessary – Beers confronts the misogyny and patriarchal biases laced throughout Orwell's writing and thought. Beers joins a wave of feminist engagements with Orwell – including Sylvia Topp's biography *Eileen* (2020), Anna Funder's memoir-cum-literary criticism *Wifedom* (2023) and Sandra Newman's novel *Julia* (2023) – which collectively act as overdue successors to Daphne Patai's *The Orwell Mystique* (1984) and Beatrix Campbell's *Wigan Pier Revisited* (1984), both landmark, but in many ways dated, studies. Beers, admirably, does not seek to rescue Orwell from his own misogyny nor rehearse personal and social contexts that rationalise Orwell as simply a product of his era. Instead, she begins with the recognition that 'Orwell was indisputably a chauvinist, even by the standards of his time' (p. 131). From that starting point, Beers sets out to explore 'what his writing reveals about his gender politics and that of many other members of the progressive left coalition in the interwar decades, and how far Western society has or has not traveled in terms of gender relations over the past eighty years' (p. 132). Early in this chapter, Beers cites Orwell's reference to feminists within a list of caricatured 'cranks' to be found in socialist circles, a motley coalition also including nudists, pacifists and Quakers. Noting that, in the 1930s, 'there were few radical feminists of any stripe' in the first place, and that the 'average feminist … was not an extremist, nor beyond the political pale', Beers concludes that 'the inclusion of feminists on Orwell's crank list was, at best, provocative' (p. 130). In this way, Orwell anticipates later associations of feminism with a kooky progressive fringe and, more specifically and recently, in the US political trope of 'the Bernie Bro', as well as in the fact that, in the UK, the Labour Party has not had a woman party leader. Exploring such echoes, Beers determines that 'the contradictions between socialism and feminism that impeded progress on gender relations in Orwell's time continue to act as a roadblock to gender equality in ours' (p. 129). This chapter's analysis yields a withering critique of Orwell and a sobering picture of the present.

At the same time, Beers acknowledges that productive, hard-earned transformations in conceptions of gender, gender relations and, in particular, gendered violence between Orwell's time and today propel hers and others' reassessments of Orwell. Citing increased recognition of Orwell's misogyny and sexual violence in Orwell scholarship as well as writing for general audiences, Beers writes: 'In the light of our current understanding of sexual harassment and assault, Orwell's casual disregard for women's bodily autonomy – in both his writing and, apparently, in his youthful practice – has become harder to ignore' (p. 157). For her part, Beers confronts these aspects of Orwell's thought, writing and character unflinchingly. However, she disavows any intention of 'cancelling' Orwell, in the sense of defaming 'previously respected or venerated individuals because of revelations about their attitudes or actions that arguably delegitimize their claims to our respect' (p. 158). Refusing to toss the baby out with the bathwater, Beers insists: 'There is still much that is prescient and valuable in Orwell's writing, both for understanding his own era and for making sense of our own' (p. 159). In short, Beers is even-handed in her account of Orwell's dismal record on women's liberation and the relationships between gender equality and other forms of equality. Even as she documents Orwell's ideological blind spots and instances of gendered violence, rightly taking him to task, Beers employs this critique not as grounds for dismissing Orwell's total body of work but, instead, as an avenue towards better comprehending Orwell, his oeuvre and legacy, and a nuanced reckoning of socialism with feminism.

The final full chapter attends to Orwell's prescriptions for democratic socialism in Britain. Drawing primarily from Orwell's long essay, *The Lion and the Unicorn: Socialism and the English Genius*, Beers unpacks Orwell's 'blueprint for a truly English revolution – how the country he loved could throw off the capitalist-imperialist yoke that he hated and build a social democratic future' (p. 162). The timing of *The Lion and the Unicorn*'s 1941 publication is significant for, as Beers writes: 'Orwell believed that the unique circumstances of the Second World War had created an opening for radical social change in Britain and the fundamental restructuring of Britain's empire' (p. 188). Beers traces Orwell's vision in the relative successes and failures of the actual welfare state that emerged in Britain following the war and Labour's 1945 landslide electoral victory. She also finds in the 2020 Covid-19 pandemic a contemporary analogue to Orwell's Second World War as both a crisis and a moment of political opportunity. Of these two juxtaposed events, Beers asks: 'Was there, in fact, a missed opportunity during either the Second World War or the recent pandemic to sustain the social cohesion that existed at the height of the crisis and usher in a permanent democratic renegotiation of the social contract toward the type of egalitarian society Orwell envisaged?' (p. 189). The chapter reflects on this core question from a number of angles, from persistent class and gendered exploitation in Britain itself to the fraught and unequal relationship between the Global North and the Global South. Across her meditations in this chapter, Beers offers valuable insights into Orwell's democratic socialism and astute analysis of recent world events, but shies away from drawing firm conclusions. Instead, she leverages her comparisons to ponder the viability of 'the types of revolutionary changes in the balance of wealth and power that Orwell advocated for' and 'whether the democratic socialist revolution that Orwell envisaged in 1941 is, in fact, within our grasp' (p. 190). Such urgent and challenging questions feed directly into Beers's Afterword, 'For freedom's sake'.

In her brief finale, Beers isolates Orwell's political purpose: 'Orwell wanted a better, more equal, and socially just world. At the same time, he wanted a world in which the personal liberties and individual freedoms that he valued so highly were safeguarded' (p. 193). As Beers details, in the decades after Orwell's death, his reception often skewed disproportionately towards the latter priority – for instance, as seen in the Western rhetoric of individuality during the Cold War and in Apple's appropriation of *Nineteen Eighty-Four* imagery to conflate computing technology with personal liberation. But, in our current moment, Beers sees an emerging opportunity to rebalance Orwell's legacy by recuperating his devotion to equality and social justice. She writes: 'Orwell's works … have much to offer us as we weigh the competing demands of truth and tolerance and free speech and fair speech in the internet age. Yet, Orwell can offer even more to the left, if the left takes him as a writer who was determined to chart a political path that would achieve meaningful social equality without sacrificing personal liberty' (p. 201). Beers detects this turn in recent work on poverty and inequality within sociology, economics and political science, all of which reflects a far broader backlash, in the wake of the 2008 financial crisis, 'against the excesses of neoliberalism [that] has led even the staunchest defenders of liberalism to support the need for the state to blunt the forces of inequality'. One might even detect this shift, if we grant a definition of 'the left' that includes the US Democratic Party, in the reclaimed rhetoric of freedom found in Kamala Harris's 2024 presidential campaign. *Orwell's Ghosts* ends on the optimistic note that Orwell's reconciliations of collective and individual freedoms, like his squaring of free expression with intellectual honesty, stand poised as the benevolent spirits of the twenty-first century. Whether one ultimately agrees with this outlook or not, *Orwell's Ghosts*, without question, provides an illuminating look at Orwell, his writings and his legacies. The book is timely, to be sure, but also offers enriching perspectives that will inform Orwell scholarship and criticism in the longer term.

**Jackson Ayres,**
**Texas A&M University-San Antonio, USA**

## 1948: A Critical and Creative Prequel to George Orwell's 1984

Brian May

University of Exeter Press, 2024, pp 188

ISBN: 9781804131299 (hbk)

With *1948*, Brian May has produced something unique in Orwell Studies that explores *Nineteen Eighty-Four* from creative, critical and pedagogical angles. The monograph includes four sections: an Introduction, a novella called 'From the archives of Oceania', a teaching supplement and an extended critical essay, 'Orwell Agonistes', that analyses Orwell's life and work with reference to 'From the archives'. I admire May's attempt to be innovative and take methodological risks. Not only does he address Orwell's relationship with modernism, his study is a kind of modernist performance that draws artistic lines of flight alongside commentary on the Orwellian condition. We could use more fanciful thought experiments of this kind in academic writing, especially given our increasingly anti-intellectual climate. That said, May's effort is encumbered by too much exposition about his procedure and his own artistic/scholarly viability. Perhaps this is a result of the publisher being anxious about his experimentation and compelling him to over-explain himself. Whatever the case, if a student of mine had written the book, I would encourage them to mind the first rule of creative writing: 'Show more; tell less.' At the same time, May seems keen on having *1948* taught alongside *Nineteen Eighty-Four* (commonly *1984* in the United States) in the classroom. The back-cover copy says it will appeal to students of dystopian fiction, 'revisionary' fiction and 'reception studies' so what feels like an excess of hand-holding to me may be ideal for formal pedagogy.

May lays the groundwork for his project in the Introduction, rightly making a case for Orwell's continued importance today in the light of 'Orwellian phenomena' such as Brexit, Putin, America First, Trump, 'fake news', alternative facts, rising anti-semitism and so on (p. 1). This rationale is subsidiary to the case he makes for *1948*, 'a work of literary criticism-*plus*, one that balances its critical discussion with a creative intervention. Both critically and creatively, it is designed to illuminate, explore and elaborate upon aspects of Orwell's post-war moment *c.*1948, as well as Orwell's responses to it, which were likewise critical and creative (pp 1-2). The subsequent description of the book's various segments is partly an extended disclaimer that approaches an apology for being interstitial. There is a palpable subtextual anxiety here: May seems worried that readers will not understand the novella, which he contextualises and explicates at great length. He begins by saying that it 'closely quotes, parodies and pastiches figures and refigures, tropes, and trumps Orwell's *Diaries* even as it creates a kind of prequel to *Nineteen Eighty-Four*' (p. 2). In terms of form, he writes: 'Part cleft palette/palate, part roman-à-clef, "From the archives" comprises a dual and dueling series of diary entries written by a renegade named Cedric B. O'Malley ("Winston Smith" but, as will be seen, not just Winston Smith) and by his sister, Avril (based upon Avril Blair, Eric Blair's younger sister)' (p. 3). Additionally, he notes that the creative impetus of 'From the archives' is undergirded by a critical refrain as a composite 'meditation on Orwell, a response to Orwell that is neither strictly critical nor strictly creative' (p. 6). This is all well and good, but overall, May seems not to want to leave anything to readers, and he even includes a short section that tells us how 'From the archives' should be read.

Technically, May is not doing anything wrong here. The introductions to scholarly monographs are meant to be explanatory. What unsettles me is the specific way he plays the dual roles of scholar and fiction writer: his bedside manner slips into over self-reflexivity, unconsciously *yearning* for his book to *work* as a hybrid text. I think it does work, but it would be much more effective if May scaled back his critical impulse to explain his creative gambit at such length.

By way of fictional documents and diary entries primarily composed by the O'Malley siblings, 'From the archives' parodies and pastiches Orwell's style, imagining what he may have written as an extension of his anti-utopian vision while mirroring the disorienting and oppressive atmosphere of *1984*. In the 'Editor's Foreword', a nameless narrator provides context for the diaries. 'Millions of the documents residing in the Archives of Oceania were destroyed in Trafalgar Square ("Victory Square," during the Oceanic era) in The Great Conflagration of 1987. This was the massive incineration of official records conducted in October of that year in reaction to the Inner Party ("IP") or so-called Blue Rebellion of 1986, the first of the three major rebellions constituting The Great Rebellion ending in 1989' (p. 19). Through the narrator, May establishes a tone and use of language that reflects *1984* with uncanny precision. Despite efforts to eradicate the archives, however, some documents survived, among them fragments of Cedric and Avril's notations. Orwell wrote most of *1984* at a farmhouse named Barnhill on the remote island of Jura in Scotland, where he moved to in 1946 – in order to recover from the trauma of World War Two and his wife's death, seeking solitude to focus on writing. Likewise 'From the archives' is set on 'planet Jura', as Cedric calls it, where the O'Malley family (including Cedric's wife Caroline and stepdaughter Gillian) has absconded from the societal collapse of Oceania (p. 26). Here and elsewhere, May riffs on Orwell's biography, which bleeds into the novella, pulling from Orwell's fiction and his own diaries.

The author's modernist sensibility may be most clearly identifiable in the prose of the O'Malleys, namely Cedric, 'a writer, humanist, [and] so-called man of Culture' whose affected, bombastic, lyrical style echoes a Joycean mode of narration. Intertextuality is not limited to Orwell. As May says in the critical supplement, for instance, it is well known that 'Orwell was particularly fascinated by James Joyce and *Ulysses*; T.S. Eliot and his "Prufrock" also impressed him' (p. 142). Orwell is also a vehicle whereby other modes are channelled. At first, the diary entries go back and forth between Cedric and Avril as they contemplate their predicament and worry about their rural lifestyle, itemising how many eggs their hens produce on a given day. The textual relationship between the O'Malleys also alludes to Orwell and his sister, who contributed to his 'literary operation', says May in 'Orwell Agonistes': 'For when Orwell was too ill to continue his diary, as he sometimes was, Avril would step in (as her first diary entry in "From the archives" mentions)' (p. 151).

Cedric refers to his diary as a 'Book of Self' (p. 81). Above all, it's a means of expression and agency, but there's no escaping the explosion of toxic humanity in an Orwellian universe. Avril initially contributes to his diary, but she soon starts her own, keeping it up until the O'Malleys are discovered and abducted, one by one. Caroline takes over the diary briefly. It's not entirely clear who composes the last three fragments, but there are clues (e.g., 'Tick tock' is a phrase used by Avril several times, although in the final fragment the speaker says he is a man). Cryptic, undated, surreal and anonymous, the fragments recount what appears to be Cedric being broken in custody just as *1984*'s O'Brien broke Winston Smith. That the voice variably sounds as if it belongs to O'Brien and/or a reconditioned Smith makes sense: Cedric is an amalgam of these characters, as May states in the teaching supplement, 'a composite figure who blends aspects of Orwell's personality, habits and situation with those of Winston as well as with those of his torturer, O'Brien – O'Brien as he was, or may be imagined to have been, before becoming the O'Brien of *Nineteen Eighty-Four*' (p. 106). Considering *1948* as a whole, I would add May to this composite Orwell-Smith-O'Brien figure, but he does not cultivate an awareness of himself as such. Like *1984*, which is categorically absurdist but hardly laughable, *1948* takes itself very seriously

BOOK REVIEW

even as it engages in semi-modernist play. This is ultimately what unnerves me about May's creative-critical-tutorial approach. A bit more self-awareness (if not light-hearted self-effacement) on his part probably would have dispelled this effect. But the book does not necessarily *need* self-awareness from May. As it stands, *1948* is a dynamic, complex engagement with *1984* that contributes to Orwellian scholarship in meaningful, provocative and insightful ways.

The teaching supplement that follows the novella is a list of eighteen questions broken into two sections, 'Connecting "From the archives' & *Nineteen Eighty-Four*' and 'Interpretive contexts for "From the Archives"'. The critical supplement is broken into sections, too, each devoted to a specific 'agoniste' relevant to the study, including Orwell's correlation with Enlightenment thought, family values, aestheticism and modernism, depictions of women, individualism, Jewishness, pastoralism, and history and memory. May begins 'Orwell Agonistes' with how he came to write *1948*, prompted by a review of William H. Gass's 2012 biography; the supplement is at once meditative, expository and scholarly. All told, Orwell and science fiction scholars will be intrigued by *1948* and find plenty of resonant material for discussion and further scholarship. I'm not so sure about the student demographic, even though they would benefit the most from May's hybrid intervention. These days, undergraduate students can barely get to the end of any book, and while Orwell's *1984* remains important and interesting, it's no page-turner. I have experienced far more enmity than amity for the novel from students when I teach it, and I am dubious about *1948* sparking greater appeal. Still, the book would work exceedingly well as a pedagogical tool, especially in a graduate literature course that centres on Orwell and/or utopian fiction.

**D. Harlan Wilson,
Dayton, Ohio, USA**

## Believe Nothing until It Is Officially Denied: Claud Cockburn and the Invention of Guerrilla Journalism

Patrick Cockburn

Verso Books, London, 2024, pp 320

ISBN: 9781804290743 (hbk)

While fighting for the Republic in the Spanish Civil War, George Orwell and Claud Cockburn had a spat. Cockburn believed that the Republican's victory depended on the unity of a central government and a professional army, and he took to denouncing in print anyone who opposed this view. In May 1937, he wrote an article for the *Daily Worker* (under the byline 'Frank Pitcairn') in which the POUM, Orwell's militia, was held up as a group of Trotskyist saboteurs and he accused them of stealing arms. Though Orwell would later cite careful evidence to the contrary, a month later the POUM was declared illegal and its members were being hunted down by Soviet security forces. Patrick Cockburn, son of Claud and author of this biography, concludes that, though 'Orwell had every reason to feel enraged by the persecution of the POUM militiamen alongside whom he had been fighting' (p. 188), his clash with Cockburn was insignificant given the inevitable victory of numerically superior Nationalist forces and the deaths of 500,000 Spaniards in the war. Claud Cockburn, tellingly, remained 'unapologetic' (p. 187) about his accusations.

Though this dispute was the extent of Cockburn's interaction with Orwell, the pair had much else in common and lived what were in many senses parallel lives. There was the same colonial infancy, the move back to Britain and to public school, the hand-to-mouth journalism in 1920s Europe, the adoption of socialism in the 1930s, the fight against fascism in Spain and the lasting success as a filmable novelist. Cockburn was the more radical, although he was less concerned with the dangers of totalitarianism than with exposing corruption inside the establishment. Having moved in similar circles to Orwell, he was connected with a startling number of literary and political figures, including Randolph Churchill, H.G. Wells and Charles de Gaulle.

Cockburn was born in Peking, as it was then known, in 1904. His father, a Foreign Office official, had lived in China since 1880. A happy childhood in Scotland preceded a memorable career at Berkhamsted School and at Keble College, Oxford, where he was secretary of the Liberal Association and editor of the *Isis* student magazine. His contemporaries included Evelyn Waugh (a cousin), Christopher Isherwood (a rival in love), Graham Greene, Anthony Powell, Henry Yorke, L.P. Hartley, Harold Acton, Cyril Connolly, John Betjeman and Robert Byron – in short, the entire cohort of inter-war Oxonians which needed only Orwell among their number to represent a complete generation of *litterateurs*.

In 1924, he and Graham Greene secured an illicit undergraduate trip to the Ruhr, by the ingenious stratagem of demanding from the German Embassy £25 cash and a letter of introduction, in exchange for a promise to write pro-German news articles on the French occupation. Germany took on a new importance when Cockburn became a *Times* correspondent in the dog days of the Weimar Republic. His Isherwoodesque existence among the Berlin upper classes included a six-year affair with Jean Ross, the model for the character Sally Bowles in *Goodbye to Berlin* (1939), who does not appear to have been as shallow and apolitical as her alter ego.

Seeing the apparent end of American capitalism in 1929 had turned Cockburn to communism (unlike Orwell he did not see 'the Soviet myth' for what it was) and much of his writing in the 1930s appeared in the *Daily Worker*. In protest at *The Times*'s violently pro-nazi position – Hitler was praised for his 'moderation and common sense' (p. 6) – he left the paper in 1933, though he could easily have stayed on and enjoyed a lucrative career.

Instead, he invested his energies in the paper which would become his greatest legacy. *The Week*, a cheaply produced guerrilla publication which tracked the dangers of fascism and warned against appeasement, was written and managed singlehandedly from a dingy London apartment, but grew quickly into a phenomenon with its regular reportage of scandal and conspiracy. The first issue, containing a leak from a cabinet meeting on German rearmament, drew attention from MI5; and it also detailed the nazi persecutions in Germany, reporting, for instance the planned seizure of Jewish property by expropriation and forced loans. Within two years *The Week* became one of the most quoted British newspapers on the world stage. In 1937 it really 'went off like a rocket' (p. 210) when Cockburn published an article on the 'Clivedon set', a network of pro-appeasers in the British establishment – in Eton, Oxford, parliament, government and big business – centred on Waldorf and Nancy Astor. Cockburn's revelations had, within weeks, been pumped across headlines the world over. It was the pithiness of the phrase 'Clivedon set' which guaranteed its success in the popular imagination. Exactly like Orwell's neologisms – Newspeak, Thought Police, doublethink – 'the phrase went marching on because it first had dramatised, and then summarised, a whole vague body of suspicions and fears' (p. 212). *The Week* was banned in wartime and ceased publication in 1941.

One thing which is not available, and which would have made a useful appendix, is a bibliography; as it is, there is no way to know precisely how much Cockburn wrote, although the excerpts quoted here give a useful sense of *how* he wrote. His prose style – lacking, slightly, Orwell's gift for metaphor – was sharp, fluent, detailed, intelligent and perfectly equipped for anecdotes and character sketches:

> He [Brenden Bracken] was a man of such all-pervading duplicity that his natural hair must come to resemble a wig (p. 151).

> A satisfactory thing about Herr von Ribbentrop was that you did not have to waste time wondering if there was some streak of goodness in him (p. 214).

The keen style equipped him for the switch in later life from investigative reporting to satire, fiction and autobiography; he was active in the 1950s on *Punch* with Anthony Powell and Malcolm Muggeridge (friends of Orwell), and in the 1960s on the magazine which became *The Week*'s closest successor, *Private Eye*, though none of this work overshadowed the legacy of *The Week* itself. He died in 1981.

Patrick Cockburn, himself a war correspondent, says that his own experiences reporting since 2000 from Iraq, Afghanistan, Libya and Syria taught him the persistent truth of one of his father's dictums – political wars are information wars – and proved that *The Week*'s moral courage and pioneering use of guerrilla journalism have grown, if anything, more timely today. Especially relevant to admirers of Orwell, this biography is lively, fluently written, crammed with memorable characters, anecdotes and adventures, and gives a living picture of a journalist who deserves to be much more of a household name than he is at present.

**Hassan Akram,**
**University of Oxford**

## AND FINALLY

# Reworkings – or Evidence of 'Convergent Evolution'?

In his latest book, *Who Is Big Brother?: A Reader's Guide to George Orwell* (Yale University Press, 2024), D.J. Taylor suggests that several of Orwell's best known works, such as 'A hanging', are reworkings of subjects in older authors (Thackeray wrote about a public hanging, for instance). Perhaps, though, Orwell exemplifies something identified in biology as 'convergent evolution', where animals long after their forebears diverged developed similar features. The Natural History Museum website has many examples, including one that Orwell would have met repeatedly: lice and mosquitoes both have blood-sucking mouths, despite having no single ancestor. Could this have happened to some of Orwell's experiences? Not everyone who has attended a hanging has written about it. Not everyone has survived being blown almost to kingdom come and written about it, but compare Joseph Conrad's memory of his first ship exploding as he spoke to a colleague (in 'Youth', 1898) and Orwell's account of his near-fatal wounding in *Homage to Catalonia* (1938) and you will find the experience is very similar.

***

War, when it gets into the leading articles, 'is apt to be waged with remarkably old-fashioned weapons', Orwell noted in 1944, citing the use of bucklers, swords and clarions. Meanwhile, in Germany, the same thing had already happened: '… the new weapon was given all kinds of different names: Hell-hound, Archangel Michael, the Flying Hamburger, Robot and Sky Avenger. None of them pleased the Minister [Goebbels, boss of secret diarist Rudolf Semmler]'. A day later, Semmler recorded the nazi broadcaster, Hans Schwarz van Berk, calling the new weapon simply 'V weapon'. To suggest that further sensational developments are on the way he proposes that they should be called V1, V2, V3, etc. The führer 'has approved the idea'. Three months later Orwell wrote '… it looks as though the doodle-bug [V1] may have a big future before it in forthcoming wars' and in December 1944, before he could escape official censorship in Britain: 'V2 (I am told that you can now mention it in print so long as you just call it V2 and don't describe it too minutely)…'. Orwell, of course, was to transform these flying bombs into the 'screamers' that fall intermittently in *Nineteen Eighty-Four*, no longer a form of artillery but, like the names dreamed in Goebbels' ministry, instruments of psychological warfare.

\*\*\*

Another tool for the student of Orwell that may have a big future before it is the Google Ngram Viewer. I was struck by D.J. Taylor (again) discussing Orwell's vocabulary. Consider, though, a word Orwell never uses even while describing the thing itself: a ziggurat. Instead, Orwell writes 'pyramidal structure' when describing the Ministry of Truth building in *Nineteen Eighty-Four*, most likely because the archaeology of Mesopotamia was still so undeveloped that the word for its defining buildings was little known. The Ngram viewer shows an occurrence of 0.00045 per cent for the word 'pyramid' in Orwell's lifetime, but no more than 0.0000080 per cent for 'ziggurat'. And just as Orwell noted that the word 'car' had reappeared to describe the now ubiquitous vehicle, so he may have noted brutalist architects erecting new ziggurats had he lived. *Nabokov's Favourite Word Is Mauve: The Literary Quirks and Oddities of Our Most-Loved Authors*, by Ben Blatt (Simon & Schuster, 2017), may provide an introduction to anyone interested in this area of numerical analysis but there is much more to be done.

\*\*\*

When Sonia Orwell and Ian Angus reprinted *The English People* in 1968 in their *Collected Essays, Journalism and Letters* of Orwell, they noted the original publisher had updated the text to omit references to the war (the book was written before 1945). Something similar happened to his friend Stevie Smith's last novel, *The Holiday*, published in 1949, to take out references to the war where it was written and set. William Vivian Butler, in his *The Durable Desperadoes: A Critical Study of Some Enduring Heroes* (1973) – an interesting book in the evolutionary line of Orwell's essay 'Raffles and Miss Blandish' (1944), Richard Usborne's *Clubland Heroes* (1953) and Claud Cockburn's *Bestseller* (1972) – noted that the thriller writers he was concerned with took a very different approach as they added to their series: for their heroes there never had been a war. 1939-1945 never happened.

New Pitcher

# George Orwell Studies

## Subscription information
Each volume contains two issues, published half-yearly.

### Annual Subscription (including postage)

*Personal Subscription*

| | |
|---|---|
| UK | £45 |
| Europe | £50 |
| RoW | £55 |

*Institutional Subscription*

| | |
|---|---|
| UK | £100 |
| Europe | £115 |
| RoW | £120 |

*Single Issue copies can be purchased (subject to availability)*


Enquiries regarding subscriptions and orders should be sent to:

> Journals Fulfilment Department
> Abramis Academic
> ASK House
> Northgate Avenue
> Bury St Edmunds
> Suffolk, IP32 6BB
> UK

Tel: +44(0)1284 717884
Email: info@abramis.co.uk

www.ingramcontent.com/pod-product-compliance
Lightning Source LLC
Chambersburg PA
CBHW080734300426
44114CB00019B/2586